PELICAN BOOKS

THE VIKINGS

Johannes Brøndsted was born in Jutland in 1890
and received his doctor's degree for research into
the relations between Anglo-Saxon and Nordic art
in Viking times in 1920. In 1922-3 with E. Dyggve
he excavated Early Christian monuments in
Dalmatia (*Recherches à Salone*, 1928). From 1941 to
1951 he was Professor of Nordic Archaeology and
European Prehistory at the University of
Copenhagen. In *Danmarks Oldtid* (three volumes,
second edition 1957-9) he has given a full statement
of the prehistory of his own country. He was elected a
Corresponding Fellow of the British Academy in
1952 and received the gold medal of the Royal
Society of Antiquaries in 1954. From 1951 to 1960
he was director of the National Museum in
Copenhagen. He died in 1965.

JOHANNES BRØNDSTED

THE VIKINGS

Translated by Kalle Skov

With twenty-four plates

PENGUIN BOOKS

Penguin Books Ltd, Harmondsworth, Middlesex, England
Penguin Books, 40 West 23rd Street, New York, New York 10010, U.S.A.
Penguin Books Australia Ltd, Ringwood, Victoria, Australia
Penguin Books Canada Ltd, 2801 John Street, Markham, Ontario, Canada L3R 1B4
Penguin Books (N.Z.) Ltd, 182–190 Wairau Road, Auckland 10, New Zealand

First published 1960
This new translation published 1965
Reprinted 1967, 1969, 1971, 1973, 1975, 1976, 1978,
1980, 1981, 1982, 1983

Set, printed and bound in Great Britain by
Cox & Wyman Ltd, Reading
Set in Monotype Baskerville

Contents

ACKNOWLEDGEMENTS

Our thanks are due as follows for permission to
reproduce the plates in this book: Plates 1C, 2A, 5A,
16A, 16B, 17A, 17B, 19A, 19B, 22A, 23B, 24B:
Antikvarisk-Topografiska Arkivet, Stockholm;
Plates 7A, 8, 9, 10, 11, 12, 20A, 21, 22B: Universitetets
Oldsaksamling, Oslo; Plates 3A, 3B, 20B: Sophus
Bengtsson; Plate 6D: Lennart Larsen, National-
museet, Copenhagen.

NOTE

Old Norse words quoted are given in the form they
assume in normalized Old Icelandic, commonly
regarded as the 'standard' dialect of Old Norse.
This may differ from that used at the time and
place appropriate to the quotation. Viking personal
names appear in several different forms. Where a
recognized English form exists, this is used, e.g.
Swein Forkbeard, Harald Hardrada. Names of
people less well known in this country are given
either in an English equivalent, e.g. Eric Bloodaxe
(Old Norse *Eiríkr blóðöx*), Harald Finehair (Old
Norse *Haraldr inn hárfagri*), or in an Anglicized form
of the Old Icelandic, e.g. Olaf kyrri (Old Norse
Óláfr kyrri). Place-names are given in either their
English gazetteer form or their local form.

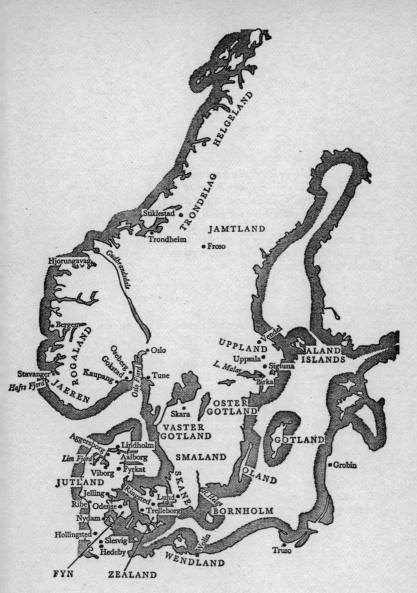

Map of Scandinavia

CHAPTER ONE

Before the Vikings

A thousand years ago in the churches and monasteries of
northern France was heard the prayer: 'From the wrath of
the Northmen, O Lord, deliver us.' This prayer was amply
justified. The Northmen were the Vikings: Danes, Norwegians, and Swedes, whose plunderings ranged from
private acts of piracy and coastal raids to formidable invasions in quest of new land to colonize. Viking activity
started before A.D. 800, and more than two centuries elapsed
before it ceased. During this period the Vikings left their
mark not only on Western Europe, but also right through
the Mediterranean from Gibraltar to Asia Minor; in what
is now western Russia, Scandinavian commercial enterprise
linked Byzantium and Arabia with Sweden.

Now how could all this happen? Why did Europe permit
the Danes and Norwegians to rule large parts of England,
Ireland, and France, and the Swedes to form a ruling class
in western Russia? Why was Scandinavia strong and the
rest of Europe weak? What inner forces led to the Viking
raids?

To answer the first question one must examine the centuries immediately preceding the Viking Age, and try to
assess the political, commercial, and social development of
the time. The most important examination of this period is
by the prominent Belgian historian, Henri Pirenne. One of
his theories is that the real dividing-line between ancient and
medieval Europe fell, not in the migration period (*c.* 500),
but during the reign of Charlemagne (*c.* 800). The break

with the past, he maintained, went much deeper in 800 than in 500. Let us examine Pirenne's argument more closely.

The lands which formed the late Roman Empire – 'Romania' as it was called in the fourth century – formed a unit surrounding the Mediterranean, the great Roman Lake. The Mediterranean did not divide countries, it linked them together. It formed the route 'along which travelled religion, philosophy, and trade'. The cults of Egypt and the Orient spread across it, the worship of Mithras, Christianity, and, later, monasticism. Along it were carried treasures and luxury goods from the east; ivory, silk, spices, papyrus, wine, and oil. In return the west sent its exports, in particular, slaves. The common currency of this immense Empire was the Constantinian gold *solidus*. This great commercial system was in the main organized and run by enterprising Syrians and Jews.

What was the effect on Romania when the Germanic migrations took place in the fourth and fifth centuries? The western dominions, including even Italy, were conquered by invading Germanic tribes, and political control over them was lost. This was a catastrophe indeed; yet it did not mean – as was once thought – the end of classical culture in the western half of Romania.

In the first place, the Germanic invaders formed only a small minority in the conquered lands. Exact figures do not exist, but historians have made the following estimates: there were about 100,000 Ostrogoths in Italy; in Spain and southern France there was a similar number of Visigoths, and there may have been a further 25,000 Burgundians in south-eastern France; the Vandal army which crossed the Straits of Gibraltar to North Africa is thought to have numbered 80,000 men – or scarcely more than one per cent of the inhabitants of the flourishing North African province of the Roman Empire into which it was absorbed. It is highly unlikely that these Germanic hosts received reinforcements from their native lands; on the contrary, their numbers were certainly reduced by the effects of an unfamiliar climate.

It is quite clear that Germanicization of the conquered territories took place only to a limited extent. It was presumably complete in those areas where Germanic languages are later found, in other words, in only a small northern strip of the Roman Empire. Apart from this, the only linguistic manifestation of Germanic influence is a number (about 300) of loan-words into French. No Romance language shows significant influence on phonetics or syntax. What evidently occurred in Italy and western Europe shortly after the migrations was that the conquering Germanic peoples were virtually absorbed into the local populations. Germanic types have to be sought for among the inhabitants of present-day Italy. Blond people still to be found in North Africa presumably descend from pre-Germanic inhabitants.

In this way Romania survived the occupation of its western part; the classical traditions – though constantly decaying – were continued. Ostrogoths, Visigoths, Burgundians, Vandals, and Franks were left to rule their new countries, which they did on exactly the same lines as the Romans before them. In these new states the King was all-powerful, as the Roman Emperors had been. The Germanic peoples conquering these countries did not destroy classical culture; quite the contrary. For centuries they had been neighbours of the Roman Empire, and had learned to respect what they saw. It was not surprising, therefore, that they copied Roman social and political institutions, at any rate in their outward forms. During this time, however, intellectual life and education declined. The Church was the only intellectual power to assert itself but, as in Roman times, the Church was subservient to the secular authority, and civil servants were recruited from the laity, not the

clergy. The new Germanic territories, like the late Roman
Empire, were ruled by absolutist governments; laymen held
the administrative offices, while the financial basis was the
king's taxes and duties collected mainly in minted gold.
These states were in fact not national states; they continued
the pattern of the former Roman satellites and provinces.
Indeed that pattern was renewed, when, in the sixth century, the armies of the Byzantine Emperor Justinian reconquered large areas of the old Western Roman Empire; and
under him the Mediterranean once again became a Roman
lake. Then came a Germanic reaction, from the Lombards.
They crossed the Alps and settled in northern Italy, but
even this event did not break the general lines of development, for they too were Romanized in the course of time.
Life remained the same. As before, the Syrians and Jews
were the main importers of luxuries from the Orient. The
Mediterranean countries maintained their close contact
with each other so that, for example, African camels were
imported as beasts of burden into Spain and France. The
small French town of Narbonne is typical of the time; in the
late sixth century Goths, Romans, Jews, Syrians, and Greeks
lived in it side by side. The Germanic rulers of western
Europe governed their countries through men of Roman
education, traditions, and habits. Latin and literacy continued, though in decline. In short, the face of western
Europe had changed but slightly under the new rulers.

Then, in the seventh century, came the real catastrophe
which was to lead to the most important event in European
history. This catastrophe was the rise of Arab power, and
swift and violent attack on the West. Mohammed died in
632 and two years later the storm broke. At this time the
Byzantine Empire, whose provinces surrounded the eastern
Mediterranean, stood at the height of its power. The Emperor
Heraclius had defeated the Persian army at Nineveh in
627 – though admittedly suffering heavy losses which left

him militarily weak. No immediate danger seemed apparent
to the eastern Roman Empire, least of all from the Bedouin
Arabs. The attack gained advantage from its unexpectedness.

In 634 the Arabs crossed the Jordan. They captured
Damascus in 635 and the whole of Syria in the following
year, Jerusalem in 637, Egypt in 641. Nothing seemed to
stop this fanatical army, whose military methods were new
and whose contempt for death was unbounded. At one stroke
it relieved Byzantium of its most valuable provinces. Later,
the Arabs ventured upon sea-borne warfare and were
checked only by the Byzantine secret weapon 'Greek fire',
a primitive type of flame-thrower.

In the following sixty to seventy years they pushed resistance aside right along the North African coast, and in 711
crossed the Straits of Gibraltar. By the next year the whole
of the Spanish Peninsula was in their power. They pressed
farther north into France, and were not decisively stopped
until twenty years later, by Charles Martel at Poitiers, and
thrust back to the Pyrenees. In the meantime, they had extended their rule to include Sicily and the southern part of
Italy. The coasts of northern Italy and southern France
were raided, and there was no fleet there to take up the
battle against the attackers. The western Mediterranean had
become an Arab sea.

There is a marked difference between these Arab conquests and the Germanic invasions of two or three centuries
earlier. The Arabs were not absorbed into the conquered
peoples, principally because theirs was a religious war.
Their Mohammedan monotheism was quite irreconcilable
with all other religions, not least with Christianity. The Germanic tribes, on the other hand, had either been Christians
themselves, or had practised a polytheistic faith which
tolerated other religions. Further, the Germanic peoples
had been culturally inferior to those they conquered, and
quite prepared to adopt their civilization. With the Arabs

it was just the opposite. They brought with them their own faith and culture; they did not require the conversion of the conquered peoples, feeling for them nothing but contempt. They demanded only unconditional surrender. Wherever they came Greek and Latin were displaced by Arabic. If the subjugated peoples wished to survive they had to accept progressively the religion and language of their conquerors.

What were the consequences for that part of Europe which had fought and avoided the Arab invasion? The Frankish Empire, the power which finally brought the Arab threat to a halt, was on the threshold of its golden age. But why did the centre of gravity of western Europe shift at this time from the Mediterranean countries with their rich and flourishing commercial life to the poorer, agrarian, Frankish territories of the north? First and foremost because of the destruction of southern trade. The Arab invasion had cut the Mediterranean in two. In the eastern half, where the Byzantine Empire survived under the protection of a strong and efficient fleet, trade still continued. In the west the Arabs had wiped it out. Western Europe's most important country, France, underwent a revolution. All the goods which until then had been imported by Syrians and other merchants from the Orient disappeared – the papyrus, spices, oil, silks, and gold. More important, many of the native traders of southern France were weakened or ruined. In their place appeared oriental merchants who acted as intermediaries between Christian and Arab worlds. An immediate consequence of the loss of trade was a sharp decline in royal revenue, leaving the king more and more in the hands of the landed nobility. This was the main reason for the political and social eclipse of the Merovingians in the seventh century. Southern France, of course, was more affected by these changes than the northern Frankish provinces: its towns decayed while the north, whose society was essentially based on landed property, held its own. It was thus from northern Frankish territory that the ancestors of the later Carolingian dynasty, of Pepin and Charlemagne, came. They were Belgian landed stock from the area round Liège, where even today the family name Pepinster survives.

Profound differences are to be observed in the condition of France under Carolingian rule in the eighth or ninth century compared with the state of things under the Merovingians in the sixth and seventh. The economy was now based on agriculture instead of commerce; silver had replaced gold as the monetary standard; the Church had ousted the laity. Latin was a learned language spoken only within the Church (oddly enough as the result of the missionary activities of Anglo-Saxon England); among the laity vulgar Latin was replaced by regional dialects. The practical, flowing, cursive script which had been commonly used for commercial purposes between individuals was replaced by an elegant, carefully formed minuscule which was to become the basis for the later medieval scripts of Europe. The so-called Carolingian Renaissance with its concentration on the language and literature of Greece and Rome was limited to scholars and did not penetrate to the ordinary man.

These views were expounded by Pirenne in his controversial book *Mohammed and Charlemagne*. Not all his claims can be accepted – for example he dates the beginning of the Merovingian decline around 640 – a time when Arab interference with Mediterranean trade had hardly begun. But on the whole his views are sound. His principal thesis is that there could have been 'no Charlemagne without Mohammed', that the development of the Carolingian Empire is only comprehensible with reference to the Arab advance into western Europe. The impulse of the Arab drive produced an agrarian and militarily powerful France, oriented now towards the north.

The strength of the Frankish Empire at the beginning of the ninth century certainly did not favour the Vikings.

Warned by the sporadic raids that occurred about 790, on the coasts of England, Scotland, Ireland, and to some degree France, Charlemagne fortified his northern coasts with a chain of watch towers, beacons, and garrisons. As a result France was free of Viking attacks during Charlemagne's lifetime, despite the fact that at this very time relations between France and Denmark were distinctly strained, indeed they were on the verge of war.

It will be remembered that Charlemagne had cruelly put down the Saxons of north-west Germany, forcibly converting them to Christianity, and so had extended his frontiers to the Elbe. Thus his lands marched with those of the western Slavs and the Danes. The Danish king, Godfred, was both audacious and active, willing to attack both the Slavs along the Baltic and the Frisians of the North Sea coasts. He did not stand in awe of the powerful Frankish emperor, and was quite ready to attack him too. But at the critical moment he died (in 810), and simultaneously Charlemagne's attention was diverted to Italy. Peace reigned again, and the northern pirates respected Frankish power as long as Charlemagne lived.

It was not to last long. At the great emperor's death in 814, his son Louis the Pious succeeded to the Empire. Gradually it began to disintegrate, the Franks became weaker and the country's coastal defences in the north were neglected. Two decades later the Viking raids began, and for the rest of the century northern France was the scene of brutal attacks, planned on a great scale and always launched from the sea. Denmark was the main source of aggression.

In the eighth century England was divided into a number of small kingdoms: Mercia, Wessex, Essex, Kent, East Anglia, Northumbria, and others. The most powerful of English kings in the last decade of the eighth century was Offa of Mercia (who took the title of *Rex Anglorum*). By the time of his death in 796 he dominated, directly or indirectly, the whole of southern England. He was the first English ruler to carry any political weight abroad. On good terms with Charlemagne, at least at times, he was a man of such strong character that had he lived longer he might well have proved a bulwark against the Viking assaults on England. But for a generation after Offa's death southern England was divided by internal squabbles until, in 825, Egbert of Wessex established control over all south-east England, and for a time even over Mercia itself. His successor was his son Æthelwulf. This royal power in the south of England was quite inadequate to keep the Vikings off. Neither Northumbria nor Scotland was strong enough in the ninth century to organize an efficient defence against Viking attack.

Ireland, a primitive and divided country, was another easy victim, as the Norwegian invasion shortly after 800 proved. The Irish certainly resisted, and their annals from 807 onwards are full of battles with the Norwegians pressing in from the sea: battles which, if we are to believe the chroniclers, the Irish frequently won. For all that, the Irish failed to keep the Vikings out, and after a generation of battles the Norwegians were firmly settled in many places in both west and east of the island.

Before concluding this review of the raids on western Europe we must consider one important point which does much to explain the supremacy of the Vikings: the fact that all their raids were launched from the sea. The Vikings were skilful navigators, more confident on the sea than either the Anglo-Saxons or the Franks, and they had far better vessels. Certainly they were not trained and unbeatable sea warriors: more than once we read about their defeats by Anglo-Saxon fleets along the English coasts. As shipbuilders, however, they were outstanding. They built fleets of fast and roomy ships designed for the transport of their armies,

and used them with speed and mobility. It was this mastery
of ships, unexcelled over most of Europe, which gave them
such decisive advantages in their attacks upon so many
coasts. The development of these Viking ships can be traced
right back to the migration period. Some of the earliest
relevant archaeological discoveries, such as the boat found
at Nydam in South Jutland, Denmark, show a large open
rowing-boat without mast or sail, and with only a rudi-
mentary keel. Of course archaeological finds are fortuitous,
and a solitary boat does not prove that such vessels were
standard. But other finds, such as the carved and painted
stones in Gotland, illustrate the slow evolution of the sail
from the sixth to the eighth centuries – from a small, not
very useful, square piece of cloth set high on the mast to the
magnificent sails of the Viking vessels. Concurrently with
this, other developments, particularly that of the keel,
turned the boat into a ship.

It is strange that the sail should have taken so long to
appear in the north, for it had been known from time immemorial by the Romans and Greeks in the Mediterranean.
From literary sources we know also that it appeared in
Holland in the first century A.D., for Tacitus tells of the
Batavian chief, Civilis, who, during a review of his fleet in
the year 70, copied the Roman custom by letting his men
use their coloured cloaks as sails. Caesar, indeed, records
that, about a century earlier, the Veneti, the seafaring tribe
of the French Atlantic coast, used sails of heavy leather.
Sidonius Apollinaris, Bishop of Clermont in 470, describes
the Saxons returning home with 'swelling sails'. It seems
strange, then, that sails took so long to reach Scandinavia,
stranger still that they took even longer to reach England.
As late as 560 the Byzantine historian Procopius wrote of
the English 'these barbarians do not use the sail either but
depend wholly on oars' – a statement that appears to be
borne out by the large, mid-seventh-century royal ship with

neither mast nor sail, discovered at Sutton Hoo in East Anglia.

It can truly be said then that the Anglo-Saxons, the Franks, and the Irish could not compete with the Vikings in seamanship or navigation. It is significant that none of these peoples ever launched reprisal attacks on the Viking countries. This supremacy at sea explains why the Vikings were able to harry and conquer such large areas of western Europe, yet it does not account for their penetration of eastern Europe, where there was no sea for them to display their mastery on, but where they nevertheless were successful.

In the eighth century the difference between Denmark and Norway on the one hand and Sweden on the other was that Sweden was already an organized and ancient kingdom (based on Uppland), strong enough to engage in colonial expansion beyond its frontiers. These extensions of its territory were partly into Latvia and Estonia, and partly farther eastwards towards the southern shores of Lakes Ladoga and Onega. The bases for these operations were Uppland (where the *Sviar* lived) and the island of Gotland in the Baltic. If such drives as these are regarded as Viking raids, then clearly the Swedish Vikings were making their mark on Europe well before their Danish and Norwegian counterparts.

Shortly before the Second World War there were discovered near the little town of Grobin (not far from Liepaja or Libau) on the Latvian coast, some prehistoric graves containing objects of Gotlandic type which were ascribed to a rather older period than the Viking Age. Swedish and Latvian archaeologists, continuing excavations on the site, unearthed an extensive burial place containing at least a thousand cremation graves whose arrangement and contents unquestionably pointed to eighth-century Gotland. Soon afterwards another graveyard almost as big as the first was found, and clearly from the same date, but this time the contents undeniably indicated a central Swedish and not Gotlandic origin. This site too had cremation graves, but with the difference that each grave was covered with a mound. The central Swedish cemetery moreover was a strictly military one, whereas in the Gotland one there were found many women's graves, and more jewellery than weapons; factors suggesting that this was a civil cemetery established in peaceful conditions. These discoveries appear to confirm existing suppositions about political conditions in Sweden in the period before the Viking raids. The Gotlanders were peaceful traders, the Swedes (*Sviar*) men of war. The Grobin discoveries suggest that a Swedish military garrison was stationed there, and that the Gotlanders were settled there as traders.

If we turn now from archaeological to literary evidence, we find in Ansgar's biography (written in the 870s by Rimbert, Ansgar's disciple and his successor as Archbishop of Bremen) a reference to the fact that the people of Courland, which we now know as Latvia, had been attacked by both the Swedes and the Danes, and that the Swedish king, Olaf, at the head of a large army, attacked and burned a town called Seeburg defended by no less than seven thousand warriors. On this evidence the Swedish archaeologist Birger Nerman, who conducted the excavations at Grobin, has posed the question whether the two cemeteries could in fact have belonged to this old Seeburg. Grobin is far more likely, however, to be the garrison town which the Swedes founded after Seeburg's destruction, but the literary and archaeological evidence cannot be fully reconciled in this particular case. Nevertheless, there is clear evidence of an eighth-century (pre-Viking) Swedish expansion eastwards, which in the course of the ninth century was to lead to colonization of the area around Old Ladoga, just south of Lake Ladoga. We shall examine the significance of these

movements towards Russia later: meanwhile let us look at
what was happening in south-east Europe and in western
Asia.

In the eighth century two powers were established in
those areas; both so strong, and both so remote from Scandinavia as to exclude any likelihood of clashes with the
Vikings. The first of these, based on Constantinople, was
the Byzantine Empire, the successor of the old Eastern
Roman Empire; the second, a relatively new one, was the
Arab Caliphate with its capital at Baghdad. The Byzantine
sphere of interest to the north lay along the shores of the
Black Sea and from the Crimea into the plains of the
Ukraine. The Arabs, who had already subdued Persia in
the seventh century, were also pressing in a northerly
direction towards the south and west Siberian steppes (the
ancient Scythia). In the eighth century these regions were
inhabited by Turkic nomads, and between them and the
Byzantines there extended, north of the Caspian Sea, the
vast independent Khaganate of the Khazars, with its capital,
Itil, in the Volga delta (their ruler bore the Avar-Turkic
title 'Khagan'). These Khazars closed the broad gap between the southern slope of the Urals and the north coast
of the Caspian, and they prevented the Turkic nomads from
spreading west, providing a peaceful frontier with the
Byzantines from the Caucasus to the Crimea. The Khazars
also checked the movement northwards into Russia of the
Bulgars, who thereupon forked in two separate directions:
one moving into the Balkans, the other settling on the Volga
bend in their own Khaganate with its capital at Bulgar.
As time went on these two Khaganates – the Khazars in
the south and the Bulgars in the north – dominated and
organized the great trade along the Volga. Little is known
of the condition of central and western Russia at this time;
the probability is that, as in the other Slav territories right
up to the Elbe, these regions were divided among loosely

related tribes lacking any political homogeneity, while the vast impenetrable forests blocked any significant movement of people or cultures.

Such, then, was the general state of Europe and western Asia in the period preceding the Viking advance. Of the three great powers of the time, the Franks were too strong for the fierce northerners, while the Byzantines and the Arabs were too remote to become involved with them. Beyond the dominions of these three powers there was weakness.

Of the background to Viking activity all that remains to be examined is the internal condition of the three Scandinavian countries during the seventh and eighth centuries. Once again we turn to archaeology for evidence, as reliable literary sources are lacking.

There is no doubt that Sweden was the most advanced of these countries, as numerous magnificent finds from Uppland and Gotland testify. There is clear stylistic influence from the southern Germanic tribes, and there must have been cultural connexions between them and the Swedes via the Baltic, despite the presence of Slavs in the intervening area of north Germany. The situation confirms the early semi-historical accounts of the ancient kingdom of Uppland. Of Scandinavian monarchies, that of the central Swedes was the oldest and most powerful. Its strength is suggested by the eighth-century expansion, mentioned above, to the lands bordering the Baltic and the Finnish-settled regions round Lake Ladoga. Uppland established contact, also, with Finland in the east and Norway in the west. Archaeological finds prove Swedish–Norwegian cross-connexions along the ancient trade route which leads through Jamtland to Trondelag. Further, in the eighth century Norway had direct sea connexions with Merovingian France, as Norwegian grave-goods show. Norway, too, seems to have had a virile and active population, though the land was divided among a number of tribes lacking unified leadership.

For Denmark the archaeological evidence is scanty, though in recent years it has been established that an individual culture existed in the eastern areas of the land – Zealand, Skane, Bornholm – distinguished by its manufacture of weapons and its artistic style. The lack of archaeological finds may be misleading. While it is reasonable to draw positive conclusions from a wealth of archaeological material, it is dangerous to draw negative ones from a lack of it. Why are the archaeological finds scanty? Not necessarily because the land was weak and thinly populated. Perhaps because custom decreed the burial of only small (symbolic) grave-goods, or even none at all; or because the religion forbade the burial of gifts to the gods; or because the appropriate settlement sites lie under modern towns. The absence of treasure hoards may just as well indicate peace and prosperity (so that there was no need to conceal possessions in the earth) as under-population. In short, poverty of archaeological material does not necessarily indicate economic poverty. Indeed, when the first gleams of light fall upon Denmark's history (c. 800), the figure we encounter is that of King Godfred, a warrior powerful enough to take up arms against Charlemagne himself. This does not suggest a weak country, and it also shows that kingship was known in Denmark at this date, though we do not know how large an area was under Godfred's rule.

We have now answered our first question about the strength and weakness of Europe inside and outside Scandinavia at the beginning of the Viking era, and their underlying causes. But what of the internal factors that were to launch the Vikings on their countless and widespread raids over a period of more than two centuries? One thing is immediately obvious, that more than one factor must have

been at work. Let us examine some of the theories put
forward by historians and archaeologists.

Over-population. This was the thesis put forward by
Johannes Steenstrup. He referred to what he called the
'Norman tradition', preserved in a number of literary
sources, both west European and Scandinavian. This
tradition applied, he thought, first and foremost to Denmark, though the rest of Scandinavia could also be included.
It was to the effect that, at the beginning of the Viking Age,
the Scandinavian lands were over-populated, a circumstance which would explain the common west-European
accounts of the enormous size of the Viking armies; like
storm-clouds, swarms of grasshoppers, waves of the ocean,
and so on. There are also many reports of the thousands lost
in battle by the Vikings. Though allowance has to be made
for natural exaggeration, these accounts must contain a
grain of truth.

The reason traditionally advanced for this over-population was the widespread practice of polygamy among the
Vikings, who rather prided themselves on the number of
sons they could beget: it was common for them to have
concubines, mistresses, and under-wives: Steenstrup also
cites as further evidence of over-population the northern
practice, particularly among the lower classes, of killing off
unwanted infants by exposure.

The Norman tradition contains two further points which,
if they are correct, may help to explain the Viking raids.
The first is the mention of compulsory exile of young men,
ordained from time to time as a result of over-population
(though this is probably not historically accurate). The
second is a point of fact. The Vikings adhered to a system
of primogeniture; and this would have created a surplus of
young men ready to seek fame and fortune outside their

home country. On the whole it is probable that Scandinavia was over-populated at the beginning of the Viking Age, and this must have been a contributory cause of the raids.

Internal Dissensions. The Scandinavian laws of succession were such that, whenever a new king, earl, or ruling chieftain secured the succession, he was likely to leave at least one ambitious and discontented 'pretender', who would go abroad to seek influential alliances or wealth, so that on his return he could press his claim with more force. This sort of situation is not a sufficient cause to account for widespread Viking invasions.

Social Differences. Under this heading comes the suggestion that certain classes or elements of the population of Scandinavia were compelled to leave their native lands. However, there is no evidence of anything of the sort happening. The early Viking raids do not seem to have been connected with social distinctions in Scandinavia.

Foreign Pressure. This can be discounted. There is no evidence for it. The early Viking raids bear no similarity to the great movements of the migration period.

Climatic Disasters. A frequent cause of migration in history has been the failure of crops, and consequent famine, due to changes in climatic conditions. This was the reason for the frequent and sustained attacks of Asiatic nomads against their neighbours. It was probably a factor in the Hunnish attack on Europe, which itself led to great migrations, and possibly in the Cimbric raid from Jutland in the time of the Roman Republic (at the close of the second century B.C.). Scandinavian geologists, working on the peat-bogs, have

discovered evidence of many variations of climate in the
north, but none datable to the early ninth century. Moreover, the early Viking raids were in no sense migratory
movements. The Vikings had every intention of returning
with their loot and glory.

Mercantile Conditions. Here undoubtedly is a major cause of
the Viking raids, perhaps the most important of all. As we
saw earlier in this chapter, when the Arab invasion dis-
rupted the trade of the western Mediterranean and southern
France, there was a corresponding growth in the mercantile
activity of northern France. The Rhine became a great
thoroughfare, and new trading opportunities developed on
the coasts of the North Sea, particularly for the commer-
cially-minded Frisians, living mainly in what is now Holland.
As early as the eighth century, Frisian trade was well established in the North Sea countries, and when Charles Martel
acquired Friesland in the year 734 he revived the Frankish
North Sea trade through the skill and experience of the
Frisians.

Up to that time it had not been easy for Denmark,
especially southern Denmark, to participate in the North
Sea trade. In the first place the Elbe was not a Scandinavian
river, and secondly there was a dearth of good harbours on
the west coast of Jutland. To reach the Baltic from the North
Sea all vessels had to round the dangerous northerly point of
Jutland – the Skaw (Skagen) – and many captains no doubt
preferred the straight run to Norway. Soon after 800 the
situation changed. The great emperor of the Franks subdued the Saxons and extended his northern frontier right
up to the Elbe. To prevent any further expansion the Danish
king, Godfred, built a mighty earthwork, which is now
called the 'Danevirke' (Danes' [defensive earth-] work).
This barrier was to serve a dual purpose: as a protection

against attacks from the south, and also to shelter a new trade-route running across the south of Jutland from the Eider in the West to the Slie Fjord in the east, which cut out the long and perilous voyage round the Skaw. This new trade-route, the eastern and more vulnerable section protected by the Danevirke, offered attractive prospects of wealth and power for the Danes.

The opportunities for getting command of trade-routes, ardently exploited as they were by the northern countries, also stimulated an activity which in the past invariably followed the large-scale development of trade – piracy. Wherever seas and coasts were not defended, pirates preyed upon commerce; and the Viking pirates were not slow to do so.

The expansion of trade, and the lure of the great riches which could be gained from piracy, were undoubtedly two of the most important factors behind the Viking raids.

In appraising these factors there is one which must not be overlooked – the Viking way of life. I am thinking here of their disposition as we know it to have been: proud, adventurous, with a yearning for glory, a desire to excel in battle, and a scorn for death. These qualities of heroism and virility, combined with their mercantile skills, made them a powerful and dangerous race. Early monastic historians, in their records of the Vikings, emphasized the cunning, cruelty, and treachery of this warlike people. The sagas, on the other hand, show them in a different light; telling of the boldness, generosity, frankness, and self-discipline of these famous warriors. No doubt in the aggregate they possessed all the qualities, complimentary and otherwise, which were ascribed to them: the Vikings were not all alike. But one thing they did all have in common: a daring resoluteness that made their period the greatest in the history of the North.

CHAPTER TWO

The Viking Raids

The exploits of the Vikings were on a grandiose scale. They embraced the whole of Europe. In the east these Northmen thrust down the great rivers of Russia to the Caspian and the Black Sea. In the west they sailed along the Atlantic coasts, past Arab Spain, through the Straits of Gibraltar, and so far and wide over the Mediterranean. Nor was this all. They reached out across the wild and unknown Atlantic, to the Faroes, Iceland, Greenland, and even to America. The direction each of the three Scandinavian lands faces, corresponds to, indeed determines, the sphere of influence its Vikings commanded.

The very names of the three countries are clues to their ancient history. Sweden is called in Swedish 'Sverige', derived from Old Norse *Svíaríki*, the kingdom of the *Svíar*. It is not fortuitous that the very name of Sweden bears a reference to royal authority and kingship. As we have seen Sweden had a well-established monarchy long before the Viking Age. Denmark means the *marc* of the Danes, *marc* having the early meaning of 'uninhabited border country'. In the present context the *marc* must be the region at the neck of the Jutland peninsula, the trackless waste south of the Danevirke, which divided the Danes from the Saxons in the south-west and the Slavs in the south-east. Gradually this name, the Danes' *marc*, contracted to *Danmark*, came to be applied to the whole of the country.* When it is con-

* This must have happened before 900. In one of King Alfred's writings, the foreword to his translation of Orosius's world history, to

sidered how much of Denmark's history was connected with this disputed southern frontier territory of South Slesvig, it must be agreed that she was aptly named.

The name of Norway also has its old roots, different from those of Denmark and Sweden. Norway became a united kingdom at a much later date than its Scandinavian neighbours: when Harald Finehair imposed unity on its many independent tribes in the early part of the Viking period. Scandinavian romantic writers of the nineteenth century sometimes used the name-form 'Norrige', but this is only an invented name modelled on 'Sverige'. Certainly Norway too has its *marc*, its northern border territory, 'Nordmarken', but this name was not applied to the whole of the country as happened in Denmark.

The name 'Norge' has a background of mercantile history, as is more evident from its English and German forms, Norway, Norwegen. It means the 'North Way', the trade route running along Norway's extensive coast, from Skiringssal (on the west side of the Oslo Fjord) in the south, to the White Sea in the north. According to King Alfred, traders from the far north brought sealskins, pelts, and walrus teeth along this route. During the Viking Age Norway was often 'Nordmannaland', the land of the Northmen, but in the long run the significant mercantile name prevailed over the simple description of the land from its inhabitants.

A geographical factor determined the part each of the three Scandinavian countries played in the Viking raids. Right down the middle of the Scandinavian peninsula runs the long mountain range Kølen (the Keel), which forms the structural spine of the country. This range is mainly harsh,

---

which we refer later, there is the first extant reference to the name Denmark (*Denemearcan*). There is nothing unusual in a local name becoming applied to a whole country: the French name for Germany, *Allemagne*, derives from the province of the Allemagni, on the Upper Rhine.

barren waste, and from the point of view of settlement divides the land into an eastward-looking and a westward-looking part.

The face of Norway was turned westward towards the great ocean and its many islands. It was principally the Norwegians, therefore, who took the lead in venturing on the vast and stormy North Atlantic with no knowledge of what might be beyond it.

Norway's sphere of interest could be said to divide into two. The southern part, and the first to be exploited, comprised the islands off the north of Scotland, which the Norwegians occupied at the beginning of the Viking period, gradually extending from them to the Scottish coasts, Ireland, the Isle of Man, and most of the coast bordering the Irish Sea – which during this period might justifiably have been called the Norwegian Sea. From these bases they penetrated deep into England, at times coming into contact with the Danes, and also into northern and southern France and so to the Mediterranean. France too was a region which Norwegians and Danes exploited side by side.

The second direction in which Norway's sphere of interest developed was to the north – to the Faroe Islands, Iceland, and Greenland – and the initiative in this development came from King Harald Finehair, who at the end of the ninth century brought most of Norway within his domain, and so forced many Norwegian nobles and free peasants to emigrate. These later Norwegian expeditions across the Atlantic were not in search of plunder, but were daring attempts at occupation of desolate and remote territory, made under special circumstances.

Sweden faces east. It is not necessary to dwell further on this basic point, as we have already dealt with its expansion across the Baltic in the early eighth century, and we shall see in a later chapter how its mercantile influence continued to penetrate through Russia and farther south to Byzantium and Arabia. Doubtless the Baltic was shared by the Swedes and the Danes.

South of the Scandinavian peninsula lies Denmark, consisting of the mainland of Jutland and numerous small islands. Jutland is physically joined to the central European continent, but in the Viking period the barren lands of south Slesvig separated Denmark proper from its southerly neighbours – the Saxons in the south-west and the Slavs in the south-east. Added to this natural barrier was the fact that the Vikings preferred to use the sea or rivers as ways of communication; which was the main reason why they expanded not south but south-west along the Frisian and Frankish coasts, and due west to England. The south-westerly advance of the inquisitive and adventurous Danes took them farther along the whole coastline of France, forcing the Straits of Gibraltar and, together with the other Scandinavian peoples, right through the Mediterranean.

The Viking raids were inspired by several motives. On that account a mere chronological account of them would produce an obscure and contradictory pattern, and an attempt must therefore be made to classify them according to their varying motives and objectives. The Swedish scholar, Fritz Askeberg, has proposed a fourfold classification:

(1) Pirate raids conducted by individuals
(2) Political expeditions
(3) Colonizing ventures
(4) Commercial penetration

Such a division, as Askeberg himself points out, cannot be universally applicable, and many of the raids doubtless proceeded from mixed motives. But, so long as it is remembered that this classification is in no sense a chronological one, it serves to put the Viking period into perspective.

Pirate Raids by Individuals

The first category, that of private acts of piracy, is the least interesting, although it is probably the one which first comes to mind when we think of the more popular tales about the Vikings. One Norwegian historian has claimed that these raids were genuine feats of exploration, and that the plunder acquired was no more than legitimate foraging, but this view approaches the naïve. Raids of this kind were numerous throughout the Viking period, but a few typical examples deserve mention. The best-known, and also the earliest recorded, of these raids in the west is the plundering and destruction in 793 of the church and monastery on the tiny defenceless island of Lindisfarne, just off the Northumbrian coast. On this Holy Island St Cuthbert had worked as abbot and bishop over a century earlier. Lindisfarne was a daughter-house of the famous Iona in the Hebrides, and widely renowned in the Christian world as one of England's most sacred places of pilgrimage. The *Anglo-Saxon Chronicle* relates that terrifying omens – lightning and flying dragons – which were witnessed in 793 were followed by famine, and that shortly after these dolorous events, in June, heathens fell upon the island community and pillaged God's house there. These heathens were Norwegian Vikings who slaughtered some of the monks, and robbed and burned the monastery. Alcuin, the, famous Northumbrian priest and scholar, who was at that time in the service of Charlemagne in France, wrote in horror to King Æthelred of Northumbria and to his colleagues in England that the murderous raid was God's punishment for the sins of the people. He found a further ominous portent in the rumour that during Lent drops of blood had fallen from the roof of St Peter's Church in York. He lamented that one of Christianity's noblest shrines in England, St Cuthbert's church, should have been desecrated by the heathens – such a thing had not been thought

possible – and implored God to save his country. This re-
sounding and bloody deed served as a suitable prelude to
Viking aggression in western Europe.

During the restoration of the ruins of the twelfth-century
priory on Lindisfarne, English archaeologists found a curious
carved stone apparently dating from soon after the assault
on the earlier monastery and illustrating the dreadful event.
On one side of the stone were carved the various symbols
of Christianity: the cross, the sun and the moon, God's
hands, and worshippers at prayer. On the other side the
attackers are seen, swinging their swords and battle-axes as
they advance in single file, dressed outlandishly in thick
jerkins and narrow trousers. This stone from Lindisfarne is
a poignant monument – carved, perhaps, by some Anglo-
Saxon monk who witnessed this early example of Viking
pillage?

At the end of the eighth century, and the beginning of
the ninth, many similar Norwegian raids took place on
Northern England, on Scotland, and on Ireland. Some of
these forays, known from literary sources, seem to have been
launched from what is now Scottish soil: from Caithness and
the Shetlands, the Orkneys, and the Hebrides. Archaeological evidence suggests that, when the Viking raids began,
the islands were already to some extent colonized by Norwegians, who had presumably found them virtually uninhabited. They were conveniently situated as bases for
raids down either side of Scotland and records of several
such assaults can be found in the chronicles. In 794 there
was an attack on the monastery at Monkwearmouth (near
Sunderland); where, incidentally, the Vikings ran into a
disastrous storm which cost them heavy loss of life. In 795
there were descents upon St Columba's monastery on Iona,
and the little Irish island of Rechru (Lambay). During this
year the Norwegians also raided the coast of Wales. In 797
they plundered Kintyre in Scotland, and St Patrick's Isle,

Isle of Man. In 802 and 806 they revisited Iona and again
laid it waste.

Such were the first pirate raids, which reached their peak
in the ninth century. They were mainly carried out by
lesser chieftains rather than by kings and earls, who had
bigger objectives in mind. The Norwegians began them, but
the Danes and Swedes soon followed suit. These minor raids
were continued throughout the whole of the Viking period.

Political Expansion

As an example of Viking activity in this section, Askeberg
names the military operations carried out at the beginning
of the ninth century by the Danish King Godfred, partly to
the south-east against the Slavs (the Wends and Obotrites)
of the Baltic coasts, partly south-east against Friesland, that
is, against Charlemagne. Godfred is said to have moved the
Slav town of Reric (probably in Mecklenburg) to the head
of the Slie Fjord in Slesvig, and shortly before his death in
810 he launched a sudden and well-planned attack on
Friesland, a province of Charlemagne's empire. With a fleet
of two hundred vessels he broke through the coastal defences
and occupied the country, imposing on it a tribute of 200
pounds of silver. This was no pirate raid and equally it
was not a colonizing venture (although as mentioned earlier
it is often difficult to distinguish between the two). It was
calculated and sudden warfare aimed at the conquest of
territories which were politically and commercially valuable
to King Godfred.

Colonization

The biggest Viking campaigns in the west were, however,
undoubtedly motivated by a colonizing impulse, and it is
these which give the great demonstrations of power of the

Viking period. They occurred in the latter half of the ninth century and the beginning of the tenth, being resumed in the early part of the eleventh century. Although the leaders were predominantly Danish and Norwegian, Swedes also played their part in them. During this period large parts of northern France, England, and Ireland, were occupied and ruled by the Vikings. The invasions were usually led not by heads of states, but by men of high rank. These leaders often held equal powers, with no one supreme commander. The Vikings insisted on this equality. When the Franks on the River Eure asked the Vikings who their leader was, they answered in the famous words 'We are all equals!'* It was invasions of this kind which penetrated to Hamburg and to Paris; which, under the sons of Ragnar Lodbrok, reached England, and, under Rollo, northern France; meanwhile Norwegian Viking chiefs attacked Ireland. The usual method adopted was for the armies to occupy base camps along the coasts during the winter months, and in spring to advance towards their goal; the colonization of the invaded country. Within the category of colonizing expeditions must be included the previously mentioned Norwegian voyages into the Atlantic, to the Faroes, Iceland, and Greenland. Here, however, there was no need to fight for colonies; it was simply a question of taking up land which was almost or completely unoccupied.

Commercial Expansion

The fourth and final type of Viking activity comprises the journeys in search of new trading opportunities. Little information survives about those to the west, but a great deal about those to the east. Swedish scholars insist that the

* Nevertheless they maintained strict discipline among their forces, especially towards the end of the Viking period; a chieftain and his warriors were obviously far from equals.

immense outburst of activity from Viking Sweden to the
south and south-east was directed to commercial ends. The
mercantile pressure maintained by the Vikings through
three hundred years, and the political significance of their
activities during this period, will be considered more closely
in a later chapter.

Origin of the Word 'Viking'

In a book about the Vikings it is natural to try to establish
the actual meaning of the word 'Viking'.

It is reasonable to suppose, although the evidence is not
conclusive, that the word is of Norse origin, because it is
rarely used in contemporary literary sources outside Scandinavia: the Frankish annals use the word *Normanni*, the
Anglo-Saxons call them *Dani*, and although these terms certainly refer respectively to Norwegians and Danes it seems
from the contexts that they were often used for Northmen
in general. In German chronicles they are called *Ascomanni*,
that is to say 'ashmen', because their ships were made of
ash. In Irish sources they appear as *Gall* ('stranger'), or
Lochlannach ('northerner'), and to the former were sometimes
added the words 'white' (for Norwegians) or 'black' (for
Danes), presumably after the colours of their shields or
mail-coats.

In Byzantine and Arabic sources the Swedish Vikings are
called *Rus*, a word borrowed from the Slavs who in turn had
taken it from the Finns, whose name for Sweden is *Ruotsi*.
According to Stender-Petersen, *Ruotsi* is a Swedish loan-
word meaning 'oarsmen', and he also maintains that the
word βάραγγοι (Old Norse *Væringjar*) given to Scandinavian
warriors by the Greeks in the late Viking period originally
meant 'trading agent capable of giving security for his part
in a deal'. In Spain the Vikings were known by the Arabic
term *Madjus* ('heathen wizards').

As to 'Viking' itself, Adam of Bremen, the German ecclesiastical historian writing about 1075, testifies that the word was used by the Danes themselves. He writes of 'the pirates whom they [the Danes] call Vikings but we [the Germans] call Ashmen'. What is the origin of the word? Is it Norse, or a foreign borrowing?

If it is Norse it may be related either to *vig* 'battle', or to *vik* 'creek', 'inlet', 'fjord', or 'bay'. The first is plausible enough semantically but doubtful on phonological grounds. Derivation from *vik* 'bay' on the other hand has found much support; a Viking was a pirate who lay hidden in fjord, creek, or bay, waiting to pounce upon passing vessels. We shall return to this explanation later. It has also been suggested that the word was related to the Norwegian place-name *Vik*, the lands on both sides of the Oslo Fjord, and so meant a man from that region; but this theory is unacceptable, as the sources show that people of this region were called *Vikverjar* or *Vestfaldingi* (the latter term, meaning men from Vestfold, is used in the Frankish chronicles which tell of the Viking attack on Nantes in 843).

If, on the other hand, the word 'Viking' is not of Norse origin, it could be related to the Old English word for camp, *wic*, Latin *vicus*. On this theory, the Vikings were, to the Anglo-Saxons, 'the camp folk'. This etymology was put forward by the great Norwegian linguist Sophus Bugge, and it is a fact that the word existed in Old English long before the Viking Age. The Swedish scholar Wadstein suggests yet another explanation; he agrees that the word originates in Latin *vicus* which he interprets 'town' rather than 'camp'. The Vikings were then town-dwellers, and as the inhabitants of the earliest towns were mostly seafaring merchants who were often enough prepared to bargain with weapons as well as money, the shift to the meaning 'pirate' would not be unlikely. Wadstein considered that the town of Slesvig provided an excellent example, the word 'Viking'

perhaps originating there; a 'Sles-viking' would be a
typical Baltic pirate of that town.

The Danish authority on the early Viking Age, Johannes
Steenstrup, differed sharply from both Bugge and Wadstein,
claiming that the word Viking is too rarely used in Anglo-
Saxon sources for it to be of Old English origin; he concluded that it must be Norse. He rebutted Wadstein by
pointing out that the inhabitants of the many foreign towns
whose names ended in -*vic* were never known as 'Vicingar'.

Several other explanations have been offered: that the
word is related to *vikja*, 'to move, turn, pass' – bringing to
mind a pirate moving off with his loot – or to the noun
wikan, 'a seal', since the Vikings were dexterous seal hunters;
but these notions have found little support.

A theory which has won considerable acceptance, being
supported, for example, by the Swedish linguist Elias
Wessén, is one which derives Viking from the Norse word
vík ('creek, inlet') already mentioned. On this theory a
Viking is one who dwells in a creek or inlet, such being the
natural hiding-place for a pirate on the watch for plunder.
Fritz Askeberg objects that there was nothing characteristically Viking about lying in a sheltered creek – all sailors
did it – whereas Vikings chose islands for places of refuge
and bases from which to launch attacks. Thus the island of
Jeufosse in the River Seine served for many years as headquarters of the Vikings in their attack upon Paris. Later the
Vikings moved to a couple of islands near Rouen, nowadays
part of the mainland, but still called Le Houlme ('the islet').
At the mouth of the Loire lies the island of Noirmoutier,
famous for its wine and salt, where in 834 the Vikings established themselves so thoroughly that the natives left. The
Vikings brought over houses from the mainland, and for a
long time used the island as a base for their raids on the
hinterland of the Loire.* Askeberg gives several other

* These Vikings were the *Vestfaldingi* mentioned above.

examples: the Île de Groix off Southern Brittany where a
Norwegian burial ship has been found; the island of Camargue where the Vikings had a permanent camp in 860;
the island of Walcheren at the mouth of the Scheldt, used
by the Danish chieftains Harald and Rorik; and Thanet
and Sheppey in the Thames, which served as winter
quarters in the year 850 during the great Danish invasion
of England. If, says Askeberg, the Scandinavian pirates were
named after the terrain they favoured in mounting their
attacks, they would be called 'Eyings' ('islanders'), not
Vikings.

Askeberg has his own hypothesis. According to him the
masculine noun *víkingr* was used only in Denmark and
the West Norse area (in eastern Scandinavia the word was
væringi). It was used, however, not only to denote Northerners, but also generally in the meaning 'sea warrior who
makes long journeys from his native land'. The feminine
noun *viking* signified 'nautical raid to distant shores'.*

The first element of 'Viking' he maintains, is not Old
Norse *vík* 'creek', but derives from *víkja*, 'to move, turn
aside'; its basic meaning is 'receding curve, corner, or
nook'. *Landi víkr*, for example, means 'the land recedes' or
'curves back'. The feminine noun *víking*, then, originally
signified 'deviation, departure, or absence', and the masculine noun *víkingr*, 'one who makes a detour', or 'one
who absents himself from home'.

However, this ingenious interpretation which fits so well
the modern conception of the Viking has not met with wide
approval, though it deserves consideration.

* Both these nouns, it must be observed, refer only to those Viking
raids which fall into the first two categories mentioned on p. 31.

EARLY RECORDS

Very little material is available in contemporary literature
about the peoples, lands, and towns of Scandinavia during
the Viking period. What there is survives rather by chance.
Three writers of quite different types have made their con-
tributions. At the end of the ninth century the Anglo-Saxon
king, Alfred the Great, wrote about trade-routes in the
North Sea and the Baltic. The much-travelled Arab merchant Al-Tartushi gave an account of his visit to Hedeby
(Hedeby–Slesvig) about the middle of the tenth century.
About a hundred years later the German ecclesiastical historian Adam of Bremen described the geography and
peoples of Scandinavia, the town of Birka, and the temple
at Old Uppsala.

Alfred the Great, King of Wessex, the great adversary of
the Vikings in England, was a highly educated man who
attempted earnestly to enlighten his people. He took it upon
himself to have translated into Old English the world history written about 400 by the Spanish monk, Orosius, and
to supplement this by an account of contemporary knowledge about the lands and peoples of northern and central
Europe. For this purpose he employed, at least in part,
primary sources; that is to say, he relied upon the experiences and opinions of travellers in those lands. As far as
Scandinavia was concerned, he related conversations he had
had with the Norwegian Ottar from Helgeland about
northern Norwegian trade and industry, the trade-routes
to the south, to Skiringssal on the west coast of the Oslo
Fjord, and thence to Hedeby. He recorded too what he
heard from the Anglo-Saxon Wulfstan of a journey he had
made eastward from Hedeby into the Baltic to the town of
Truso, at the mouth of the Vistula river. Such early accounts
are obviously of the greatest importance.

Ottar told King Alfred of his home in the remote north,

of his reindeer herds, of the tribute he gathered from the Finns – walrus teeth, bearskins, and birds' feathers – of the lengthy journey he had made round the North Cape to the White Sea. The walrus, Ottar says, has fine strong teeth, and from its skin excellent rope can be made. Here is the 'North Way', the great trade-route, which he knows so well; particularly the southern stretch from Helgeland to Skiringssal, a voyage which takes more than a month, even with favourable winds. Ottar's descriptions of the countries and islands are, in their main features, reliable, and he gives a splendid general picture of the geography and natural characteristics of northern Norway: the broad wastes to the east and the narrow habitable coastal strip to the west. He ventured as far south as the Oslo Fjord and Slesvig simply because he knew that the markets for his goods were much better there; both Skiringssal and Hedeby were thriving market towns; but let us hear in King Alfred's words what Ottar said of the passage south from the Oslo Fjord:

From Skiringssal he said that he sailed in five days to the port called *aet Haeþum* [Hedeby], which lies between the Wends, Saxons, and Angeln, and belongs to the Danes. As he sailed from Skiringssal Denmark lay to port, while to starboard for three days was the open sea; and after that there was a further two days sailing before Hedeby was reached, during which time Gotland [Jutland] and Sillende [South Jutland] and many other islands lay to starboard. Here the Angles had lived before they came to this country [England]. During those two days islands belonging to Denmark lay to port.

Also through King Alfred, we hear from the Anglo-Saxon trader Wulfstan about his journey from Slesvig eastwards into the Baltic:

Wulfstan said that he left Hedeby and came to Truso after seven days and nights, and that the ship was under sail all the time. Wendland lay to starboard, while to port were Langeland, Lolland, Falster, and Skane, all of which belong to Denmark.

After that Burgendaland [Bornholm], which has its own king, was seen to port, and, after that, first the land called Blekinge, then More, Oland, and Gotland, all belonging to the Swedes. Right up to the mouth of the river Vistula, Wendland lay to starboard all the way.

Like Ottar's, this description is a reliable geographical account of one of the early trade-routes; and together they constitute our first real knowledge of the north.

Another and slightly older source of information (from *c.* 880) is Rimbert's biography of Ansgar, whom he succeeded as Archbishop of Hamburg and Bishop of Bremen. Included in it are several valuable eyewitness accounts, particularly of the Swedes, but also of the Danes. The biography of Rimbert himself can also be mentioned, although it follows the rather stereotyped pattern of hagiographical works.

About the year 950, Hedeby was visited by an Arab merchant Al-Tartushi from the Caliphate of Cordova. Although the oriental must have felt completely out of his element under those northern skies, he did provide us with a short description of Hedeby–Slesvig, the town at the head of the Slie Fjord.

Slesvig is a large town at the very far end of the world ocean. It has freshwater wells within the city. Its people worship Sirius except for a few who are Christians and have a church there. A feast is held to honour their deity and to eat and drink. Any man who slaughters a sacrificial animal – whether it is an ox, ram, goat, or pig – fastens it up on poles outside the door of his house to show that he has made his sacrifice in honour of the god. The town is poorly provided with property or treasure. The inhabitants' principal food is fish, which is plentiful. The people often throw a newborn child into the sea rather than maintain it. Furthermore women have the right to claim a divorce; they do this themselves whenever they wish. There is also an artificial make-up for the eyes; when they use it their beauty never fades, on the contrary it increases in both men and women.

Later he adds:

I have never heard such horrible singing as that of the
Slesvigers – it is like a growl coming out of their throats, like
the barking of dogs only still more brutish.

We are here provided with a number of specific facts
about Hedeby, which there is very little reason to disbelieve.

Adam of Bremen wrote his history of the Archbishops of
Hamburg about 1075. Some of his information on the Scandinavian countries was possibly first-hand, but it is evident
that most of his knowledge, particularly that about Denmark, was obtained from his superior, Archbishop Adalbert
of Bremen, and from his personal friend the Danish king,
Swein Estridsson. Historically speaking, Adam's works are
far from reliable, yet it is worth reporting here some of the
material of his fourth volume covering the geography and
ethnography of the north.

Denmark consists almost entirely of islands; its main part,
Jutland, stretches north from the river Eider, and from there it
takes five or seven days to reach Aalborg. The shortest crossing
to Norway is from the Skaw at the tip of Vendsyssel. The barren
soil of Jutland is sparsely cultivated, and large towns exist only
where fjords cut into the land. Fyn is separated from Jutland
by a narrow strait which stretches from the Baltic to the town of
Aarhus, whence one can sail to Fyn, to Zealand, to Skane, or
right up to Norway.

A further fifteen Danish islands are mentioned.

When one has passed the Danish islands a new world opens
up in Sweden and Norway: two vast northern countries still
very little known to our world. The well-informed King of
Denmark has told me that it takes a month or more to travel
through Norway, and that one can hardly journey through
Sweden in two.

Adam comments upon the fertile Swedish soil producing

rich crops and an abundance of honey, and upon the cattle-breeding which, he says, surpasses that of all other countries. Many foreign goods are imported, and the Swedes are short of nothing. He then enthuses over the virtues of the Swedes in a fashion which brings to mind Tacitus's description of the Germans; but he adds, however, that the Swedes are very intemperate about women. Every Swede has two or three or more women according to his means, and the wealthy and the princes have many more. They are excellent fighters on land or sea, and although they have rulers of ancient lineage the monarchy depends upon the will of the people. Among Swedish towns mentioned by Adam are Birka, Skara, Sigtuna, and Old Uppsala. Of the last named he describes the famous sanctuary which will be referred to again in Chapter 14.

Norway, says Adam, is the remotest country in the world and stretches north to an extreme latitude. Its rugged mountains and intense cold makes it the least fertile of lands, only suitable for cattle-grazing. The herds pasture far out into the wastes. The Norwegians are brave warriors not softened by luxurious living: 'Forced by the poverty of their homeland they venture far into the world to bring back from their raids the goods which other countries so plentifully produce.' They are frugal in their eating as they are simple in their life and habits. Adam also mentions the forest and the arctic fauna of Norway, the aurochs, elk, blue fox, hare, and polar bear. Of the towns he refers only to Trondheim. Finally, he mentions Helgeland, Iceland, Greenland, and Wineland (in North America) as the northernmost countries of all.

CHAPTER THREE

The Ninth Century

THE DANES

King Godfred, the impetuous and ruthless ruler of Denmark, was murdered in 810, while daring, under the very eyes of Charlemagne, to lay hands upon the coast of Friesland. His death put a temporary stop to the Danish plans, but the Godfred episode must have been a lesson to Charlemagne because he instigated an extensive coastal defence programme to protect his northern frontier. His son and successor, Louis the Pious, continued these precautions, and Frankish fleets were stationed in river mouths not only in Friesland, but all along the north-east coast of France, including the Seine; and near Boulogne an ancient watchtower of the time of the Emperor Caligula was converted into a primitive lighthouse. For the first twenty years of his reign Louis the Pious managed to safeguard the country from northern attacks – except for two minor Viking skirmishes in 820, one in Flanders, the other at the mouth of the Seine. France was weakened not by invasion, but by internal conflict between the Emperor and his sons, which gradually drained its resources. In 834 when Louis, by strenuous exertions, had once more established his position, the first large-scale Danish attack since the death of Godfred was launched on the coast of Friesland. The coastal defences were completely overrun, and the Danes without hesitation turned on Dorestad – the trading centre of Friesland – which was captured and looted.

The wealth and property of Dorestad had long been a severe temptation to the Danish Vikings. The town was situated almost in the centre of Holland, south-east of Utrecht, not far from the point where an ancient tributary, the Lek, joined one of the arms of the River Rhine, 'the winding Rhine'. The rivers run in different courses nowadays, but a small town near to where the junction used to be is still called Wijk bij Duurstede ('the little place near Dorestad'). Dutch archaeologists have found the site of a Carolingian fort built before Viking times, probably by Charlemagne himself. Between the fort and the fork of the Rhine lay Dorestad, a place stretching for over half a mile along the river, protected by palisades and gates.

In early texts Dorestad is called *Emporium* which means 'market-town'. In the early Viking period it and Quentovic (perhaps the modern Calais) were the Frankish Empire's main trading ports on the North Sea coast. Quentovic was the centre of the trade with England; having both a customs house and a mint. Dorestad was no less important: here was minted Charlemagne's famous 'Dorestad coinage', eagerly sought and, indeed, copied by the Northerners. From Dorestad, too, sailed the stout big-bellied Frisian vessels carrying the products of France to Norway and the Baltic countries. In its prime, the fifty years or so from 780 to 834, Dorestad was reputedly the largest trading centre in northern Europe.

The Danish storming of Dorestad in 834 was followed by several others, in spite of every effort on the part of the Franks to restore the coastal defences. Repeatedly the inhabitants had to stand by and watch their town ravaged and plundered by the Vikings. However, it took more than fire and looting to destroy the old towns. As long as the reason for their existence remained it was quite simple to rebuild the simple wooden houses and repair the palisades and earthworks. Dorestad survived for another generation. Then in 864 the real catastrophe struck the town – but not in the shape of yet another Viking raid. A series of tidal waves, followed by extensive floods, put a decisive end to this defiant town. Large parts of Friesland and Holland were inundated, and the vast sand dunes which had formerly stretched out from the coast towards England were swept away. This calamity was described in the chronicle in these words:

Strange portents were observed in the sky, and these were followed by plagues, gales, tidal waves, and floods. The waters of the Rhine were forced back by the sudden inrush of the sea, drowning masses of people and animals in Utrecht and all over Holland. From then on, the River Lek was embanked with dikes, and the Rhine changed its course towards Utrecht, while at Katwijk it completely silted up!

In other words the river which was the artery of Dorestad's trade failed it; this was Dorestad's real death-blow. Its place was taken by other towns with more stable river conditions, such as Utrecht and Deventer.

It was not only the strength of the Frankish Empire which had kept the Danes in check until 834. Trouble at home in Denmark also played its part. There was strife between King Godfred's sons and a pretender called Harald, who had ingratiated himself with the Emperor Louis the Pious by becoming a Christian. In 827 Harald was finally driven out of Denmark* by Godfred's son, Horik, who remained king until his death in 854.

Horik did not favour individual pirate ventures; he wanted any Danish Viking raids to be under his direction. In 845 he dispatched several hundred vessels up the Elbe to ravage Hamburg, and at the same time sent Ragnar Lodbrok with a smaller fleet up the Seine to capture Paris.

---

* Before his banishment however, Harald managed to secure, though only for a short time, a foothold in Denmark for that great missionary of the North, Ansgar.

A few years before these events the Emperor Lothar had
been forced to cede the island of Walcheren at the mouth
of the Scheldt to two Viking brothers called Rorik and
Harald – the latter being in all likelihood the pretender
banished from Denmark in 827.

Louis the Pious died in 840, and the Frankish Empire
entered a period of decline and division which was ended
when the Treaty of Verdun of 843 divided the Empire up
between the Emperor's three sons: the east being allocated
to Louis the German, the west to Charles the Bald, and the
centre to Lothar. However, they were not on the best of
terms with each other, and, moreover, had difficulties
in controlling their feudal subordinates. Here was the
perfect opportunity for the Vikings, and they promptly
seized it; the great invasions of France by Danes and
Norwegians began. From 840 onwards their armies swept
across France: Rouen, Paris, Chartres, and Tours were
the principal objectives, and the occupying forces were
strong enough to winter in France. Soon Charles the Bald
was forced to come to terms by buying-off the invaders with
danegeld.

Back in south Denmark Horik still reigned, and evidently
in a most shrewd and far-sighted fashion. Although he
himself was not a Christian, he realized the diplomatic advantages which could be gained by allowing Christian missionaries to have access to his country, and in many ways
he was most obliging to Ansgar, whose two visits to the
Swedish town of Birka were brought about only through
Horik's intervention. Finally, however, his enemies proved
too strong, and in 854 he was killed with almost the whole
of his family, except for a young son also called Horik.
A few years later the Viking Rorik (mentioned above in
connexion with Harald), with the help of the Franks, gained
a foothold in southern Denmark, the part 'which lies between the River Eider and the sea' – in other words the

region at the neck of the Jutland peninsula controlling the trade-route to the Slie Fjord. Exactly how long he held sway in this strategic position is not known.

As for the young Danish king, Horik, he is said to have been sympathetic to Christianity, and to have banished from Slesvig the anti-clerical earl, Hori. After him, and indeed throughout the second half of the ninth century, history does not tell of any Danish rulers of importance. It was as if during this period Denmark was applying all her energies abroad. Her leading figures were independent princes rather than monarchs: chieftains who made convenient and profitable alliances with each other in order to fulfil their aspirations to foreign conquests and pillage. During this period the invasions of northern France and eastern England were primarily carried out by these Danish Vikings, although even then there was some participation by Norwegians and Swedes.

A summary of developments in France about 900 will be useful at this point. From about 860 a seven-year campaign was waged by the Danish and Norwegian Vikings against the Franks in the region of Jeufosse, the island in the Seine north-west of Paris, mentioned earlier. Charles the Bald decided to dislodge the Northerners entrenched there, and was joined in this effort by his brother Lothar. Large Frankish forces descended upon the island, but to no avail; and in the meantime the third brother, Louis the German, invaded France from the south-east, forcing Charles to leave the Vikings. Subsequently, however, another Viking marauder, Weland, commanding two hundred vessels, offered to clear the Vikings from Jeufosse for Charles, for a fee of 5,000 pounds of silver, plus sufficient rations for the operation. This kind of offer was by no means rare among the Vikings, who were frequently willing to fight as mercenaries against their own countrymen. In the ninth century there were many Viking chiefs who cultivated the habit of wintering abroad and selling their services, like the Italian *condottieri*, to the highest bidder.

The Franks, and not least Charles the Bald, sought other methods than the payment of danegeld to keep the Vikings out. Fortifications seemed to be the answer, especially when they included stone or wooden barriers thrown across the rivers which were the Vikings' favourite approach. The Vikings never really relished attacking strong fortified positions, and much preferred to take them by ruses and stratagems. The famous stories of the mock burial* of Hasting in Luna, which, by the way, the Vikings believed was Rome, in north Italy, and of the Vikings' use of birds, bearing fire beneath their wings, against wooden fortresses, illustrate their cunning.

Charles the Bald set about constructing a bridge across the Seine at Pitres, south of Rouen, which would prevent the Viking ships from penetrating farther into the Seine valley; but this barrier does not appear ever to have been completed. Meanwhile, the Vikings were busy elsewhere in northern France: in the west, south of Brittany, for example, where Norwegian raiders forced their way up the River Loire. Worse was in store: there lay ahead the great thirteen-year devastation which was to afflict France, Flanders, Belgium, and western Germany. This invasion was, in fact, started off in England, where Alfred the Great's resolute defence culminated in his victory at Edington in Wiltshire in 878. When this news reached a newly-arrived Danish fleet in the Thames, a majority of its leaders decided to turn towards the Continent. Reinforced by other hordes in the neighbourhood, the 'Great Army' sailed for Belgium, and in April 878 reached the Scheldt, with Ghent as their first goal. During the thirteen years which followed, 'there did not exist a road,' says the chronicle, 'which was not littered with dead, priests and laymen, women, children,

* See p. 60.

and babies. Despair spread through the land, and it seemed that all Christian people would perish.' It cannot be said that the Vikings did not meet any resistance; both the eastern and western Frankish kingdoms (roughly equivalent to the Germany and the France of today) defended themselves fiercely. These two countries had been created following the agreement in Meersen in 870, when Lothar's empire was divided between two new kings, both named Louis. The eastern Louis (III) was not very successful in his clashes with the Vikings. He lost his only son in the battle of Thuin, fell sick himself, and died a few years later, leaving the Rhine and Moselle valleys at the mercy of the Northerners. The western Louis, a grandson of Charles the Bald and son of Louis the Stammerer (apparently the Carolingians named their kings after their shortcomings rather than their strong points) was more successful. In 881 he defeated the great army at Saucourt, near the Somme. The Franks triumphantly sang 'Lord, preserve and honour him'; but this prayer was not answered. Shortly afterwards this brave soldier, not yet 20, was killed – though not in battle. The story has it that he caught sight of an attractive young girl and spurred after her; to save herself she fled through a low gateway, and he in pursuit rode into it, killing himself. When his brave and capable young brother Carloman died in 884, also as the result of an accident, the responsibility of defending western Franconia fell upon the inadequate shoulders of Charles the Stout. He had already shown his incapacity when, in 882, he faced the enemy with a huge army behind him, at Elsloo, near Maastricht – and bought them off instead of waging battle. Three years later, when the Vikings were making no headway at all in their siege of Paris, which was stoutly defended by Count Odo, Charles the Stout arrived on the scene with a strong force, and once again played the poltroon. First he again paid danegeld in return for renewed promises from the

Vikings to leave the country and, secondly, he allowed
them to pass the two bridges blocking their further progress
up the Seine, and spread over the whole land. The Vikings
proceeded to loot and burn the entire countryside for a
further number of years. Not until 892 did the great army
meet its match – in the form of a great famine and pestilence.
The Vikings quickly gathered what was left of their men
and ships, and returned to their bases in Kent, where their
army was dissolved a few years later. France's respite from
the Viking invader was only brief, and in the summer of
896 Viking vessels were once again sailing up the Seine,
their number gradually increasing; until the Frankish king,
Charles the Simple, was at his wits' end. About the year
900, however, the character of the Viking invasions of
Frankish territory changed. From being purely marauding
raids they began to assume a more settled and pacific purpose, and in fact became deliberate efforts at colonization.

In England the infiltration began in 835 with a Danish
raid on the mouth of the Thames. During the next thirty
years these assaults continued, with varying results for the
Northerners. The islands of Thanet and Sheppey were commonly used as bases for these attacks; from his camp on
Thanet the Danish chieftain Rorik (who had settled in
Friesland) plundered both Canterbury' and London about
850. The next year, however, he was defeated by King
Æthelwulf of Wessex, who ruled most of southern England,
and who for some years was able to instil into the Vikings
a healthy respect for the West Saxon fighting man. On the
whole it is clear that southern England was capable of defending itself and at times even of defeating the Vikings in
their own element – the coastal waters. In 865, therefore,
when the Viking attacks were intensified, they were
launched in a more northerly direction and based on East
Anglia. This was the starting point of an attack by a united
heathen army led by the three sons of Ragnar Lodbrok,

Ivar the Boneless, a most clever strategist, Ubbi, and Halfdan. This army turned towards Northumbria, and captured York on 1 November 866. In 867 it invaded Mercia and took Nottingham, after which the Mercians paid danegeld and the Vikings retired to comfortable positions behind the Roman walls of York, where they spent the winter. From here the army proceeded south-eastwards towards Peterborough and Ely, capturing and killing King Edmund of East Anglia. It was now the turn of Wessex, which was defended by King Æthelred and his brother Alfred, the latter being the famous leader who was to prove in the long run the only man able to keep the Vikings at bay.

On 8 January 871, the English came off best at the battle at Ashdown though the victory was not decisive; three months later Æthelred died and was succeeded by Alfred who, to gain time, was at first content to buy the Vikings off. During 871-2, they wintered in London, and Halfdan emerged as their army's supreme commander. A couple of years later they moved northwards again and divided their forces. One part under Halfdan moved into Northumbria, and with York as a base began a definite system of colonization, the first Danish effort of the kind to occur in England. Halfdan divided the land among his men, took part in several battles against the Picts and Britons in southern Scotland, and then vanished from history. One surmise is that he went across to Northern Ireland and met his death there.

The other part of the Viking army, led by three chieftains, made its headquarters at Cambridge, and from there in 876 resumed violent attacks on Alfred's kingdom of Wessex. Their land assault from the north was reinforced by naval attacks on the Channel coast; and their combined pressure on Alfred was so intense that according to the legend he became a fugitive, sheltering in the forests and swamps. However, in the most difficult circumstances, he eventually managed to raise fresh forces, and set upon the Danes at Edington (Wiltshire) in the spring of 878, and decisively defeated them. The Vikings fell back into East Anglia where their king, Guthrum (who had become Christian at Alfred's instigation), followed Halfdan's example by distributing land among his men in an effort at colonization. London remained in Danish hands until Alfred liberated it in 886.

Alfred was now the acknowledged leader of free England. He still had to fight battles, however, and particularly after 892 when the 'Great Army' returned from the Continent; but four years later, in 896, the Viking forces dispersed. Alfred, one of England's great rulers, died three years later, in 899.

The position in England at the time of his death was this: the whole of southern England, including London, was free, under the leadership of Wessex. North of the Thames, as far as Chester, and to the east of a line roughly coinciding with the old Roman Watling Street, was the region occupied and colonized by the Danes and called the Danelaw – comprising parts of Mercia and Deira as well as East Anglia. In these areas the Vikings settled down as farmers, a society of free men with their own laws, customs, and language – the latter still evident in the place-names of this part of the country. The centre of the Danelaw was the area round the 'Five Boroughs': Lincoln, Stamford, Leicester, Nottingham, and Derby – more or less the area from the Humber and the Wash in the east, to Wales and western Mercia in the west. Farther to the north, the area centred on York was also occupied by Vikings, but these included many of Norwegian origin. Judging from the traces which still survive in the dialect and place-names, Lincolnshire must have been a centre of Danish colonization. Country folk speaking the local dialect still use many Danish words in their speech: 'lathe' for 'barn', 'bigg' for 'barley', and 'bairn' for 'child', to mention only a few. Danish place-names are abundant: well over half of the early settlement names in Lincolnshire are of Danish origin, particularly noticeable being those ending in '-by' and '-thorpe', meaning 'village'. Even today farmers in Lincolnshire call the homestead a 'toft', the meadow an 'eng'.

The Scandinavians introduced into Anglo-Saxon England their own territorial divisions, and the names of these, too, survive in places. For instance in many northern areas hundreds (as they are elsewhere called) are known as 'wapentakes', which derives from Old Norse *vápnatak*, a word used at the sessions of the ancient Thing or assembly. The assembled people showed their agreement with a decision taken or a sentence passed, by striking their shields or rattling their spears, and this was called *vápnatak* 'grasping of weapons'. Later this word was applied to the place where the Thing was held, and then to the whole of the region from which the Thingmen were gathered. Both Thingoe (Old Norse *þinghaugr* 'assembly mound') and Thingwall (Old Norse *þingvöllr* 'assembly field') are to be found among place-names in the north and east of England. Yorkshire to this day is divided into three Ridings, East, West, and North; Riding derives from Old Norse *þriðiungr* 'a third part'.

The Vikings of the Danelaw no doubt helped themselves to the more substantial properties, and the native inhabitants had to take second place within the farming community. There is no reason, however, to believe that the Anglo-Saxons were pushed out or enslaved by the invaders, though very little evidence is available on this point.

THE NORWEGIANS

Norway in the ninth century was not unified by powerful monarchs as was Denmark. Danish kings apparently exercised considerable powers in the first half of the century: indeed King Godfred's domain included parts of southern Norway. Norway itself at the same period, and indeed much later, was divided between numerous local kings and earls. In the second half of the century, at a time when Danish kings are little heard of, a monarchy in Norway began to develop. This was directly related to Harald Fine-hair's great victory in 872 (or possibly a few years later) at Hafrs Fjord and the subsequent rise of his power. It was his régime, indeed, which is said to have led to the Nor-wegian colonization of the Faroe Islands and Iceland, as the men who joined these expeditions were malcontents and refugees from his tyranny. On the other hand, the first Norwegian raids on the Scottish islands and mainland and on Ireland were ordinary pirate attacks, which only later changed into efforts to annex new territories.

The treeless islands of Shetland, Orkney, and the Hebrides had long been inhabited when the Norwegians landed on them at the end of the eighth century. This is proved by buildings still in existence – the towers known as brochs for example – as well as by archaeological investigation. However, the Pictish population could not put up any effec-tive resistance, and soon these archipelagoes became Nor-wegian bases for attacks upon the Scottish mainland, and more particularly upon Ireland. In the last quarter of the ninth century the situation was changed by the unification of Norway under King Harald Finehair, who pursued his enemies right across the North Sea, seizing the Orkneys and establishing a strong earldom there under his direct sovereignty.

Long before that, however, Norwegian Vikings had settled in Ireland. A green island with a mild climate, it was a prize well worth fighting for. The Viking raids on Ireland increased in intensity after 800; the earliest record in the Irish annals dates from 807. The country was divided into

numerous petty kingdoms which were consolidated, theoret-
ically at least, into two alliances – the south-west and the
north-east – conditions favourable to a swift and successful
advance in the island. Within twenty years the Norwegians
were the masters of many parts of the country in both the
east and the west; they had come to stay. Ireland had been
Christian for some four hundred years, had been the centre
of classical education in Europe during the migration period,
and a base for extensive and fanatical missionary activity
on the Continent. Its innumerable monasteries were rich in
art treasures, many of which now fell into the hands of the
Vikings. In 839 the Norwegian chieftain Turgeis arrived
with a large fleet in the north of Ireland, and declared himself, as the annals relate, 'King of all foreigners in Erin'.
He was an active soldier and a confirmed pagan. He
founded Dublin and tried to replace Christianity by the
worship of Thor; in Armagh, the holy of holies of Christian
Ireland, he officiated as pagan high priest. The Irish, however, gradually learned to put their resistance in better
order; in 844 they captured him and drowned him in
Lough Owel.

A few years later Danish Vikings made their appearance
in Ireland. The Irish cunningly took advantage of the
enmity between the Danes and Norwegians, and allied
themselves with the newcomers. Together they inflicted a
heavy defeat upon the Norwegians in 851; but later in the
same year their luck changed. There arrived on the scene
another chieftain from Norway, Olaf the White, who reconquered Dublin, restored Norwegian supremacy, and finally
chased the Danes out of Ireland. For the next twenty years
Olaf ruled in Dublin, and his brother Ivar in Limerick.

These were hard times for the Irish. Their hatred of the
intruders, expressed in typically flowery and colourful language, can be seen in the following passage from a contemporary chronicle:

If a hundred heads of hardened iron could grow on one neck, and if each head possessed a hundred sharp indestructible tongues of tempered metal, and if each tongue cried out incessantly with a hundred ineradicable loud voices, they would never be able to enumerate the griefs which the people of Ireland – men and women, laymen and priests, young and old – have suffered at the hands of these warlike, ruthless, pagans.

That the Vikings in Ireland were mainly Norwegians is proved beyond question by the written sources, but even if such proof were lacking the evidence of place-names and archaeology would establish that conclusion. Ninth- and tenth-century graves in Norway contain many objects and jewels of Irish origin; scarcely any similar finds have been made in Denmark and Sweden.

In 870 Olaf the White was recalled to Norway, and the government of Dublin was taken over by his brother Ivar. The rest of the century the Norwegians spent in fighting; partly among themselves, and partly against the Danes under King Halfdan in northern England. Finally, in 901, the Irish captured Dublin from the Norwegians.

The Norwegians were also active in other areas around the Irish Sea. Large tracts of south-west Scotland and north-west England were in their power, and their prolonged occupation in this and the next century is shown by the abundance of Norwegian place-names in Cumberland, Westmorland, Lancashire, and even farther east in Northumberland and Yorkshire. The Isle of Man did not escape them either, and here too, especially in the north of the island, there are many place-names which testify to Norwegian settlement.

The Norwegian raiders went south as well. No doubt they participated with the Danes in the great battles of northern France, but their favourite hunting grounds in France were along the Atlantic coast, particularly the Loire estuary which served as a gateway to the centre of France.

One of their many raids was on Nantes in 843, when that
flourishing town was sacked and burned by the Vestfaldingi
(the Norwegians from Vestfold in the Oslo Fjord). Subsequently they made a lengthy stay on a small island in the
mouth of the Loire called Noirmoutier (New Monastery),
from where they were able to control the extensive trade of
the area, which mainly consisted of wines and salt. Also,
from this convenient base they were able to penetrate the
lower reaches of the Loire, and meddle in the affairs of
northern France. One would have thought that these
achievements would have satisfied the Norwegian desire to
expand along the coasts of western Europe, but neither
Norwegians nor Danes called a halt. Ahead of them lay
Spain and the Mediterranean, where the two nations appear
to have operated together. This was a direct continuation of
the work of the Norwegian Loire-Vikings, while the Danes
operated in the Mediterranean under two leaders, Björn
Ironside, son of Ragnar Lodbrok, and Hasting.

Literary sources (Arab among them) mention two campaigns to the Iberian peninsula: the first in 844, the second
a few years later (859–62); the latter penetrated to the
western Mediterranean.

The earlier expedition of 844 followed the coast of Galicia
to the Christian town of La Coruña; but here the Vikings
were out of luck. The natives proved too strong, and the
Viking ships with their red sails (as the sources relate) passed
on. They sailed along the Portuguese coast, and eventually
reached and captured Lisbon. Shortly afterwards Cadiz and
even Seville suffered the same fate, a remarkable feat, considering that these towns were in the very centre of the
mighty Caliphate of Cordova. At this point, however, the
luck of the Vikings changed; and after a heavy defeat they
were happy to exchange their prisoners for food and clothing,
and soon the whole fleet was homeward bound.

The later venture was far more ambitious: under the

leadership of Björn Ironside and Hasting a fleet of sixty-two vessels set out from Brittany. This time, however, they found the coasts of Spain heavily guarded, and they were only able to sack Algeciras just inside the Straits of Gibraltar. From here they crossed to Nekor in Morocco, and eight days later sailed north past the Balearic Islands to the southern shores of France, where they set up camp on the island of La Camargue in the Rhône delta. Here they remained for some time, causing great annoyance and detriment to the inhabitants of the coastal and delta areas. In 860 the Vikings turned east into northern Italy, where they pillaged Pisa. To this campaign belongs the story related by Frankish historians, of how Hasting arrived at an Italian town, now vanished, called Luna, which he mistook for Rome itself and which he captured by the famous ruse of the mock funeral.* In 862 the expedition was back in Brittany via the Straits of Gibraltar and the Spanish coast. An Irish source recounts that the Vikings brought back with them to Ireland a number of black prisoners, which seems quite feasible.

We must still consider the ventures of the Norwegians into the North Atlantic. These were no doubt begun before Harald Finehair came on the scene, though conditions created by him in Norway must have stimulated the colonization of the Faroes and Iceland. The first settlement in the Faroes, according to such medieval Scandinavian sources as the *Saga of the Faroe Islanders* (in the *Flateyjarbók*) and Snorri's *Saga of King Harald*, occurred during the reign of Harald Finehair, in other words in the latter part of the ninth century. Contemporary foreign sources do not mention the Faroe Islands, although it has been pointed out that

* The Vikings said that Hasting had died as a Christian, and they claimed a Christian burial for him in the city church. But during the ceremony Hasting suddenly arose, killed the bishop, and sacked the town, backed by his men who had been secretly armed all along.

the Irish geographer Dicuil, who lived in France, was probably referring to the Faroes when he mentioned, in a document dated about 825, 'the many islands in the northerly part of the British Sea which can be reached from the north British islands within two days if the wind is favourable'. And he continues: 'These islands, unnamed and uninhabited from the beginning of time, are now abandoned by the hermits who had sought seclusion there, owing to the arrival of northern pirates. These islands are full of sheep and many varieties of sea birds.' These references fit the Faroes admirably; and the thought that the Celtic hermits, in their pious wanderings – which history so often records – through the northern seas, should have reached this isolated group of islands and settled with their Christian religion and their sheep, is not at all unlikely. When the land-starved Norwegian emigrants arrived in these distant islands about 800 they evidently found them not wholly waste, and the ejection of the Celtic hermits who had sought sanctuary there must have been an easy matter. This early colonization of the Faroes by the Norwegians took the form of casual and intermittent arrivals by emigrant groups or families, and was, therefore, not important enough to be mentioned in the later, Icelandic, literature of the thirteenth century. This records only the settlements which occurred after Harald Finehair had driven large numbers of dissidents out of his united kingdom. Thus, the *Saga of the Faroe Islanders* says: 'There was a man called Grim Kamban. He was the first man to settle in the Faroe Islands – in the days of King Harald Finehair. At that time many people fled [Norway] because of the king's tyranny. Some settled in the Faroe Islands and built up farms there; others went to other uninhabited lands.' There is also the story of the outlaw called Nadd-Odd who took land in the Faroes apparently towards the middle of the ninth century. In Iceland too there is reason to suppose some sparse Celtic habitation before the

arrival of the Norwegians, despite Snorri's assertion that the
colonization of Iceland from Norway was due entirely to
pressure brought to bear by Harald Finehair. Here too we
can refer to the work of the Irishman, Dicuil, who says that
Irish monks had found their way to Iceland. And finally, it
is related in Ari Frodi's *Íslendingabók* (*c.* 1130) that the
Norwegians in Iceland encountered Irish Christians, called
papar, who soon left 'because they would not live alongside
heathens'.

Scandinavian written sources mention three distinct men
as being the first to reach Iceland. Who really did get there
first is not known. There was Nadd-Odd, mentioned above,
who on a voyage from Norway to his home in the Faroe
Islands was thrown off course by a gale, and came upon an
unknown land – Iceland – which on his return he called
'Snowland'. The second was the Swede, Gardar, who was
also driven off his course north of Scotland, and so found
Iceland. He wintered there, and on his return to Sweden
named the island which he had discovered 'Gardarsholm'
after himself. The third was a Norwegian, Floki, from
Rogaland, who had heard of Nadd-Odd's discovery of
Snowland and started off in three ships in search of it, sailing
via the Shetlands and the Faroes. He reached his destination
and wintered there, twice in difficult conditions, but found
the place little to his liking, and upon his return named it
'Iceland'. These three journeys in all probability occurred
just before Harald Finehair's rise to power in Norway.

The most important source of information on the settlement of Iceland in the late ninth and early tenth centuries
is the famous Icelandic *Landnámabók* (the book of the taking
of the land), which dates from shortly after 1200. In this
are mentioned the names of some four hundred settlers, and
in several cases the places they came from. They were mostly
from western Norway, but quite a few came from the
Norwegian colonies on the northern Scottish islands and in

Ireland. Only a few came from eastern Norway and Sweden, and none at all from Denmark. It is important to notice the influx from Ireland, as it supports the opinion expressed by the Norwegian archaeologist Shetelig, that 'the Celtic elements may have done much to make the Icelanders distinct from the Norwegians, and they certainly made a valuable contribution to later Icelandic literature'.

The correct and traditional manner in which a colonist chose his settlement-site in the new country was to throw his 'high-seat pillars'* overboard and follow them as they drifted at the will of the gods. Where they landed the emigrant would take land for himself and his followers, build his house and a temple for the gods. By the end of the century several thousand settlers had made their homes in Iceland. One of the earliest of these, the Norwegian Ingolf Arnason, found that his 'high-seat pillars' had drifted ashore on the south-west coast of Iceland, at a spot where there were warm steaming springs. He settled there, naming the place *Reykjavik*, which means 'bay of smoke', and today this is the capital of the country. This new community of Iceland retained a Norwegian legal system and the Norwegian language, but it was not long into the next century before the Icelanders began to consider themselves as independent Nordic people.

THE SWEDES

We now turn to Sweden. In an earlier chapter, reference was made to Volga Russia during the eighth century, with its two Khaganates (or empires) – the Khazar in the south, and the Bulgar in the north. The situation here made it a

* The wooden beams framing the seat-of-honour of the master of the house.

logical task for active Scandinavians to link up, by way of
the Volga, these two great powers, and to exploit to the full
the obvious trading possibilities. The Swedes were just the
people for this task. Their colonizing and mercantile ventures, begun in the Baltic, were later developed, still in an
easterly direction, towards Lakes Ladoga and Onega. The
steady development of trade brought about a meeting between northern and southern cultures, not only by way of
the Volga, but also by the much nearer (though possibly
more dangerous) route down the Dnieper to the Black Sea
and Byzantium. This meeting – not of course a single one
under specific circumstances – took place in the early
decades of the ninth century. That it really did happen is
proved by two convincing pieces of evidence, one archaeological, the other literary. To the north of the little modern
town of Staraya Ladoga (Old Ladoga) close to the southern
end of Lake Ladoga, Russian archaeologists have excavated
a large settlement. The deepest and oldest layers of this site
prove to be Finnish. On top of these were found the remains
of square log-houses with stone hearths, quadrangular wells
of wood, stables, etc., and other remains which establish
with certainty that from the early ninth century to the
middle of the eleventh there was on this site a large settlement of Swedish origin. When the Swedish colonists or
'Rus' arrived in the land which now bears their name, it
was here that they first settled.

The Old Norse name of this place was Aldeigjuborg; let
us consider for a moment the situation of this town with
regard to its communications with the south and east. Between Lake Ilmen and Lake Ladoga runs the River Volkhov; Aldeigjuborg stood about six miles south of the river's
entry into Lake Ladoga. In the Viking period anyone
wanting to travel south would follow a route from Aldeigjuborg along the River Volkhov to the town of Novgorod
(Old Norse *Holmgarðr*). From there the way continued

across Lake Ilmen and along the length of the River Lovat. By this route the area east of Polotsk was reached, near which three great rivers have their source: the Dvina, which runs into the bay of Riga; the Volga, which flows to the east; and the Dnieper which runs due south to Kiev and the Black Sea. If, on the other hand, the traveller from Aldeigjuborg wished to journey to the lands to the east, he could either go by the rivers Syas and the Mologa to the Volga bend, north of Rostov, or he could sail up the River Svir, which joins Lakes Ladoga and Onega, and from Onega follow the river to the almost circular White Sea, where he would reach the trading centre of Byelosersk, and go farther south along the Syeksna towards the Volga. From Aldeigju- borg, therefore, both these ways provided openings for bold, adventurous men, in search of trading opportunities. The furs, the honey, and the slaves went through territory held by Finnish and Permian tribes down to the Khaganate of the Bulgars. From there they continued, carefully guarded, by way of the Volga, to the Khazar Empire, to Itil and across the Caspian Sea to join the caravan routes to the Caliphate of Baghdad.

The literary evidence for the contacts via the East between Sweden and the distant south comes, oddly enough, from a western European – Frankish – source. It exists be- cause of the chance occurrence that, in the spring of 839, messengers from the Rus to the Byzantine Emperor, Theo- philus, were prevented from returning the way they had come by unrest among tribes on the Dnieper. A Byzantine mission was about to set out, sent by Theophilus to the Frankish Emperor, Louis the Pious, and this took the mes- sengers under its protection as far as the town of Ingelheim on the Rhine where Louis was residing. We know about it from a chronicle written some twenty years later by the Frankish bishop, Prudentius, who was possibly in Ingelheim at the time. He writes that Louis, who had suffered from

Viking attacks on his empire, insisted on examining the Rus messengers in order to satisfy himself that they were not Viking spies. Whether they cleared themselves Prudentius does not tell us, but he does disclose two items of the greatest interest to historians. The first is that the Emperor Theophilus, in his letter to Louis, said that the messengers declared that they had been sent from the Khaganate of Rus. The second is that the messengers themselves told Louis that they were not Swedes, though they were 'of Swedish origin'. The Danish scholar Stender-Petersen, was the first to recognize the significance of this evidence. Prudentius tells us no more about the messengers' home country, but the main point is clear: the men were from a northern Khaganate of Rus wherever that may have been. Before the middle of the ninth century, therefore, the colonizing Swedes had created in northern Russia a settlement so independent that they could send their own ambassadors to the distant Byzantine Emperor.

Stender-Petersen suggests that these emigrant Swedes, the Rus, were originally farmers who, recognizing the important possibilities of trading with the East, decided to develop them first by way of the Volga and later the Dnieper. This interpretation is open to doubt, but there is no altering the fact that Swedish expansion was essentially mercantile in character. Between Viking activities in western Europe and Swedish enterprises in the east, there is this difference; the Swedish journeys were undertaken in search not of plunder but of new markets. How independent of its homeland (the kingdom of Uppsala) this Rus Khaganate in northern Russia may have been, is difficult to say.

The many oriental coins and other objects, particularly from the tenth century, found on Gotland and in the Uppland trading-centre of Birka, suggest that the Swedish kingdom had a deep interest in its affairs. Scandinavian archaeologists and historians commonly hold the well-

founded belief that from the end of the ninth century
Sweden was politically active in developing trade between
eastern and western Europe by securing for itself control,
not only of the long routes through Russia, but also of the
port for the North Sea, Hedeby, which came into Swedish
hands in about 900.

To call this complex activity 'the foundation of the Russian Empire' is to provoke violent disagreement among
eastern and western European historians. Such an expression
is in any case misleading, implying as it does the establishment of the Great Russian state. In eastern Russia along
the Volga, there were independent Khaganates which owed
nothing to Swedish colonization, and many independent
states too in southern Russia side by side with Byzantine
territories. Yet it is interesting to note how the traditions of
their origin developed a fixed form in the literature of the
Rus themselves, a kind of birth myth of the nation with a
kernel of historical truth. The *Russian Primary Chronicle*, or
Nestor's Chronicle, dating from shortly after 1100 and said to
have been compiled by the monk Nestor in the cave
monastery of Kiev, gives the following account of the origin
of the Rus people:

The Varangians came from beyond the sea and demanded
tribute from the Finnish and Slav peoples. They were driven off,
but in due course dissension broke out among the peoples,
and became so acute that they said 'Let us find a prince who
will rule us and judge justly.' So they went across the sea to
the Varangians, to the Rus (for the Varangians were called Rus
as others were called Swedes, Normans, Angles, and Goths),
and they said to the Rus 'Our land is large and fruitful but it
lacks order. Come over and rule us.' Three brothers were chosen
as rulers, and these three agreed to go over, taking all their family
and all the Rus people with them. It is further related that the
eldest brother, Rurick, came to Ladoga and built there the town
of Aldeigjuborg [Old Ladoga]. The second, Sineus, settled near

the White Sea [at Byelosersk], and the third, Truvor, at Isborsk
in southern Estonia. Two years later the younger brothers died,
and Rurick assumed full power, after which he went south and
built on the shore of Lake Volkhov the town of Novgorod (Holmgarðr). From here the Rus people spread south, to Smolensk
among other places.

From this account in *Nestor's Chronicle* it is fair to assume
that when the Khaganate of Rus sent ambassadors to the
Byzantine Emperor in 839, its capital was Novgorod, although Stender-Petersen is of the opinion that the Khaganate came into existence at an earlier date, and in the
upper Volga region of north-east Russia. So far there is no
conclusive evidence for either contention.

Nevertheless, it is certain that the Rus folk penetrated
rapidly south along the Dnieper as far as Kiev. We know
the names of two of their rulers: Höskuld and Dyri. By 860
this advance had already progressed so far that the Rus
were able to attack Byzantium itself, which, however, was
quite capable of defending itself. Soon after this we hear of
more friendly contacts between the Greeks and the Rus.

The Rus prince Höskuld who captured Kiev adopted the
Christian faith, but his example does not seem to have been
followed extensively by the Rus people, and his successors in
Kiev maintained paganism for a long time.

Apart from the Khaganate of Novgorod, which originated
as we have seen, from Aldeigjuborg, there was another line
of Scandinavian expansion, beginning at Polotsk on the
Dvina. Headed by a man called Rögnvald, Vikings ventured south along the Dnieper, and in doing so came into
conflict with the Novgorod Rus.

Side by side with these ninth-century Scandinavian probes
into Russia – in east and west, warlike and peaceful– there
gradually developed a widespread commercial activity
whose leaders were the 'Varangians'. Scandinavian names
appear in records of the area, more or less influenced by

Russian forms; Helgi becomes Oleg; Yngvar, Igor; Valdemar, Vladimir; etc. There is no colonization in the sense that the Swedes took over land intending to settle permanently on it. Their motive was to establish (often by violence) trade-routes linking market centres which in due course became towns. This is confirmed by the Arab writer, Ibn Rustah, who reports of the Rus in the mid tenth century, 'they have no lands, but live entirely on what they import from the countries of the Slavs'.

By 900 Swedish influence had become a very important factor in Eastern Europe; an extensive network of river routes had been established, and at least two permanent Scandinavian Khaganates set up, one based on Novgorod and the other on Kiev.

CHAPTER FOUR

The Tenth Century

THE DANES

The early part of the tenth century seems to have been a lean time for the Danes. Their protracted conflicts in France and England, especially the serious defeats which they suffered in Brittany in 890 and at Louvain in 891, had sapped their strength, so that when the Swedes attacked southern Denmark about 900 the Danes were unable to put up an effective defence. The king of Denmark at that time was Helgi (if he is not a mythical figure). He was defeated by 'Olaf, who came from Sweden and took possession of the Danish kingdom by force of arms'. Our authority for this is Adam of Bremen, who records it in 1075, quoting as his source his contemporary, the Danish king, Swein Estridsson. The Swedish Olaf ruled over southern Denmark for some time with his sons Gnupa and Gurd, and they were succeeded by Gnupa's son Sigtryg. Gnupa's wife Asfrid set up two rune-stones in memory of Sigtryg, which have been found not far from Hedeby at the head of the Slie Fjord in Slesvig. These two inscriptions (together with the testimony of Adam of Bremen) offer ample proof that a Swedish royal house reigned in southern Denmark for a generation. We next hear of Gnupa in 934 when, as we shall see, he was involved in conflict with the Germans. In the light of what has been said in the last chapter about European trading conditions, it is not surprising that the Swedes were anxious to control Hedeby. It was the connecting link between the North Sea

and Baltic trade. The Swedes could now combine the two
activities, and even extend them to their own great centre,
Birka, on Lake Malar.

How were the Danish Vikings in northern France faring
in the years just before and after 900? Historical sources are
very reticent on this matter. The St Vaast Annals cease
about 900, and the monk of Reims, Flodoard, does not
begin his narrative until some twenty years later. Dudo, the
canon of Saint-Quentin, who a hundred years later wrote
his fulsome panegyric on the dukes of Normandy, is not
always reliable. What is certain, however, is that Rollo,
later to become the first Duke of Normandy, spent the first
decade of the century with his Vikings fighting battles in
the Seine valley with varying turns of fortune. His nationality is uncertain : Dudo declares he was a Dane, but Scandinavian sources call him a Norwegian. His army was no
doubt predominantly Danish. Rollo established himself
firmly in northern France, and in spite of occasional setbacks and defeats was not easily got rid of. It is most probable that he was the real ruler of Normandy for some time
before the Frankish king, Charles the Simple, made it over
to him on condition that Rollo swore him allegiance and
protected Normandy against further Viking attacks. Rollo's
official elevation to the dukedom, which took place at St
Clair-Sur-Epte in 911, marks an important stage in the
history of France ; Rollo kept his promises to Charles and
defended the country against his compatriots. He settled his
men on the land to cultivate it and stood by Charles in
subsequent troubles. When turbulence racked the King's
territories, Rollo, in alliance with his Norwegian friends the
Vikings of the Loire, kept order in Normandy until Charles
could re-establish his authority.

In this way the dukedom of Normandy sprang up as a
Scandinavian colony on the banks of the lower Seine, extending in the north-east to Picardy (at the River Bresle),

and in the south-west to Brittany (at Saint-Malo), while just across the Channel lay the tempting and prosperous south of England. Rollo's duchy comprised approximately the modern Departments of Seine Inférieure, Eure, Calvados, Manche, and most of Orne. The place-names of the province bear ample testimony to its Scandinavian origin, especially near the Seine, the waterway along which the Vikings arrived. There are numerous village names with the Norse second elements -*tofte*, -*garde*, -*lond*, -*torp*, and others have as their first elements Norse personal names such as Thorbjörn, Asmund, Ulf, and Ragnar. Rollo was baptized as early as 912, and by that time the great Viking invasions of Frankish territory were over. One or two smaller raids occurred in the tenth century, but in general Rollo and his successors made themselves widely respected.

In England, during the first decades of the tenth century, the Danish Vikings did not fare at all well. Edward, the eldest son of Alfred the Great, was a stubborn and skilful warrior who, in alliance with his sister Æthelflæd (called 'the Lady of the Mercians'), now successfully made war on the Danelaw. His strategy was to establish and garrison a number of strongholds which served as bases for attacks on the enemy. The Danes were driven back, suffering one defeat after another; no reinforcements from their homeland were forthcoming. In the north of England also the Danes were hard pressed, sometimes by the Anglo-Saxons, and sometimes by Norwegians and Britons penetrating from north-west England and Scotland. By 918 the losses and the withdrawals of the Danes had become so considerable that the Anglo-Saxons were masters right up to the Humber. In the north the Norwegian Rögnvald, who had come from Ireland and had captured York, was forced in 920 to make a hasty peace with the invincible Edward who, after his sister's death in 918, had added the whole of Mercia to his kingdom.

In 924 Edward died and was succeeded by his son Athelstan, another brave warrior, who in 927 conquered the whole of Northumbria and York as well. Ten years later he met the combined forces of his enemies in the north and north-west, led by Olaf of Dublin, and defeated them at a place called Brunanburh, which has never been located. Athelstan became one of the greatest kings of Wessex and England; King Harald Finehair sent to him an embassy with the gift of a magnificent Viking ship. When Athelstan died in 939 he was ruler of Wessex, Mercia, Northumbria, York, and the Danelaw, and parts of Cornwall. In the 940s his brother and successor, Edmund, ran into severe trouble, and was involved in battles with Norwegian invaders from Dublin. At this time the Danes appear as bitter enemies of the Norwegians whom they resisted in alliance with the Anglo-Saxons. In 945 Edmund was murdered by a returned outlaw, and his brother Eadred inherited the throne. A few years later the Norwegian Eric Bloodaxe appears on the scene as king of Northumbria and later of York, battling against, among others, one of the Dublin kings. He was ousted, in 954, and his domains taken over by Eadred, who died childless the following year. For some years to come England was untroubled by Vikings, and at this point we turn to consider what was happening in Denmark itself.

In the thirties of the tenth century Swedish rule in southern Denmark was drawing to a close. It was not the Danes who were mastering the Swedes, however, but the Germans. In 934 the Swedish king of Hedeby, Gnupa, attacked the coasts of Friesland: an unwise venture which evoked immediate retaliation by the German king, Henry the Fowler, who raided Hedeby, defeated Gnupa, and forced him to accept baptism. Two years later Henry died. Adam of Bremen (quoting Swein Estridsson as his authority) gives the following account of the end of Swedish rule in Denmark: 'When he [Sigtryg, son of Gnupa] had reigned a

short while, Hardegon, son of Swein, who came from Nortmannia, took his royal powers from him.' Now Nortmannia
can mean either Normandy or Norway, so it is impossible
to say where this Hardegon came from, or who he was.
Swedish rule came to an end soon after 936, and the next
dynasty of kings of Denmark was connected not with
Hedeby–Slesvig, but with Jelling in South Jutland.

At Jelling, about 940, lived the first known king of this
line, Gorm the Old, and his queen, Thyri, whose runic
memorial stone honours her as *Danmarkar bót*, which means
'Denmark's restorer' – a distinction which tradition attributes to Thyri's improvement of the great rampart, the
Danevirke, along the southern frontier. The inscription
reads: 'King Gorm made this memorial to his wife Thyri,
Denmark's restorer.' Hans Brix has read the inscription so
that the phrase 'Denmark's restorer' referred to Gorm himself, but philologists in general do not accept this. Gorm
was a pagan, and a wooden burial chamber was built in a
huge mound at Jelling as a double grave, doubtless for him
and his wife. Connected with this mound, which still
exists, the Danish archaeologist Dyggve has traced a large
triangular plot of ground framed by upright stones marking
a consecrated place. It can be assumed that Gorm died
sometime in the 940s; we know no more of him. Of his
famous son Harald Bluetooth we know much more, because
under him Denmark regained its former strength. However,
this recovery did not begin immediately. To start with, there
was clearly a strong German influence in Denmark, which
revealed itself in the establishment of Denmark's first three
dioceses. Adaldag, the German Archbishop of Hamburg,
became Primate of the kingdom. Thus Christianity was
officially introduced to Denmark about the middle of the
tenth century, when Harald himself was still a heathen. In
due course, no doubt under German pressure from Otto I,
Harald was baptized by the priest Poppo, who, in the

presence of Harald, endured the ordeal by fire as a demonstration of the power of Christianity. This must have occurred about 960. About this time too, Harald took up arms against Norway, incited by his sister Gunnhild, widow of the Norwegian king Eric Bloodaxe who had been exiled to England. Gunnhild wanted to recover the throne of Norway from her late husband's younger brother, Hakon. Harald Bluetooth agreed to help in this project, but at first had no success. Hakon not only drove him back but took the offensive, and in 957 raided Jutland and Skane and even took possession of the whole of Zealand. After this episode the tide turned in Harald's favour; he drove the Norwegians out of Denmark, invaded Norway, and in a decisive battle in Hordaland defeated and killed Hakon; shortly after 960 he was sole monarch of both countries.

It is this achievement which King Harald Bluetooth, with justifiable pride, stressed on the stone he set up at Jelling in commemoration of his parents, King Gorm and Queen Thyri, and in his own honour. This, the famous Greater Jelling Stone (Pl. 18B), is a remarkable work of art, decorated with intricate carvings in which the figure of Christ crucified and a great lion surrounded by interlaced, ribbon-like ornament, occupy dominant positions. Its runic inscription reads: 'King Harald had this monument made in memory of his father, Gorm, and his mother, Thyri. Harald who won all Denmark and Norway and made the Danes Christians.' This memorial has been called 'the Danes' certificate of baptism', and certainly the consolidation of Christianity in Denmark was the most lasting of King Harald's three great achievements.

Unrest soon began to develop in Norway. Harald Greycloak (a son of Eric Bloodaxe) held power for some time, but the banished Earl Hakon whose father, Sigurd, Greycloak had had burned alive, sought refuge with Harald Bluetooth, and they succeeded in killing Greycloak in a battle

on the Lim Fjord in Jutland. Norway was now divided,
Earl Hakon settled in the north as an independent ruler,
and governed the west as liegeman to Harald Bluetooth,
while in southern Norway Harald himself was king. This was
the situation immediately after 970. Then, however, a
serious danger confronted Harald Bluetooth, coming this
time from the south. In 974, in revenge for Danish attacks
on Holstein, the German Emperor, Otto II, assaulted the
Danevirke and Hedeby. King Harald summoned assistance
from Earl Hakon but, even then, could not keep Otto at
bay. Otto penetrated the Danevirke and mastered the whole
district, establishing there a strongly garrisoned fortress.
This defeat produced quarrels between Harald and Earl
Hakon, disputes deepened by the fact that Harald had insisted on the latter's being baptized. The result was that
Hakon assumed independence in his part of Norway, while
Harald's rather weak efforts to subjugate him from southern
Norway proved fruitless.

To add to Harald's troubles, his son, the violent and virtually heathen Swein Forkbeard, now began to assert himself, although Harald was still nominal ruler of Denmark.
The Danes turned on the Germans in the south, breaking
their power. In 983 the fort which Emperor Otto II had built
near the Danevirke was carried by a ruse and burned down,
and after that Hedeby was besieged. Two rune-stones from
the Hedeby region commemorate warriors killed on that
occasion. One inscription refers to the time 'when men sat
round [besieged] Hedeby'; the other stone, also naming the
Hedeby battle, proclaims itself erected by King Swein –
which must refer to Swein Forkbeard who, presumably as
his father's deputy, commanded the Danish forces in this
battle. Soon afterwards an open breach occurred between
Swein and Harald, and the latter escaped wounded to a
Viking stronghold – possibly built by himself – on the Baltic
coast of Germany; Jumne or Jomsborg, where Wolin now

stands. And here the great Harald Bluetooth died about
986, 'wrongfully wounded and banished for the sake of
Christ', as the pious Adam of Bremen writes. He was buried
not in Jelling but in his own church of the Holy Trinity in
Roskilde. In Jelling, Harald had previously erased his father
Gorm's heathen sanctuary, by raising over its southern end
a great memorial mound, and had, as it seems, prepared a
transfer (*translatio*) of his parent's remains from the wooden
chamber of the northern mound to a Christian burial place.

Swein Forkbeard was a powerful and ambitious ruler.
Without being a Christian himself he tolerated Christianity
and supported the bishop of Jutland, Odinkar, but for political reasons only. His first action, after securing the
southern border of Denmark, was to attack Norway, an
effort in which he was assisted by the Joms-Vikings from
Wolin, led by Earl Sigvald; but the attempt failed. Earl
Hakon won a decisive sea battle at Hjorungavag in western
Norway, which must have taken place about 990. There is
also an unauthenticated story to the effect that Swein Forkbeard waged unsuccessful war against the Swedish king,
Eric the Victorious, who occupied parts of Denmark, and
that Swein was captured by Slavs and finally ransomed at
great cost. In the final decade of the tenth century, Swein
Forkbeard's attentions turned towards England.

After Eadred's death in 955 there was a prolonged period
of peace in England lasting at least a quarter of a century.
Eadred's handsome successor, Eadwig, 'the all-fair', died
young, and his brother Edgar became king. His coronation
was delayed, but when it did take place, at Bath in 973,
the solemn ceremony of the anointing was combined with
an event of great splendour. Acting as oarsmen in the king's
boat were Scandinavian and Celtic princes, and Edgar
adopted the proud title of 'King of England and ruler of
the kings of the islands and the sea'. He is known to have
allowed the Danelaw some degree of autonomy. With his

death in 975 the peace was broken and bad times returned
again. His eldest son, Edward, a violent and turbulent
prince (who nevertheless was later recognized as a saint),
was murdered after only four years of rule by the retainers
of his half-brother Æthelred. So this young man, weak,
inconsistent, haunted by the guilt of his brother's murder
(for which he was certainly not responsible), became king,
to be nicknamed Æthelred Unræd – Æthelred 'No-Counsel'.
An irresolute ruler was the last thing that was needed now
because the Viking raids were resumed and intensified. Between 980 and 982 there were minor descents on the south
and west coasts, but from 988 onwards the attacks were
heavier, and were made not only by the Danes but, particularly in the west, by the Norwegians as well.

The year 991 was a particularly disastrous one for
England, for then began the fatal method of buying-off the
Vikings by payments of danegeld – thousands of pounds of
silver year by year which brought no more than temporary
respite. In reality the Vikings sailed from place to place and
sold local peace for cash payments. In the south the Normans
observed with sympathy and interest this successful policy of
their Scandinavian relatives and, indeed, made their harbours available to them if necessary. This form of support
was checked by a papal negotiator, who made a treaty
between the English and the French, ratified at Rouen in
March 991, though this proved short-lived. In the same year
the Viking raiders on English shores included the famous
Norwegian chief Olaf Tryggvason (by then already baptized). When he arrived on the Thames in 994 he was accompanied by the Danish king, Swein Forkbeard. With a
joint fleet of about a hundred longships, and presumably at
least two thousand men, they attacked London; but the city
beat off the assault, and the Vikings had to be content with
plundering south-east England and finally accepting sixteen
thousand pounds of silver to leave. Olaf Tryggvason left for

good to take up the task of conquering Norway; Swein Forkbeard returned to England – though not for about nine
years. His return will be discussed later. Meanwhile the
Viking raids along the coasts of England continued inter-
mittently throughout the 990s.

THE NORWEGIANS

In Norway too, the tenth century brought troubled times
and varying fortunes for the different rulers, interspersed
occasionally with periods of peace and progress. In the 30s,
three years before his death at a great age, Harald Finehair
resigned his throne to his son Eric Bloodaxe, who was
evidently more Viking than king. He retained the throne
for only a few years and preferred, when his youngest
brother Hakon, Athelstan's foster son (later called 'the
Good'), was recalled to Norway, to leave the country without a blow being struck. He went to England, where he
twice held thrones, but was killed shortly afterwards. His
widow, the Danish Gunnhild, Harald Bluetooth's sister,
returned to Denmark and, as mentioned above, incited the
Danes to attack the Norwegian king, her brother-in-law,
Hakon Athelstan's foster son. In the second of these attacks,
in 960, Hakon was killed. He had proved a good monarch,
he drew up legal codes – the laws of the Gulathing and the
Frostathing – and organized a militia, which enabled him
to retain only a small personal guard of armed men and yet
be assured of support in cases of sudden attack. He was sen-
sible enough to refrain from forcing Christianity upon completely heathen peasants. All in all he seems to have
deserved the title 'the Good'.

The sons of Eric Bloodaxe, now returned from England,
among them Harald Greycloak, who became King of

Norway and proved a sharp contrast to Hakon the Good, in
both character and actions. He was harsh to great and
small alike. He was so hostile to heathen sacrificial practices
that he sought to suppress them by force, and his reign was
accompanied by storm, failure of crops, and famine. Greycloak did not rule for long; as mentioned above he was
slain on the shores of the Lim Fjord in Denmark, fighting
against Earl Hakon who, with Harald Bluetooth's aid,
avenged the murder of his father, Sigurd. After this event,
which occurred about 970, Norway was divided into three
parts. We have seen the sequel to this division: how Harald
Bluetooth, assisted by Earl Hakon, was defeated by the
Germans at the Danevirke, and how enmity subsequently
developed between Bluetooth and Hakon. Earl Hakon returned to his own domain the heathen he always was, and
some years later, at Hjorungavag, successfully beat off an
attack on western Norway by the Joms-Vikings. He finally
met his end when Olaf Tryggvason, the most picturesque
figure of all the Norwegian Vikings, returned from England
in 995, newly confirmed in his Christian faith by the English
king at Andover, and fully determined to conquer and convert Norway. Earl Hakon was murdered by one of his own
servants, and Olaf proclaimed king by the people of Trondelag. His problem now was to weld together the long
straggling territories of Norway. What happened up at
Trondelag in the north was very different from what might
be done or said in the south and south-west, especially in
Olaf's own homeland, the province of Vik.

In his endeavours to unify and consolidate, Olaf came up
against the demands and pretensions of the Danish king,
Swein Forkbeard, who asserted a traditional Danish supremacy over southern Norway. It was inevitable too that Earl
Hakon's two sons, Eric and Swein, should become Olaf's
bitter enemies. Olaf Tryggvason seems to have been more
warrior than diplomat. In any event he failed to prevent

Swein Forkbeard from winning over to his side, by a series of skilful marriage alliances, the Swedish king, Olaf Skotkonung, son of Eric the Victorious. He married one of Earl Hakon's sons, Swein, to Skotkonung's sister; and the other, Eric, to his own daughter; and to round-off the relationship Swein Forkbeard himself married Skotkonung's mother, the widow of his one-time enemy Eric the Victorious, thus creating a cleverly spun web of alliances.

His quarrel with Olaf Tryggvason came to an end at the naval battle of Svöld in the year 1000. It is disputed whether the location for the battle was in the Oresund, or off the Baltic coast of Germany. There were two aspects to Olaf Tryggvason's situation. One was his failure to hold together his supporters – he was betrayed both by those in Norway and by Earl Sigvald, leader of the Joms-Vikings. The other was his superb personal bravery. Despite his huge longship, the *Long Dragon* – the biggest warship ever seen in the north – Olaf's fleet proved too weak. He was defeated and killed by a superior force. Swein Forkbeard now became overlord of the whole of Norway, although the two earls Eric and Swein, who had been his allies, exercised authority under him in the north of the country.

This, then, was the situation about the year 1000 in Norway and Denmark. Let us look at what took place in the tenth century in the Norwegian sphere of interest in the west, in the old Viking hunting grounds along the Atlantic coasts and islands, and, to begin with, at what happened in Ireland and in the Irish, Scottish, and English areas. We completed our last survey of these regions with the Irish conquest of Dublin in 901. This was a hard blow to the Norwegians. From their bases in the north of England, especially in Northumbria, they prepared their revenge. They struck back, twice in fact – in battles at Confey in 916, and Climashogue in 919, where the Irish were defeated in a gruesome massacre – and by these victories secured the control of great parts of Ireland for over half a century. This was the period when the Ivar dynasty flourished in the kingdom of Dublin, a dynasty which included such famous names as Sigtrygg, his son Olaf Cuaran, and Gudröd. It was during Olaf Cuaran's time, says an Irish chronicler, that Ireland was really penetrated by Norwegian influence: 'There was a Norwegian king in every province, a chief in every clan, an abbot in every church, a sheriff in every village, a warrior in every house', a most effective way of billeting. Besides controlling much of Ireland, Olaf Cuaran, like Sigtrygg, fought extensively in north and north-west England. Christianity now spread among the Norwegians in Ireland: Olaf Cuaran himself died as a monk, in 981, in the monastery of Iona. The year before this the Norwegians suffered a heavy defeat at Tara – the first Irish victory of any importance for many years. With this the Irishmen's fortune improved, and in Brian Boroimhe they found a ruler of remarkable political as well as military prowess. Shortly after 1000 he managed to secure the sovereignty of all Ireland, including Dublin.

In northern England, and particularly in Northumbria, the Norwegians had greatly strengthened their positions, against both the English and the Danes, during the tenth century, largely as a result of the leadership of such warriors as Rögnvald and Sigtrygg (who died a Christian). After 926, however, Northumbria was incorporated into England. Olaf Cuaran later invaded north-west England, to be beaten finally, as already related, at the battle of Brunanburh in 937. In the 940s he and Eric Bloodaxe were alternately kings in York; then came a long period of peace in England under King Edgar. Before we leave this résumé of Norwegian influence in English, Irish, and Scottish regions, mention must be made of Sigurd the Stout, mightiest of the Orkney earls, who became the sovereign of all Scottish and Irish islands, including the Isle of Man, whose tenth-century stone crosses display a significant mixture of motifs, and traditions – Norwegian and Celtic, pagan and Christian.

South towards France, from Ireland and the Irish Sea, went the Norwegian Vikings in the tenth century as they had done before. Reference has already been made to the part the Norwegians played in colonizing Normandy – Rollo may have been a Norwegian. On the Île de Groix, off the south coast of Brittany, one monument of Norwegian activity along the Atlantic coasts has been found in the shape of a burial mound erected over a Norwegian Viking about 900. The mound contained relics of a cremation: a ship, shields, weapons, household articles, tools, fragments of gold and silver thread that had been interwoven in cloth, and various other things. On this spot some far-voyaging Viking, perhaps from Northern Ireland, had died and been buried with heathen rites. During an Irish raid on a Norwegian settlement at Limerick in 968 there were captured, according to the chronicler, 'the Vikings' most treasured possessions; their beautiful foreign saddles, gold and silver, exquisite woven cloth of all colours and kinds, satins and silks in scarlet and green'. It sounds like a treasure hoard where the Vikings stored the spoils captured in raids upon the Orient and Spain.

The Norwegians were also active in the Loire region during the tenth century, as we know from their alliances with Rollo's Vikings from the Seine. We also know of raids on the Spanish peninsula in the 960s: on the territory around Lisbon and on Asturias, where the pilgrim shrine of Santiago de Compostela was attacked. Evidence of contacts with the Arabs in the western Mediterranean has been provided by finds in western Norway of Arab silver coins minted in southern Spain and Africa. There is no doubt that the Norwegians' penetration was extensive.

We must not overlook the North Atlantic 'sphere of

interest'. In the first place, Iceland. On the evidence of the *Landnámabók* the emigration to Iceland was coming to an end about 930; each family arriving on the island needed to claim and settle a substantial piece of land. Iceland was a strange country – some parts good, some parts bad – it was treeless, and most difficult to cultivate, but it had tracts of good grassland. Birds and eggs were plentiful on the rocks, there was an abundance of fish in the rivers, no lack of seals and whales along the shores, and driftwood was plentiful on the beaches. Large flocks of sheep were gradually spreading in the interior, and one man, it is said in the *Landnámabók*, began counting his sheep but had not the patience to continue when he reached 2,400. The number of horses, too, increased as time went on.

Some of the more important early settlers set up their own law courts, but it soon became necessary to organize justice on a wider scale, and it is said that a man called Ulfljot was sent home to western Norway to study methods of law and justice. Three years later he returned to Iceland, and in 930 the Althing was set up, and Ulfljot became Iceland's first *Lögsögumaðr* (law speaker). The annual session of the Althing was held in the summer in a place called Thingvellir in the south-western part of the island. Here the people gathered to hear the laws proclaimed, to lodge their suits, to worship their gods, to display their skills, and to buy and sell. Several local Things were established over the island.

The story of how Iceland became Christian is as dramatic as everything else in the history of the saga island. It began with several unsuccessful endeavours at the end of the tenth century. First, in 981, the Icelander Thorvald returned to the island accompanied by a Saxon priest called Fridrek. Their ardent missionary efforts, however, ended in killing, outlawry, and their banishment from Iceland. The zealous, fanatical Olaf Tryggvason sent missionaries to Iceland on two occasions. First he dispatched Stefni in 987; but Stefni seems to have been a man of Olaf's vehement temper, for he too was chased off the island. Olaf's next missionaries, in 997, were an Icelander and a German (Thangbrand) who, after some initial progress, found themselves involved in killing and banishment. At last came success. Two Icelanders, Hjalti Skeggjason, and Gizur the White, arrived from Norway. They began boldly by pulling down a shrine to the gods, and then with a crowd of followers went to the Thing and proclaimed Olaf Tryggvason's message, calling upon the islanders to accept Christianity. At that moment a volcanic eruption occurred, and was promptly interpreted as a sign of the wrath of the ancient gods. A skirmish developed, but the law speaker, Thorgeir, in whose hands the case was placed, proved himself master of a difficult situation. On the third day he called the people together and warned them sternly of the division that would destroy them, if they could not reach agreement. The people understood the issues involved and, says the Icelandic source,

it was then agreed by law that all should become Christians, and that all who were not baptized must become so; but certain ancient laws were retained, such as the practice of exposing children and the eating of horseflesh. Sacrifice in secret to the old gods was also permitted, but if witnessed by others incurred the sentence of banishment from the island for a period of three years. A few years later this relic of heathen practice was abolished.

The decision to retain secret sacrifices for a time may seem naïve, but it no doubt served as a safety valve. Thorgeir, himself a heathen, knew exactly what he was doing. This remarkable occasion, probably unique, on which an entire people, although a small one, decided to change its religion, suggests that the situation was ripe for such a radical change of faith, and that the traditional religion had lost its power. In this simple yet dramatic manner Iceland adopted Christianity in the year 1000.

About a hundred years before this incident took place, Greenland was discovered by a Norwegian called Gunn-björn. His visit was involuntary: he was sailing from Norway to Iceland, but was blown off his course and sighted eastern Greenland presumably only at a distance. He felt no temptation to get to know it better, and on his return to Iceland he called it Gunnbjörn's Skerry. Almost a hundred years were to elapse before that land was again reached. In 982 a man called Eric the Red, born in Jaeren in Norway, was outlawed from Iceland for three years for committing a murder. He decided to spend his period of banishment travelling, not to the south or the east, but in a westerly direction, to take a closer look at these rocks, which people still talked about. So he found Greenland, and it must be presumed that with his companions he worked his way south down the icebound and impenetrable eastern coast of the great island, rounded Cape Farewell, and eventually reached the more accessible and hospitable south-westerly part of the island. Somewhere here the daring band of men wintered, and in the following summer made a camp at a fjord which Eric the Red consequently named after himself. He went farther along the west coast towards modern Godthaab, 'giving names to many places'. He stayed in the country two more winters, and then, his banishment over, returned to Iceland from his resourceful expedition. Wishing to return to the discovered country accompanied by as many people as possible, Eric named it Greenland, hoping that this attractive name would induce people to go with him. He succeeded, for there were many in Iceland still anxious to travel, possibly because there was already a dearth of land there. So in the following summer, with a fleet of twenty-five vessels carrying the emigrants, their women, and domestic animals, they set out; and in 985 or 986, after a

hazardous journey, a small majority reached their destination. We may assume that further colonization occurred
rapidly in the succeeding years. Greenland and Iceland
were alike, offering more or less the same means of livelihood, and the climate there was approximately the same
as it is at its best today (i.e. milder than in the later Middle
Ages). Eric the Red chose to settle at the head of Eric's
Fjord, where he built his farm (Brattahlid) which was excavated by the Danish archaeologist Poul Nørlund, in 1932.

At an early stage the colonization of Greenland was concentrated in two large and separate districts, the 'Eastern
Settlement' in the south, where Brattahlid and the Thing-
place Gardar were located (near modern Julianehaab); and
the 'Western Settlement' in the north, south of modern
Godthaab. Danish archaeological investigations have unearthed the remains of some two hundred farms or holdings
in the Eastern, and about a hundred in the Western Settlement; quite a substantial total, though not all these places
were established in Eric's time. Agriculture was never
widely practised in Greenland, and the people lived off
their domestic animals (cows, horses, sheep, pigs, and goats)
and off the products of these animals (butter, milk, meat,
and cheese), as well as from hunting and fishing. Eric the
Red's farm in Brattahlid, where he lived for the rest of his
life, consisted of a house with several rooms, built of stone
and turf, and a great hall (with a well in the middle), round
which were the stables and stores. Thick walls of turf kept
out the biting cold, and a little farther up in the mountains
were the barns and sheepfolds.

The introduction of Christianity to Greenland, and the
Norse discovery of America, were both effected in 1000, by
one and the same man: Leif Ericsson, the son of Eric the
Red. We shall return to him later.

THE SWEDES

Sweden at the beginning of the tenth century was as strong
as Denmark was weak – hence the Swedish occupation of
parts of southern Denmark at that time. We know from
Wulfstan's account that not only Gotland but also Oland,
and Blekinge were under Swedish rule. This sphere of
Swedish domination was now extended to south Slesvig,
where a Swedish prince settled at Hedeby and controlled
its transit-trade. Between Wulfstan's description, which
makes no mention of Swedish rule in southern Denmark,
and Hardegon's eviction of the Swedish King Sigtryg from
Hedeby shortly after 936, there is a period of about forty
years representing the span of Swedish domination of
southern Denmark. How large an area of Denmark the
Swedes occupied is not known. Significant perhaps is the
distribution in Slesvig and the southern Danish islands of a
place-name type with a personal name as its first element,
and the second element -*by*. This type is common in the
area round Lake Malar, which suggests that the Swedish
domination was not a local conquest with mercantile aims,
but a real attempt at colonization and permanent settlement. It is, however, unlikely that a short stay of less than
fifty years should have left such lasting traces – unless one
assumes that the Swedish population remained in south
Denmark after the fall of its kings.

On political conditions and events in Sweden itself in the
early tenth century the sources say very little. Two rune-
stones from Skane describe in similar terms a battle at
Uppsala which ended in a defeat for the Danes. One of
them says of Toki 'he did not flee at Uppsala'; the other
says of Asbjörn, 'he did not flee at Uppsala but fought as
long as he had weapon'. This information, combined with
what is revealed by later Icelandic sources, suggests that the
Swedish kingdom of Uppsala under Eric the Victorious was

violently attacked by the Danes, and by Eric's nephew, the famous Viking Styrbjörn, who sought the Swedish throne, but that Eric won a decisive victory in the battle fought on the plain of Fyris, near Old Uppsala.* Sweden fought another famous battle soon afterwards: the battle of Svöld, where, as related earlier in this chapter, Eric's son, King Olaf Skotkonung, and his allies defeated Olaf Tryggvason.

When we come to consider Sweden's enterprises abroad in the tenth century – whether these were in waging war or developing commerce – we find, as we did earlier, that her expansion lay primarily to the east. Yet she undoubtedly took an active part in several developments in western Europe: for example, there were Swedes with Rollo in Normandy. Russia was the main centre of Swedish activity abroad in the tenth century. The great Volga route through the Khaganates of the Bulgars and the Khazars was still navigated by Swedish merchants; and by a lucky chance an Arab eyewitness noted what he saw of the doings of the Rus in the Volga regions. This was Ibn Fadlan who, shortly after 920, was special ambassador of the Caliph of Baghdad to the Khaganate of the Bulgars, and stayed for some time in their capital, Bulgar. His spirited narrative describes his strenuous journey via Samarkand and Bokhara, and recounts how, on the Volga, he met Rus traders and their women, whom he discusses in a lively and vivid manner (see p. 264-5).

Judging from the quantity of Arab coins found in Swedish soil, the stream of silver from Arab sources in the southern parts of Central Asia dwindled during the tenth century and stopped altogether at the beginning of the eleventh. The silver mines were worked-out, and commerce found other routes. For the Swedes in Russia, this meant a more extensive use of the western trade-routes, especially that

* Adam of Bremen's statement that Eric also took Denmark from Swein Forkbeard is not considered trustworthy.

along the Dnieper to the Black Sea and Byzantium. In two treaties, from 911 and 944, between the Rus and the Byzantines there appear several Scandinavian names – more in 911 than in 944. The impression emerges that the Swedes were gradually becoming assimilated with the Slavs.

In 965 the prince of Novgorod, Svjatoslav (or Sveinald), conquered the Khazar stronghold of Sarkel. Of his two sons, Vladimir (or Valdemar) was given Novgorod, while Jaropolk received Kiev. With the help of reinforcements from his Swedish homeland, Vladimir advanced on Kiev in 980, and succeeded in killing his brother. The two Rus Khaganates were now combined, and Kiev became the capital of a Rus kingdom which extended over the whole of western Russia, from the Dnieper to Lake Ladoga. Vladimir was baptized in 987, and became an ardent Christian. After his death, in 1015, he was proclaimed a saint. During his reign the friendly connexions with Byzantium were maintained.

CHAPTER FIVE

The Eleventh Century

THE DANES AND THE NORWEGIANS

In Denmark at the beginning of the eleventh century, Swein
Forkbeard stood out as the undisputed ruler. Since his
assaults on London in 994 and the ensuing raids on southern
England, that country must have been frequently in his
thoughts. From a Viking point of view, conditions were not
unfavourable for realizing these dreams of conquest. Æthelred Unræd had committed a tactical error – which has been
described as a political crime, and which was certainly a
political *bêtise* – by ordering the massacre of all Danes in
his country, an event which occurred on 13 November 1002,
Saint Brice's day. This massacre, in which Swein Forkbeard's sister, Gunnhild, was murdered, aroused violent
anger, and Swein launched two punitive expeditions in 1003
and 1004 into Wessex and East Anglia. Other raids followed
in the ensuing years, although not under Swein's direct
leadership. From 1009 the Danish raiders in England were
commanded by Thorkel the Tall (perhaps a brother of Earl
Sigvald, of Jomsborg) who eventually came into Æthelred's
service. Then, in 1013, Swein Forkbeard resumed command
and with fleet and army launched a rapid and skilful campaign. In a short time he overran Æthelred's kingdom and
then advanced on London, now defended by Thorkel the
Tall. The city held out, and Swein decided to waste no time
besieging it, but turned on Wallingford in order to secure
his hold on Wessex, and from there went on to Bath. Then

London surrendered and Æthelred fled to his brother-in-law, Duke Richard II of Normandy, with whom his wife Emma had already taken refuge. Thorkel the Tall remained in England, but with a force so far inferior to Swein's as to cause him no further anxiety. Swein's task was now accomplished, and he was generally accepted as the sovereign of England. But, on 3 February 1014, he died suddenly at Gainsborough.

The immediate consequence of his death was that the Anglo-Saxon nobles in England turned again to Æthelred in Normandy, and made a pact that, under certain conditions, Æthelred should return home and resume the battle against the Danes. The Danish leader in southern England was now Cnut, Swein's son, who had been campaigning with his father in England while his elder brother, Harald, stayed in Denmark. He was undertaking a big task for such a young man, made the more arduous by the fact that Æthelred's bellicose son, Edmund Ironside, was now one of England's commanders. In these circumstances Cnut decided to return to Denmark in order to raise, with his brother Harald's aid, fresh forces for a decisive attack on the English. He was in luck. For one thing, he was unexpectedly joined by Thorkel the Tall, who for some time had been in Æthelred's service and was a most experienced warrior and a valuable ally, more because of his cunning than the strength of his fleet. Perhaps best of all was the active support of his brother-in-law Earl Eric of Norway.

In 1015 Edmund Ironside, acting against his father's wishes, seized power in the Five Boroughs, and therefore in the Danelaw. Shortly after Cnut and his brother Harald arrived with a large fleet off the south coast, and found facing them Edmund Ironside and Eadric of Mercia – the latter a most unreliable character who, during subsequent developments, changed sides more than once. Battles between the rival forces had varying results, with Cnut making good progress in Wessex, and (via Mercia) also in Northumbria, where the Anglo-Saxon earl was deposed and replaced by the Norwegian earl, Eric. Then Cnut, avoiding the Danelaw, where Edmund was too strong, went back through Mercia to Wessex and prepared for a summer offensive against London, where Æthelred and Edmund were both camped with their armies. Æthelred died there in April 1016, and Edmund was chosen by the Londoners as his successor. Before Cnut had time to cordon off the city, Edmund broke out, and reconquered Wessex; upon which Cnut, leaving a force to besiege the capital, went after Edmund. Edmund, however, proved to be as good a warrior and strategist as his opponent, and, after Cnut's failure to capture London, Edmund defeated him in a battle at Otford gaining the upper hand to such an extent that the opportunist Eadric of Mercia changed his affections from Cnut to Edmund. This proved a doubtful gain: in the following October the two armies fought a pitched battle at Ashingdon in Essex; here at a most critical moment Eadric and his forces fled, transforming an impending victory for Edmund into a heavy defeat.

Both sides were by now exhausted and the time was ripe for a settlement. This was reached when they met on an island in the River Severn and in most solemn surroundings concluded a treaty, whereby Edmund was to have Wessex, and Cnut the rest of England, including the unconquered London. Hardly was this peace concluded, when the brave Edmund, who had lived up to his nickname 'Ironside', died suddenly, in November 1016. The consequence was that Wessex now acknowledged Cnut, who thus became king of the whole of England. Under him Earl Eric ruled in Northumbria, Thorkel the Tall in East Anglia, and the treacherous Eadric, who was soon after assassinated at Cnut's instigation, in Mercia. To begin with Cnut assumed direct

rule of Wessex himself, but soon afterwards divided this
province (and Mercia as well) into smaller earldoms.

As early as 1018 Cnut made it clear that he wanted
England to be regarded and treated not as a colony, but
as an independent kingdom with himself as its chosen ruler.
He took two important measures to demonstrate this. He
dismissed the great fleet and sent it back to Denmark, paying
off its men with the biggest danegeld ever levied in England
—10,500 pounds of silver from London itself and 72,000
pounds from the rest of the country. He retained for himself
a small personal fleet of some forty ships, which was later
reduced to sixteen. Next he summoned a national assembly
at Oxford, where it was agreed that the new constitution
should be an acceptance on oath of the laws of King Edgar's
time. Soon after, Cnut's brother, King Harald, died childless in Denmark, and in 1019 Cnut returned to his homeland, partly to assume the throne there, partly to ensure
that no new Viking raids against England should be
mounted. Having achieved both these objects he was soon
back in England, where, for reasons we do not know, he outlawed Thorkel the Tall, who returned to Denmark. It was
soon apparent to Cnut, however, that it was far too dangerous to have as an enemy a man with such powerful connexions as Thorkel had in Denmark, and in 1023 Cnut
returned to that country and was reconciled with Thorkel.
The terms of agreement reveal the strength Thorkel wielded:
these were that Thorkel should govern Denmark in Cnut's
absence, and that each of them should adopt the other's son
as a foster-child (i.e. as a hostage). After Thorkel's death
(probably in 1024) his place in this curious pact was taken
by Earl Ulf, who was married to Cnut's sister Estrid; thus
the only son of Cnut and Emma, Hardacnut, became Ulf's
foster-child.

About this time Cnut was threatened by a new danger,
this time from Norway. Here one of Harald Finehair's

descendants, Olaf, son of a Norwegian noble Harald
Grenski, was making trouble. In his youth he had gained
experience in Viking raids on England, under Thorkel, as
well as in service with Duke Richard of Normandy. While
Earl Eric was in England he saw his chance to seize control
of Norway; he began in the south, and by 1016 he had
defeated Eric's brother Earl Swein in Trondelag in the
north of Norway. Thereafter Olaf Haraldsson, later called
St Olaf, was master in Norway, although he made many
enemies who, displeased with his rigorous rule, frequently
appealed for help to Cnut in England. Cnut, however, had
his hands full, and decided to defer his settlement with
Norway. This gave Olaf a respite, which he was not slow
to take advantage of.

His natural ally was Sweden, whose ruler king Önund
Jacob, a son of Olaf Skotkonung, was most concerned about
the change in the Scandinavian balance of power which
would result if Denmark, England, and Norway were all
under one king; and Önund's interest in the situation was
increased by the fact that his sister was married to Olaf. The
year 1026 was chosen for their joint attack on Cnut, and
Olaf and Önund were counting a good deal on the strained
relations which had developed between Cnut and his
brother-in-law Earl Ulf, to make the latter a potential ally.
As the place of battle the Swedes and the Norwegians chose
the mouth of the River Helge in eastern Skane, and to this
rendezvous came Önund's ships from the north-east and
Olaf's from the west, followed by Cnut's fleet which came
from the Lim Fjord across the Kattegat. Seldom has such an
important battle been reported in such contradictory
accounts. The Swedes are said to have held their own, but
all the military and political consequences of the battle
point emphatically to Cnut as the victor; the Swedes were
checked, Olaf returned to Norway, and Denmark was no
longer threatened by them. A rune-stone of this period from

Jutland, set up over a man called Full, perhaps refers to this battle in the words 'who met his death east across the sea, when kings were fighting'.

Shortly after this battle, the tension between Cnut and Ulf was resolved by Ulf's murder at Roskilde at the instigation of Cnut, who atoned for the deed by bestowing large estates on Ulf's widow, his own sister Estrid. At Easter 1027 Cnut was in Rome for the coronation of Conrad II as Holy Roman Emperor, and was received as one of the world's leading monarchs. He made friends with Conrad, and came to terms with him about the southern borders of Denmark. All that remained for him to do was to secure his North Sea empire, where the only remaining problem was Norway.

Here Olaf Haraldsson still reigned, although he was now in open conflict with the Norwegian nobles, one of whom he had killed. The situation was ripe for intervention, and in 1028 Cnut brought a combined Danish and English fleet into action, landing at a number of places along the Norwegian coast, and taking the entire country without a blow being struck. Olaf retreated to the Oslo Fjord and from there fled east to Gardariki (Russia). Cnut now summoned a parliament at Trondheim (Nidaros), and there proclaimed his son Hardacnut as king of Denmark, and Earl Eric's son, Hakon, as king of Norway.

In the winter of 1029 Cnut left Norway, taking with him a suitable number of hostages to ensure that the peace was not disturbed. Nevertheless, there were disturbances and during the same year Hakon was drowned whilst visiting England; in his place Cnut installed his young illegitimate son, Swein, as the ruler of Norway, though under the guidance of the boy's mother Ælfgifu. She, however, failed in her attempts to introduce the Danish systems of taxation and justice into Norway. Almost before she had begun her unsuccessful government of the country there was a sensational event: Olaf Haraldsson, at the head of an army, returned via Sweden to regain Norway. He was defeated by the peasants of Trondelag in the famous battle of Stiklestad in 1030 (of which more later). Soon after this the Norwegians seem to have regretted their hostility towards Olaf, the zealous, though harsh, champion of Christianity. Such an intense national feeling developed against Ælfgifu and her son that they were compelled to retire, first to southern Norway in 1033 and later, in 1035, to Denmark. The successor to the Norwegian throne was Magnus, the son of St Olaf, who had been brought home from Russia by Norwegian nobles.

There is no doubt that Cnut the Great was a powerful personality. He was not his father's son for nothing. There was a streak of violence in him which not infrequently revealed itself; but first and foremost he was a statesman of profound acumen. So far as his principal kingdom, England, was concerned, he worked towards two ends: first, to consolidate good relations with the Church; and second, to cultivate the principle that this government was a continuation of the national Anglo-Saxon government of King Edgar's time. He was internationally-minded as well; he prudently secured Denmark's southern frontiers, and towards the end of his life arranged a diplomatic marriage between the Emperor Conrad's son and his own daughter Gunnhild. He safeguarded and improved the pilgrim routes from England and Scandinavia to Rome, and developed amicable relations with the ruler of Aquitaine. The only power with which he failed to get on good terms was Normandy, where Richard II, who died in 1026, was succeeded a year later by the ambitious Robert, who was not well disposed towards Cnut.

Whether Cnut really expected his North Sea empire, comprising three widely separated countries, to survive him, it is not possible to say. Even a man of Cnut's determination found extreme difficulty in ruling this union. It was hard, for example, to eradicate from the Anglo-Saxon mind the feeling that he was a foreign conqueror, when he was obliged on practical grounds to surround himself with his 'housecarles', a Scandinavian bodyguard whose strict discipline made them supremely efficient. The process of assimilation might have been completed if Cnut – who in any case had promulgated a comprehensive law code for England – had lived longer; but he died in 1035, and almost at once the process of disintegration began.

Two sons were now candidates for the English throne. One was the Danish King Hardacnut; the other was Harald Harefoot, one of Cnut's sons by Ælfgifu. In 1035 Hardacnut was in Denmark, Harald in England, and both mothers, Emma and Ælfgifu, pressed their respective sons' claims in England. After a period of turmoil Harald was made King of England in 1037 (though without a coronation or anointing), and Queen Emma, Hardacnut's mother, was exiled to Flanders. Cnut's North Sea empire was thus split again, although Hardacnut in Denmark still nursed his ambition for the English throne. This he showed in 1040, by sailing to his mother in Flanders with a strong fleet, on his way to attack Harald Harefoot; but Harald died suddenly and Hardacnut now succeeded without difficulty to the throne of England. However, at the same time he lost control in Denmark, which was taken from him by King Magnus of Norway. A Danish attempt soon afterwards to overthrow the new régime – led by Swein, a son of Earl Ulf and Cnut the Great's sister, Estrid – ended in complete failure. Moreover, Hardacnut was not fated to enjoy the English throne for long: he died in 1042, and was succeeded by his half-brother (whom he had presumably nominated), Edward the Confessor, son of Æthelred II.

With Hardacnut's death the period of Danish rule of England came to an end, but it was far from the end of

Danish Viking raids on the country. As we shall see, not even the Norman conquest of 1066 put a stop to them.

In Denmark the Norwegian Magnus occupied the throne; and under him Swein Estridsson ruled as Earl of Jutland. He was with Magnus when he crushed a powerful Wendish army in South Slesvig. In the middle of the 1040s, St Olaf's half-brother, Harald Hardrada, returned from Byzantium and presented to Magnus his claim to a share in the Norwegian throne. At the same time he formed an alliance with Swein Estridsson, who had now broken with Magnus and was living in exile in Sweden (where he had been brought up in the royal house, and from which he still received support). Magnus and Harald came to terms, and agreed to share the royal powers in Norway. Just as things began to look really black for Swein Estridsson, Magnus was killed (in 1047) by a fall from his horse. Swein immediately had himself proclaimed King of Denmark in Jutland, and there now followed a trying period of seventeen years (with an interval in the 1050s) during which Harald Hardrada attacked Denmark in a series of raids which Swein was unable to ward off. Yet, although he was continually defeated, he showed an uncanny knack of surviving all setbacks, having great toughness and persistence. At long last, in 1064, peace of a sort was reached with Harald, who was preparing an attack on England where he was killed two years later. Swein was able to turn his attention to the rebuilding of his country and to the policy of the Danish church, which was striving for independence from both Germany and England. He remained an astute and capable sovereign of Denmark right up to his death in 1076, by which time the Viking period was over.

A few words now about England. In the 1060s two serious campaigns were launched from Scandinavia: the first in 1066 just before the Norman Conquest, was from Norway, headed by the Norwegian king Harald Hardrada. We will return to this later when we survey conditions in Norway. The second campaign, in 1069, was started from Denmark, by the shrewd Swein Estridsson, who, eagerly though he wished to renew Swein Forkbeard's and Cnut the Great's conquests of England, was not disposed to commit all his forces to such a venture; it was too risky for him. He compromised by dispatching against England a fleet of 250 vessels commanded by his brother Asbjörn. Three of Swein's sons took part in this campaign, which was also joined by many Norwegians. Arriving off the coast of Kent the fleet turned north along the coast to the mouth of the Humber, where the army went ashore and was joined by a large Anglo-Saxon force which had been mustered in the hope of overthrowing William the Conqueror. The combined armies marched upon York, which the small Norman garrison promptly set on fire. The invading armies won a victory, and, had they been better led, they might well have altered the course of history; but they took to plundering and, when a rumour arrived that Duke William was approaching, the Danes went back to their fleet and entrenched themselves in the Isle of Axholme. William therefore turned upon the Anglo-Saxon army, and while he was so engaged the Danes advanced on York again and captured it. William then decided to leave York alone for the time being, but set about methodically laying waste large areas of Yorkshire by fire and destruction, so as to drive away the inhabitants and prevent future risings against him in those parts. He applied this ruthless 'scorched earth' policy against Mercia and Northumbria – again to ensure that future invasions should attract no local support. Meanwhile, the Danish fleet lay in the mouth of the Humber, and here King Swein himself arrived from Denmark in 1070. In the spring, Danish and Anglo-Saxon forces captured Ely and Peterborough, but during the summer Swein and William the Conqueror reached an agreement, for which William

probably had to pay a consideration. Ely was given up by
the Danes and Swein returned home with the fleet the same
year.

After his death in 1076 Swein Estridsson was succeeded
by his five sons in turn. The second of these, Cnut (later
called St Cnut) planned, in conjunction with his father-in-
law, Count Robert of Flanders, and the Norwegian king,
Olaf Kyrri, to conquer England. A large fleet was assembled
in 1085, in the Lim Fjord, in Jutland; but before it could
sail a rebellion broke out in Denmark, in the course of
which Cnut was killed. With him perished the last threat of
Scandinavian invasion of England.

THE NORWEGIANS

In Norway, as we have seen, conditions after the crucial
battle of Svöld enabled Swein Forkbeard to hold supreme
sovereignty over the whole country, and exercise direct rule
in the south, while under him Earl Swein governed Vestland, and Earl Eric Trondelag. These earls were the sons of
Earl Hakon. This arrangement displeased many, particularly the young and ambitious chieftain, Olaf, son of the
south Norwegian noble, Harald Grenski. After the death of
Swein Forkbeard in 1014, and while his son Cnut, together
with Earl Eric, had more than enough to do in England,
Olaf returned to Norway, made rapid progress in the south
(his native soil) and in 1016 attacked and defeated Earl
Swein in a great naval battle at Nesjar in the mouth of the
Oslo Fjord. For the next decade he was king of Norway, and
proved a harsh ruler who made many enemies, not least by
his zealous advocacy of Christianity in opposition to traditional forms of religious worship. Olaf, expecting an attack
from Cnut the Great, allied himself with the Swedish

monarch Önund Jacob, and this led to the battle, already
mentioned, of the three kings at the River Helge, in which
Cnut triumphed. Olaf remained in Norway, for the time
being in conditions of constant unrest, and when at last
Cnut the Great moved against Norway in 1028 with his
massive Anglo-Danish fleet, Olaf had to give way and
flee. He went to Russia but, as early as 1030, he returned
home via Sweden, where Önund Jacob helped him with
forces and equipment. Olaf, who was soon to give up his
material nickname 'the Stout' in favour of the more
spiritual St Olaf, marched west through Jamtland, in north
Sweden, determined to regain his lost kingdom of Norway.
Since in centuries to come Olaf was to be regarded by
Norwegians and by their church as their greatest sovereign
and saint, we will now consider this crucial campaign in
Norwegian history in some detail.

Anyone travelling today in Jamtland, westwards along
the ancient route from Sweden to Norway, will pass the
little island of Froso (the isle of the god Frey) which stands
in the middle of Lake Stor (Storsjön), the holy lake of the
Jamt people. On it is an open-air amphitheatre, beautifully
situated; a grass-clad slope falls towards the west, and far
below lies the tiny stage, across and above it the eye looks
west over the lake, over the low blue hills until it is held
by the distant barren mountain range of Kølen, which
marks the gateway of Norway. On this open-air stage there
is often performed nowadays the musical drama *Arnljot*,
which takes a theme from St Olaf's campaign. Arnljot was
a Swedish warrior, mentioned by Snorri, outlawed for killing
at the holy Thing place of Froso. He volunteered to join
Olaf, became a Christian, and fell fighting under Olaf's
banner at the great battle of Stiklestad. This open-air
pageant affords modern travellers in northern Sweden an
excellent introduction to the saga of Olaf.

Trondelag is accessible from Sweden by three routes, as

in Olaf's time. These all start near a great mountain 4,500 ft high, called Areskutan, a mass which projects between the valleys and affords, towards the east, a view over half Jamtland. From here King Olaf set out for Norway, with an army of probably 2,000 men. Snorri records that he chose the middle one of the three routes, that which nowadays passes numerous mountain huts and crosses the Kølen range down into the Norwegian Inn valley south of Stiklestad. On the Norwegian flank of the Kølen near Sul they met a peasant who complained to the King that the soldiers were trampling down his crops. From now on, the King predicted, the fields would give a splendid yield, and so it proved! When Olaf crossed the Kølen he saw, in a vision, the whole of Norway laid out before him. Then he went to meet his fate on the battlefield he chose himself, Stiklestad.

He arrived there with his mercenaries a few days ahead of the enemy, determined to break the nobles and peasants of the Trondelag. Their army, led by the great land-owners Kalf Arnason and Thori Hund, was much bigger than Olaf's – a factor which determined the result of the battle. Stiklestad, as Brøgger noted, was the first land battle known to the history of Norway. All through the ninth and tenth centuries major engagements took place at sea; Harald Finehair, St Olaf's great-grandfather, conquered Norway from his ships. Land engagements there had been, but on a small scale. The strategy of a land battle followed this pattern: both sides let off a hail of arrows – as dense as possible 'so that the sky was darkened'. After this volley (the discharge of artillery, so to speak) came the hurling of spears, and finally the hand-to-hand mêlée, with sword and axe. Snorri relates vividly and tersely the progress of the battle of Stiklestad. The narrative contains such unforgettable incidents as the death of Thormod, Olaf's skald, in the 'field hospital' after the battle. He pulled an arrow out of his

chest, saying dryly: 'Well has the king fed us; I still have
fat round the roots of my heart!'* King Olaf, Snorri tells
us, had carefully selected the battlefield. He took up his
position on slightly higher ground, from which he led such
a vehement charge that it almost carried him to victory;
but numbers began to tell, and before long King Olaf was
hemmed in and fell under his banner, slain by blows from
all the Vikings' three main weapons: sword, spear, and axe.
His half-brother, the 15-year-old Harald Hardrada, who
was to become the last and perhaps the fiercest of all
the Viking kings, was 'blooded' on this bitter occasion,
but managed to escape after the battle. Stiklestad was
fought on 29 July 1030. When Snorri declares that the
sun was darkened during the battle we must correct him;
the eclipse of the sun did not take place until the following
year.

Norwegian historians have disagreed violently on the
nature and significance of this battle. Earlier scholars asserted that Olaf's enemies in Norway were the nobles and
land-owners, and his supporters the peasants and com-
moners; they idealized Olaf as a man motivated by faith
in the future of his country and willing to give his life for
this belief. Authorities of later generations, however, maintain that Olaf's friends were the lesser nobles who joined
him against the great nobility like the earls of Lade. They
find no particularly idealistic motives in Olaf, but rather a
passion for revenge and a Viking unruliness. He promised
his troops, who were by no means all Norwegians, rewards
of land and property in Norway when victory had been
achieved. Olaf's last battle was certainly not fought in the
cause of religion; in fact, Christians were represented in
the army of Trondelag peasants which defeated him at
Stiklestad, and indeed a Danish bishop harangued them

* Snorri's narrative gives interesting sidelights on the medical skill of
the Vikings, their skilful diagnosis of wounds, etc. See p. 255.

before the fight began. By that time Norway was already Christian; Olaf's campaign cannot be considered a crusade against a heathen horde. We get nearest the truth perhaps by regarding the men of northern Norway as the natural defenders of Trondelag – and therefore, of the realm of Norway – against a Viking king bent on revenge.

Snorri's *Saga of St Olaf* does not disclose any saintly qualities in its hero. He seems no more sympathetic a character than most Viking leaders – certainly less so than Olaf Tryggvason. Yet shortly after Stiklestad the legend developed which transformed Olaf the Stout into St Olaf. There is talk of miraculous cures, etcetera. At this point the Church took a hand in the game. It was on the verge of a notable accession of strength in Norway, and its rising fortunes could be strengthened by a saint, especially one of royal blood. The Church certainly contrived to get such a one in Olaf, and the result may be calculated by the estimate that 200 years later there was a priest in Norway for every 150 inhabitants – 2,000 of them in all. St Olaf was a powerful factor in the church's attainment of such power. Near Stiklestad lies the old royal estate of Haug, and some time after the battle Olaf's son, the young king Magnus, was discussing the fight with two chieftains, Einar Thambarskelfi and Karl Arnason. Snorri relates what happened: 'Go with me,' said Magnus, 'to the battlefield and show me where my father fell.' Einar answered, 'You had better ask your foster-father, Kalf, for he fought there that day!' When they came to the place Kalf said, 'Here he fell.' 'But where were you then, Kalf?' 'Here,' said Kalf, 'where I now stand!' Magnus's face darkened: 'So your axe could reach him?' 'But it did not touch him,' cried Kalf – and he leapt on his horse and galloped away. The same night he fled the country, as Thori Hund, the other great leader of the peasants, had done some time before. Now King Magnus

embarked upon a campaign of extermination against those
who had led the men of Trondelag against his father at
Stiklestad, so that discontent grew in the area. The situation
was taken care of by Sighvat, who had been Olaf's favourite
skald. He composed a poem – the equivalent of a modern
open letter in the newspapers – in which he warned King
Magnus not to make a deep division between throne and
people as Olaf had done. The warning was heeded and
Magnus changed his course of action. He compiled the law
code known as *Grágás*, became popular among his people,
and gained the sobriquet 'the Good', which his father
had never enjoyed. Magnus did not assume full powers until
1035, when Ælfgifu (nominated regent for her son Swein
by Cnut the Great) was driven from Norway. Magnus left
behind him a good name in his own country as well as in
Denmark, which he conquered. About 1045 his father's
half-brother, Harald Hardrada, returned home from Byzantium, famous and rich, and shared the kingdom of Norway
with Magnus until the latter's death two years later. Then,
for nineteen years, Harald held supreme power, and became
the most feared warrior of his time. He had a passion for
fighting, and engaged in frequent raids against Swein
Estridsson in Denmark; he succeeded, indeed, in burning
and completely destroying Hedeby in 1050. Finally he
made peace with Swein, and turned his turbulent attentions to a campaign against England, this time from the
north.

Harald assembled his ships and men in the Orkneys,
and from there sailed south in September 1066, aided partly
from Scotland, and also by the exiled Anglo-Saxon Earl
Tostig, brother to the English king Harold Godwinesson,
who had succeeded Edward the Confessor. Aided by that
same north wind which was delaying William the Con-
querer's armada in the estuary of the Somme, Harald
Hardrada now proceeded southward along the Scottish and

English coasts with a fleet, it is said, of three hundred vessels, entered the Humber, and anchored in the River Ouse. Landing there, the Norwegian army marched towards York, and on 20 September, won a battle at Fulford, south of the city, whose inhabitants had some sympathy for the invaders. Harald now returned to his fleet, after making an agreement with the people of York for their future assistance in his attempt to conquer England. He now summoned hostages from several places, and received these in his camp at Stamford Bridge, a few miles east of York. Meanwhile, the English King Harold was far from idle. By rapid marches he advanced from the south, reached undefended York on 24 September and the next day took the Norwegians completely by surprise at Stamford Bridge. This admirably executed campaign gave Harold a complete victory, in which both Harald and Tostig were killed. Harald's son Olaf was compelled to make terms, and to sail back home with the remnants of the expedition, having given his word that he would never again attack England. The valiant and skilful Harold had but brief enjoyment of his brilliant victory: three days later, Duke William of Normandy made his fateful landing in the south of England; Harold immediately made another forced march to meet him, and in the Battle of Hastings, on 14 October 1066, Harold was killed. The Norman Conquest had begun.

Harald Hardrada's son and successor in Norway, Olaf Kyrri, reigned for over twenty-five years, almost to the turn of the century, and proved himself a man of peace. With him the Viking period, as far as Norway itself was concerned, came to an end.

We must now take a look at the Norwegian 'spheres of influence' in the west, and note the course of Viking activities in those quarters. The Orkneys, in about 1000, were ruled by the powerful, independent Earl Sigurd Digri

(the stout), married to the daughter of the Scottish king,
Malcolm. He exercised his powers not only over the Orkneys
themselves but also over Caithness, the Hebrides, and the
Isle of Man.

In Ireland in 1012 Brian Boroimhe (Irish: 'tribute'), the
supreme monarch, fell foul of the King of Leinster, who
allied himself to another of Brian's under-kings, Sigtrygg
Silkybeard, the Norwegian ruler of Dublin. Sigtrygg, fearing
that Brian Boroimhe would recapture Dublin, called upon
Sigurd Digri for aid. A fierce and bloody battle was fought
at Clontarf, on 23 April 1014, in which the Irish prevailed,
but both Brian Boroimhe and Sigurd Digri died on the
battlefield. Dublin itself was not attacked and Sigtrygg, who
had not himself taken part in the battle at Clontarf, continued to reign as King of Dublin for many years. Incidentally, he was the first monarch in Ireland to mint coins.
Sigtrygg, like his father, ended his life a penitent monk in
the monastery of Iona.

In Ireland during the rest of the century there was a
succession of skirmishes and affrays between the Norwegians and the Irish, from which no outstanding personality emerged. Towards the middle of the eleventh century,
however, the Orkneys provide us with just this in Thorfinn
the Mighty, a descendant of King Malcolm of Scotland.
Embroiled at this time in a quarrel with a relative, Rögnvald, whom he managed to kill, Thorfinn was for the next
twenty years the great earl of the Orkneys, until, by the
time of his death in 1064, he had become acknowledged
ruler of the whole of north-west Scotland.

The Isle of Man also had its strong 'king' (about 1080–95)
in the Icelandic-born Godred Crovan, who succeeded in
extending his rule to Dublin and Leinster. On three occasions at the end of the century a king of Norway visited
these old Viking stamping grounds. This was Magnus Bare-
foot, son of Olaf Kyrri, who brought the Orkneys, the

Hebrides, and the Isle of Man under Norway. He fell in
1104 during a campaign in Ulster.*

ICELAND AND GREENLAND

The further development of the independent Icelandic
Christian state in the eleventh century can be told briefly.
The adoption of Christianity went smoothly, for the people,
as we know, had chosen it of their own free will. It may be
assumed that the heathen sanctuaries soon disappeared and
were replaced by simple turf-built churches. In the eleventh
century Iceland had three eminent Christian administrators
of a single family: father, son, and grandson. The first of
these was Gizur the White, who was present at the decisive
meeting of the Althing in 1000, when Christianity was
accepted. He sent his son, Isleif, to Germany for an
ecclesiastical training; and in 1056 Isleif was consecrated
by bishop Adalbert of Bremen to be Iceland's first native
bishop, with his see at Skalholt. He died in 1080, worried (the
story goes) over the manifold difficulties which beset a bishop.
His son, Gizur, followed as bishop (1082–1118), and proved
well endowed with wisdom, persuasiveness, and authority.
He was evidently one of those admirable prelates in whom
physical and spiritual strength and courage are matched.
During his time, it is said, there was peace throughout Iceland; people could move about without weapons; and so
great was Gizur's prestige that 'everyone, young and old,
poor and rich, women and men, did as the bishop ordered'.
This period of tranquillity, which lasted not only throughout

* The link between the Orkneys and Norway was maintained with
occasional breaks until the fifteenth century, when King Christian I of
Denmark–Norway made over the islands as security for his daughter's
dowry to King James III of Scotland.

bishop Gizur's time but through most of the eleventh century, cannot be entirely attributed to the achievements of
a few men. What other factors operated it is difficult to say,
for there was no lack of trouble both before and after. Iceland's constitution, established in 930 on a Norwegian pattern, had an Althing consisting of the legislative assembly
presided over by the law-speaker, and a judiciary divided
into four groups, one for each quarter of the island, supple-
mented after the year 1000 by an appeal court. In spite of
this the country had not enjoyed peace. The authorities
responsible for legal decisions had not the powers to ensure
that they were implemented. Thus in the century or so from
930 the country had been racked by blood feuds and strife.
Then, for another hundred years there followed the period
of peace, and after that the strife and bloodshed of the
twelfth and thirteenth centuries. It is time, however, to leave
Iceland for the most remote of Scandinavian colonies,
Greenland.

Though sources do not always agree, it is said that Leif,
son of Eric the Red, visited Olaf Tryggvason in Norway in
the autumn of 999. There he was baptized, and ordered by
the king to return to Greenland and straightway preach and
proclaim the Christian faith. For this mission he was given
two assistants. Leif accepted the task without enthusiasm,
and soon found that his evangelism displeased his father,
who presumably never accepted Christianity. His mother,
on the other hand, was allowed to build a small chapel
where she and the other converts could gather for prayer.
Thus Christianity was introduced to Iceland and Greenland
almost simultaneously about the turn of the century, though
it was not until the twelfth century that Greenland had its
own bishop.

THE DISCOVERY OF AMERICA

One final Viking achievement must be recorded, one which occurred in the remotest confines of the Norwegian 'sphere of influence': the discovery of North America. According to the sagas, Bjarni Herjolfsson and his associates left Iceland for Greenland in the year 986, but lost their course on the journey and three times sighted land, though they did not go ashore. The first land they saw was a well-wooded coast and so was the second; but their third landfall was a rocky island with glaciers.

Some time later Leif Ericsson bought Bjarni's ship and left Greenland, probably in 992, with thirty-five men to find and explore the land which Bjarni had discovered. He first found the glacier island, and between the shore and the ice there was nothing but stone; the island, which he named 'Helluland' ('Stoneland' or perhaps 'Slateland'), seemed to him to be 'without any good qualities'. Next he reached a flat and forested land which Leif named 'Markland' ('Forestland'); and two days later they came to an island on which they found abundant grass and sweet dew. Between this island and a headland they entered a strait in which their vessel grounded on a sandbank at low tide. They freed the ship at high water, and brought it into a river, deciding to winter there, since there was good timber available from the adjacent maple forest, for building their huts. In the rivers and the sea they found salmon bigger than they had ever seen before; there were no frosts in the winter, and the grass scarcely withered at all. Day and night were of much more equal duration than in Greenland and Iceland. On the shortest day the sun rose at the *eyktarstaðr*, and set at the *dagmálastaðr* – whatever these terms may mean.

Leif now divided his company so that some stayed by the camp, while others went to reconnoitre the surrounding

districts. One evening a man called Tyrki, a German, one
of Eric the Red's old friends and Leif's foster-father, was
reported missing. They started a search and came across
him near at hand. He was clearly in a state of great excite-
ment – babbling in his German mother-tongue, grimacing,
and rolling his eyes. He had found vines and grapes, he
said, and he would certainly know, as he was born in a
country where vines were common. The next few days they
collected grapes, cut vines, and felled timber, loading all
this on to their ship; and in the spring they broke camp and
sailed home from the land which they christened Vinland
('Wineland'). On their way back they rescued some ship-
wrecked men from a rock, and safely reached Brattahlid,
Eric the Red's farm at Ericsfjord in Greenland. Elsewhere
it is told that after his voyage Leif was called Leif the Lucky.

The saga continues with the tale of Leif's brother Thorvald, who, borrowing Leif's vessel, sailed away with thirty
men and safely reached Leif's huts in Wineland, where they
settled down for the winter. The following summer they
explored the west coast of the country, which they found
very beautiful, with forests, white sandy beaches, numerous
islands, and shallow waters. On one island they came across
a kind of wooden shed, but otherwise found no sign of
human activity. In the autumn they returned to their base
at Leif's hut, and they spent the next summer in exploring
the east and north coasts. Their keel broke in a storm while
rounding a headland, and after fitting a new one they set
up the broken one on the headland which they called
Kjalarnes ('Keelness'). Continuing their journey to the east
they came upon wooded fjords, and lay alongside a promontory so beautiful that Thorvald exclaimed, 'This is a fair
land; here I will establish my farm.' On the beach, however,
they came across three skin boats with nine men, and a
fight developed in which eight men out of the nine were
killed. Soon afterwards they were attacked by a large

number of men in skin boats, and these *Skrælingar* ¸
them but finally fled. Thorvald, however, was wound
one of their arrows and died from his injuries. They bu
him on the promontory, as he asked, erecting crosses at h
head and feet; and called the place *Krossanes* ('Crossness').
They then returned to Leif's huts for the winter. They collected grapes and timber for cargo; and when spring came
they sailed for home, reaching Ericsfjord 'with great tidings
for Leif'.

Another narrative tells how the Icelander Thorfinn Karlsefni ventured to Wineland with three ships and 160 men.
They first reached 'Stoneland', and after that 'Forestland',
and then, after sailing along strange, long, sandy beaches,
reach the promontory with the ship's keel, 'Keelness'. Near
here they turn up a fjord and dispatch two scouts – two
Britons, man and wife, noted for their speed in running –
these return three days later with grapes and self-sown
wheat. They continue into another fjord with an island at
its mouth, where there nest so many birds that a man can
hardly put a foot between the eggs. A powerful current
flows round the island and so they name the fjord *Straum-*
fjörðr and the island *Straumey* (*straumr*: 'current'). They
winter here with their cattle. There is enough grass, but
little food for human beings. In their hunger they pray to
God: one of their company, Thorhall the Hunter, on the
other hand, appeals to Thor. A whale is stranded near by,
of a variety unknown even to Thorfinn Karlsefni, who was
knowledgeable about whales. It proves to be uneatable, and
they all become ill and throw the whale meat back into the
sea. As spring comes they manage on birds' eggs, hunting,
and fishing; but by this time Thorhall the Hunter is discontented and anxious to return to Greenland, and therefore he sets off taking one ship and nine of the men. They
are driven by a westerly gale to Ireland, and there Thorhall
dies. Thorfinn's party sail south for a long way, until they

reach a river running through a lake into the sea; only at
high water can they get into the river. They call the place
Hóp. Here on the low ground grows self-sown wheat, and on
the higher ground vines; and every brook teems with fish.
At high water-mark they dig pits, and when the tide ebbs find
halibut in them. The forest abounds with animals of many
kinds, and they decide to spend winter here, where no snow
falls and cattle can be left out of doors all year round. Now
they encounter the inhabitants of the country, the
'Skrælings' and at first barter peaceably with them, giving
them red cloth and milk (which was unknown to the
natives) in return for furs. A quarrel, however, arises as a
roaring ox frightens the natives, who now arrive in their
hordes in skin boats, terrifying the Scandinavians by fling-
ing great stones, sewn into painted skins, from tall poles.
Men fall on both sides; the Skrælings fight with slings and
stone axes, and are astonished at the iron axes of the Scandinavians. After this Karlsefni decides it is too dangerous
to remain in the land of Hóp, and, abandoning the idea of
settling, returns to Straumfjord half-way between Hóp and
Keelness. Leaving most of his people there, he takes one
ship north to look for Thorhall and after a vain search
returns to winter at Straumfjord where a son, Snorri, is
born to him. Next spring they all return home via Markland, where they capture and take along with them two
Skræling boys. One of their vessels, which turns out to be
worm-eaten, founders, but Karlsefni's own ship finally
reaches Ericsfjord in Greenland.

The last story in the Wineland sagas tells of Freydis, a
violent Viking woman who was an illegitimate daughter
of Eric the Red. She sets out on a voyage to Wineland in
two ships, accompanied by two Icelandic brothers, Helgi and
Finnbogi. They reach Leif's huts in Wineland, where they
winter, but here trouble breaks out. Freydis carries out a
plan to murder both brothers, and, moreover, with her own

axe cuts down all the women. Early next summer she returns to Greenland.

This is in the main what the sagas tell about Wineland. Earlier scholars tended to be sceptical of this material and to reject the whole story as fiction, but this attitude has now been abandoned. In its place there is recognition of the truth that is hidden behind these tales, namely, that the Norsemen of Greenland, somewhere round the year 1000, really did discover and explore an extensive non-arctic country which can only have been part of the North American continent. But where was it? Where did Wineland lie? Much has been written on the subject, though there is no generally accepted conclusion; there is not enough evidence – nautical, astronomical, or anthropological – in the sagas to pin-point the locality of Wineland. Nor has North America provided any archaeological material which will stand up to critical examination. To my mind, there is no reason whatsoever to doubt that the Norse colonists of Greenland did find America at the close of the Viking period or in the later Middle Ages, and did endeavour to establish a permanent foothold there. In the latter effort they evidently did not succeed. America, unlike Greenland and Iceland, was not uninhabited when the Norsemen discovered it, but had a population which was apparently hostile – for which it is certainly not to be blamed, considering the behaviour of the Scandinavians! The sagas make it clear that the men from Greenland made serious efforts to colonize North America, but that the task was too much for them. The lines of communication with their home bases were too extended and the bases themselves too weak. However, the attempt may be regarded as a final expression of Viking adventurousness and energy. It failed because the source of energy was too distant and too weak; otherwise world history might have developed differently in several ways.

It would be interesting if we could trace Wineland by locating the sites of Leif's huts, or finding remains of other Norse houses like those which have been excavated in great numbers in Greenland by the Danish archaeologist Poul Nørlund – for example, the ruins of Eric the Red's own farm at Brattahlid. Such discoveries would confirm the presence of Norsemen in America long before the days of Columbus. It would be worth while conducting a systematic search for such evidence, along the treeless Atlantic coast of North America, by aerial survey from low-flying and slow-moving planes, on the lines of those carried out by Danish archaeologists in Greenland.

THE SWEDES

Of Sweden's political history in the eleventh century little is known as sources are scarce. We have already mentioned Olaf Skotkonung who, with Danish and Norwegian aid, fought Olaf Tryggvason at Svöld in 1000, and his son Önund Jacob who, in company with Olaf Haraldsson, was defeated by Cnut the Great in 1026. Both these Swedish kings were Christians, and so, too, was King Stenkil forty years later. It must not, however, be assumed that Sweden as a whole adopted the Christian faith in the early part of the eleventh century: on the contrary, religious strife seems to have continued after 1100. Of the three Scandinavian countries, Sweden was the last to give up its paganism. As we shall see later, the pagan temple at Uppsala was flourishing when Adam of Bremen wrote in the 1070s.

The Swedish 'sphere of influence' in Russia had changed much during the eleventh century. The two Rus Khaganates of Novgorod and Kiev were amalgamated into a single Christian West Russian Empire, in which Swedish elements gradually gave way to Slav, and where Byzantine influence was continually increasing. The eastern trade-route along the Volga had lost its importance, owing to the fall-off in the production of silver in the Caliphate of Baghdad; from the Swedish point of view the major trade-route was now the Dnieper, leading to the Black Sea and Byzantium. The Eastern Roman Emperor in Constantinople recruited a bodyguard of Scandinavians – the Varangians – of which Harald Hardrada had been a member; and the word 'Varangian', which had formerly signified a merchant guarantor, now meant a Viking warrior. These Swedes got as far as Athens. The big marble lion found in the harbour of Piraeus, and now set up in Venice, has a Swedish runic ribbon curving round its shoulders, though the inscription on it has unfortunately weathered away.

In late Icelandic literature we are told of an outstanding Viking feat – an expedition launched from Sweden, around 1040, against Mohammedan countries in the East ('Serkland') led by Yngvar the Far-Travelled, Emund's son. His campaign is commemorated on a number of rune-stones from Uppland, Sweden (the so-called 'Yngvar stones'), but there are no reliable records of it. During the reign of St Vladimir and his son Jaroslav (who was married to Ingigerd the daughter of Olaf Skotkonung) in the first part of the eleventh century, the Kiev Empire was powerful enough to make the Dnieper route safe against attacks by eastern nomads.

Later two factors combined to weaken the West Russian Empire based on Kiev: the Crusades brought oriental trade directly across Europe, instead of by the more devious route of the Russian waterways; and the Asiatic nomads – the Kumans – increased their raids upon the west, so that the Dnieper route became increasingly dangerous. However, when we look back on the achievements of the Rus, we can truly say that it was Swedish activity that created the following Russian towns: Novgorod, Izborsk, Polotsk, Byelosersk, Rostov, Murom, Smolensk, Chernigov, and Kiev.

This extensive development of the eastern routes by Swedish merchants and warriors in the eleventh century had a profound effect upon Sweden itself, as archaeological evidence shows the many thousands of Arab coins found in Swedish soil – the Kufic *dirhems* – must nearly all have been brought along the Volga route; they belong to the ninth and tenth centuries, and, significantly, there are scarcely any from the eleventh. By that time the Volga route had become increasingly insecure, and the Baghdad caliphate had lost its silver mines to eastern invaders. On the other hand Sweden obtained a substantial share of the English danegeld from the end of the tenth century and throughout the first half of the eleventh; thousands of Anglo-Saxon coins of this period have been found in Sweden, especially in Gotland.

CHAPTER SIX

Weapons and Tools

WEAPONS

A Viking's weapons of attack consisted of sword, axe, spear, and bow and arrow. Of these the sword and axe took pride of place: any self-respecting Viking bore them about him always.

The Viking's sword is well known from numerous finds in Scandinavia – over two thousand in Norway, many in Sweden, but comparatively few in Denmark. To some extent this distribution is accounted for by the fact that these swords are usually grave-finds, and that Christianity, which forbade the burial of weapons with the dead, came earlier to Denmark than to Norway or Sweden. The sword was undoubtedly the Viking's principal weapon, with the axe a close runner-up. During the period immediately preceding the Viking Age, the most popular kind of sword, especially in Norway, was of the single-edged type, but the Vikings preferred the long, usually broad, two-edged iron sword, with the hilt made up of four elements: nearest the blade a cross-piece (the guard or lower hilt), then the flat grip narrowing away from the blade, a further cross-piece (the upper hilt), and finally a triangular or semi-circular, often segmented, pommel. The guards were most commonly straight, but curved forms also occur. The blade may be pattern-welded and sometimes inlaid; and the hilt is often richly chased and gilded, or inlaid with gold, copper, silver or niello; so that the Viking sword was often a weapon of

great splendour. The Vikings, indeed, loved richness and
colour in their weapons, harness, and clothes. The scabbard
is seldom found, but its bronze chape often remains: it is
triangular and often carries openwork animal-ornament.

Early Viking swords are quite simple; the later ones tend
to develop longer guards and to accentuate the segmenta-
tion of the pommel. Scandinavian archaeologists have made
a careful typological study of these Viking swords, and
classified them into more than twenty categories: Norwegian, Danish, Swedish, and common Scandinavian; early
and late. Specimens have also been unearthed in the various
Viking 'spheres of influence' – in England, Ireland, France,
Russia, etc.

Where were these Viking swords manufactured? In Scandinavia, or abroad, or perhaps both? The probable answer
is that some were home-produced, others imported. A sword
is a complicated product, and its various parts were not
always made by the same craftsman. There may well have
been different specialists for blades, hilts, and other features
of the assembly. For example, it is to be supposed that a hilt
decorated with a distinctively Scandinavian design, with a
'gripping beast' or something in the Jelling style, is far
more likely than not to have been made in Scandinavia
itself. On the other hand, a blade bearing the factory-mark
ULFBERTH or INGELRI, was certainly forged abroad,
apparently in France. No doubt Scandinavian smiths had
in general the technical skill to manufacture swords; the
quantities of iron and smith's tools found among Viking,
particularly Norwegian, remains bear witness to the importance of the smith's craft among the Vikings. A second
question then arises: who made the best swords? There is no
doubt about the answer, the Franks. For this there is literary
evidence. First, the repeated embargo on the export of
swords and other weapons, imposed by Charlemagne and
Charles the Bald, even to the extent of the death penalty for

infringement. Charlemagne's ban applied to both east and
north – both the Avars and the Vikings – and the attention
of the clergy was specifically drawn to it, which suggests
that weapons were often forged in the smithies of monasteries. Charles the Bald's prohibition was expressly directed
against the Viking market : why should his craftsmen supply
these blood-thirsty robbers with the choicest weapons in the
world?

An illustration of the superiority of Frankish over Scandinavian swords is to be found in the anecdote told in *Gesta
Caroli Magni* (the History of Charlemagne) of the Frankish
Emperor, Louis the German, sitting on his throne receiving
gifts of homage from 'the kings of the Normans'. Among
these gifts were Scandinavian swords, which Louis tested
with his experienced hand; only one sword passed. The
anecdote may well be an invention, but even so it has made
its point. Another indication of the same kind occurs in the
report of the Arab, Ibn Fadlan, who specially noticed the
swords which he saw the Rus merchants carrying in Bulgar :
with broad, flat, grooved blades 'after the Frankish pattern'.

The region of the Rhine and Cologne, in particular, was
an important centre of manufacture. England is said to have
imported 'good Cologne swords'. Other Arab writers testify
to the importation of swords to the Orient, partly from
France (through Jewish middlemen) and partly from the
Rus. They record, however, that the Arabs sometimes
robbed the graves of Rus warriors to filch the splendid swords
buried with the dead; from the statement of Ibn Fadlan
just quoted it is likely that both the Rus-imported swords
and the Rus grave-goods were Frankish weapons. The
Arabs, who were themselves no mean swordsmiths, would
scarcely have given such praise to Scandinavian blades.
These observations have archaeological support, too. A
Swedish scholar has brought to light a Viking Age find from
Oland in the Baltic, consisting of five damascened sword

blades bearing the manufacturer's mark (ULFBERTH).
Apparently these blades were imported from the Franks to
have hilts fitted in Sweden, as the Scandinavian craftsmen
were traditionally famous for their production of inlaid or
chased bronze hilts.

Whereas the sword was common to all countries in the
Viking Age, the axe was a characteristically Scandinavian
weapon. In the Viking period the battle-axe was, if not
obsolete, at least archaic in Europe generally, and was
degenerating into a ceremonial, heraldic, or decorative
weapon. In the Nordic countries, on the other hand, the
battle-axe achieved a renaissance. To the much-afflicted
peoples of western Europe the long-handled broad-edged
battle-axe became the distinctive symbol of the blood-
thirsty Viking. The Lindisfarne stone bears a carving of
Vikings in column of march carrying their two principal
weapons, axe and sword, raised high above their heads. The
Viking battle-axe had many varieties of form, but there
were two main types: the older one, called the *skeggöx* or
'beard-axe' was an inheritance from the eighth century,
while the broad-axe with its corners more symmetrically
extended to a wide, curving edge first achieved popularity
about 1000. The cutting edge of the broad-axe was often
made of specially hardened iron, welded on to the weapon.
Both types of axe had angular necks, and were sometimes
decorated with exquisite silver inlay on blade and neck. One
exceptionally beautiful silver-inlaid broad-axe was found
during the excavations of the Danish Viking fort at Trelleborg.

The spear, too, was in common use among the Vikings: it
can be called their third weapon. No shafts have been preserved, only the iron spearhead. These are blades of an
elegant shape with a sharp mid-rib and a hollow conical
socket to fit the end of the shaft. Sometimes this socket has
short side-lobes or 'wings'; these 'winged' heads are

undoubtedly Frankish. Some later specimens are richly inlaid with geometrical silver patterns across the base of the blade; doubtless these spears would be carefully returned to their owner after the battle, were he lucky enough to be alive.

Finally there is the bow and arrow, an ancient weapon which, as the sagas confirm, played an important part in many a Viking battle. Neither the bows themselves (certainly of a long simple kind) nor the arrow-shafts survive. In contrast arrow-heads are quite commonly found in graves (including women's graves); strong, dangerous points, which must have possessed a considerable penetrative power when released from a strong bow. Sometimes they are found alongside the dead in bundles of anything up to forty. They were carried in cylindrical quivers.

Another Viking weapon – which also served as a tool – was the iron knife. The single-edged knife, with a handle of wood or bone, was carried by men at their belts and by the women (as Ibn Fadlan relates in his Volga report) on a chain worn on the breast. In graves from the Viking Age it is common to find the dead woman lying with her knife on her breast or by her waist.

The most important defensive equipment of the Vikings was the wooden shield, the iron coat of mail, and the leather or iron helmet. Few specimens have been found, but they are known from pictorial records and from literary references. The shield was round, flat, and not very thick, often painted and reinforced at the centre by a round iron boss. Shields of this kind hung in rows along the gunwales of the famous Norwegian Viking ship from Gokstad. Mail-coat and helmet were worn only by the nobles, and fragments are all that have survived, but pictorial records show helmets, probably of leather, of roughly conical shape. This pointed shape is possibly borrowed from oriental models. Woven tapestries from the Norwegian Oseberg ship depict white-coloured mail-coats covering the whole body and topped with a hood.

An analysis, some years ago, of the weapons recovered from Danish graves revealed the fact that the full equipment of attacking weapons – sword, axe, spear, bow and arrow – was never found in a single grave; and only in one case did sword, axe, spear, and shield accompany a warrior. As a rule only one or two weapons were found with the body; most commonly the axe, then the sword, and thirdly the spear. This investigation, however, only covered Danish discoveries, which are far fewer than Norwegian and Swedish ones.

While on the subject of Viking weapons it is perhaps appropriate to refer to that strange species of Viking warrior known as the 'berserk'; the violent half-mad fighter who possessed terrifying strength while battle-fever, *berserksgangr*, was upon him, only to relapse afterwards into stupor and lethargy. Snorri, in the *Ynglinga Saga*, speaks of this kind of warrior as being inspired by Odin's rage. He writes:

Odin could bring it about that in battle his enemies were struck with blindness, deafness, or terror, so that their weapons cut no better than sticks; whereas his own men refused to wear mail-coats and fought like mad dogs or wolves, biting their shield-rims; they had the strength of bears or bulls. They cut down the enemy, while neither fire nor iron could make an impression on them.

The word *berserk* has been derived from 'bare sark', 'shirtless' – that is to say, without armour; or from 'bear sark', a reference to the belief that man could take on the appearance, and then the nature of beasts.* These berserks are quite often mentioned in Old Norse literature; Nils Lid is of the opinion that they are to be regarded as a sort of psychopath selected for their exceptional strength and ferocity and formed into special corps in the service of a

---

* There were other fanatical fighters called *ulfheðnar*, 'wolfskins'.

king or a chieftain. Thus, during battle they would incite each other to mad frenzy.

The favourite animal of the Vikings was the horse, and a warrior's charger (and his dog) were often buried with him. The rider's outfit – spurs, stirrups, bridle, bit, reins, saddle, collar harness, buckles, etcetera, afforded ample opportunity for fine ornamentation. In a grave at Birka, Sweden, there was found a bridle made of leather decorated with studs of silvered bronze, and on the south Danish island of Lange-land was a chieftain's grave containing spurs and stirrups adorned with superb silver inlay of elegant pattern. A Viking horseman in all his splendour must have been a sight well worth seeing. Across the horse's mane lay the carved collar-harness: a bronze-mounted piece of wood with holes through which the reins were passed (Pl. 3c). The saddles found in Norway are of wood and seem to have been placed well forward on the horse, so that the rider's legs pointed forward. Stirrups – originally invented on the steppes of Eurasia – appear in Viking Age Scandinavia in two forms, both of iron, but deriving from primitive types in leather and wood. One is an iron version of the simple narrow leather strap; the other copied in iron, often finely inlaid, the same type of strap together with its inset rectangu-lar wooden foot-rest. The vertical bars of the stirrups were frequently decorated with silver or copper inlay (Pls. 3A and B). Another item in the riding outfit, according to Norwegian evidence, was a kind of rattle, whose noise was probably intended to keep evil spirits at bay.

TOOLS

That the Vikings were skilled craftsmen is shown by the numerous archaeological finds of home-manufactured goods

– ships, carts, sledges, textiles, jewellery, as well as numerous
tools for the use of artisans. The most important of all craftsmen was the blacksmith: his skills were basic; without the
iron tools he fashioned ploughing, house-building, and
weapons would have been poorer; in short, there would
have been a much lower standard of living. The three
Scandinavian countries had long known how to extract iron
from bog ore. In this they were self-supporting, as the finds
of hidden dumps of raw material (hundreds of home-made
iron bars) prove. The blacksmith was a highly respected
member of the community, whose tools would be buried
with him for use in the other world. *Egil's Saga* tells how
Egil, on the death of his father, Skallagrim, built a mound
for him at the far end of a promontory and laid him inside
it, with his horse, his weapons, and his blacksmith's tools.
Even the chieftain mastered smithing; but it seems likely, as
Sigurd Grieg has suggested, that each village had its own
professional blacksmith to perform the jobs which were too
difficult for the layman. Grave-finds, in Norway, illustrate
the tools of the Viking blacksmith; light and heavy
hammers, tongs with bent or straight heads, files, chisels,
scissors, anvil, and a number of tools for special purposes.

The equipment of many other kinds of artisan has also
come to light in Swedish and Norwegian graves – such as
the carpenter's knives, chisels, drills, axes, planing-irons,
awls, and saw-blades. Agricultural implements found include coulters, scythes, sickles for cutting grass and corn,
and knives for cutting branches and leaves from trees;
fishing gear includes hooks, spears, gaffs, and stones for
sinking the nets. Of women's household equipment there
have been found most of the things necessary for sewing,
spinning, and weaving – needles, spinning-wheels, slays,
loom-weights, scissors, smoothing irons – and the full battery
of kitchen utensils, such as bronze or iron cauldrons, racks
and chains, frying-pans, spits, grills, hooks, wooden bowls,

and pots made from soap-stone. Swedish and Norwegian
finds have been especially fruitful. In Norway old soap-stone
quarries have been excavated so that it has been possible
to trace the technical processes of this ancient industry,
from the ring-shaped cuts in the rock wall where the talc
was quarried, through the various rough processes, right
down to the completed, finely smoothed bowls and pots.
Only one ancient craft, one which had formerly been skilfully practised in the North, seems to have been neglected
in Viking times – ceramics. In Norway pottery almost disappeared, to be replaced by wooden vessels, soap-stone pots
and iron cauldrons. Some Danish pottery of the period
exists – mainly hemispherical bowls with rounded bases, in
smoothed black or brown ware, without handles or legs.
Only in Sweden has better-class pottery been encountered –
well fired and decorated. Some of this is from Birka, perhaps
imported from Finland. The fact that in Birka and Hedeby,
which were both Viking Age trading centres, there has been
found excellent pottery, often painted or with plastic ornament, which was imported from the Rhineland and Friesland, cannot conceal the truth that the potter's art was
neglected in the Viking homelands, although less in Sweden
than in the rest of Scandinavia.

   Finally there remain two other fields of Viking craftsman-
ship: glassware and coins. In Hedeby crucibles and other
witnesses to glass production have been found – although
this does not invalidate the view that the finer glass found
in the graves of the nobles had been imported. As for coins,
it has been established that the Scandinavian countries were
minting them as far back as the ninth century, but more
of that later.

CHAPTER SEVEN

Dress and Jewellery

DRESS

How did the Vikings dress? We would love to be able to see Viking men and women, observe the cut of their clothes, get a general impression of their clothing, of the fashion or fashions of Viking times. This is not completely impossible. Three types of source can be used. First, archaeological discoveries, which fall into two separate groups: fragments of Viking dress which afford clues to technique and detail, and Viking representations of themselves, which give the general picture. The second source is provided by European finds outside Scandinavia; and the third comprises descriptions of Viking dress in literature.

The Scandinavian archaeological find which affords the best impression of Viking costume in the ninth century is the ship from Oseberg in south Norway, a splendid treasure brought to light more than fifty years ago and still revealing new features and new details. In this ship was found a tightly packed bundle of textiles which, after years of patient treatment of the badly damaged materials, has revealed its contents: a woven tapestry designed to hang in the great hall. Such wall hangings were common in the Viking Age. The best-known parallel outside Scandinavia is the famous embroidery known as the Bayeux Tapestry. In Old Norse a band of tapestry such as that from Oseberg was called *refill* or *tjald*. The Oseberg specimen is only eight inches high, a fact which Robert Kloster has explained by saying that it had to be so placed in the hall that people sitting around could see and study it. If it were hung high in a dark and smoky hall it would not be seen at all; if it were hung too low it would be obscured by the heads of the people at the table. There was not much room to play with, hence the narrowness.

The original colours of this Oseberg tapestry were mainly red and yellowish brown. It had numerous figures on it, and a simple decorative frame. Clearly the themes of the tapestry were drawn from myths, tales, and heroic poems. We see warriors in plenty, berserks in chain-mail, Valkyries, horsemen; there are two-seated open carts and covered wagons, the latter looking like prairie wagons. Between these pictures, as space-fillers, we find birds, zigzag lines, swastikas, knot-like patterns, and so on. The weapons depicted are mainly spears and arrows, but there are also swords and axes. The predominance of the spear is striking – it is found everywhere, not only in the warriors' hands but also standing free. At first glance the horses seem to be in a grove of tall tulip-like flowers; it is not a flower-grove, but a dense forest of deadly spears. The scenes on the Oseberg tapestry undoubtedly represent a land battle – no ships are in sight. They are difficult to interpret, but one of them, a particularly vivid battle scene, with spears, shieldwall, berserks, and a solitary warrior in a chariot has been explained by Bjørn Hougen as an illustration of the battle of Bravalla, with King Harald Hilditönn in the chariot.

The costumes on the Oseberg tapestry are very interesting. Some men wear helmet and coat of mail, and have white oval shields and spears; but some seem to be in civilian clothes, though they too carry the indispensable spear. Their clothes consist of an apparently thick woollen coat reaching half-way down the thigh or a little higher. The sleeves are long, and the coat, though occasionally belted, usually hangs loose. Yet it seems to be tailored: it fits neatly at the waist. This coat or jacket is familiar from other Viking finds in the North; for instance from carved stones from Gotland, a Norwegian stone, and a bronze statuette from Skane. It is the same kind of coat that is shown on the Lindisfarne stone mentioned above.

Two kinds of trousers are depicted in the Oseberg tapestry: they are either long and tight (again as in the Gotland and Lindisfarne stones) or else wide and baggy, rather like plus-fours – the same type of trousers, though with a rather different cut, as appear on some of the men shown on the Gotland stones. The Arab, Ibn Rustah, in the tenth century, said of the Rus traders that they used very full trousers, gathered at the knees. The two Vikings shown on the Smiss-i-När (Gotland) stone are engaged in a duel, and their wide trousers stick out horizontally below the knee to such an extent that one is inclined to believe they are supported on some sort of frame like a crinoline. Trousers of this baggy kind, which used so much material, would of course be appropriate to rich and noble persons who liked to display their wealth. It is a common-place that, always and everywhere, fashions are dictated not least by vanity and the desire to flaunt the wearer's riches.

There is yet a third garment, depicted on the Oseberg tapestry. This is a long cape or cloak ending in two points reaching almost to the ground, and worn either of two ways – with the points at either side or else at back and front. This cloak, again, is well represented on the Gotland stones. We are reminded of Ibn Fadlan's report that the Rus traders wore their cloaks thrown over one side so as to keep one arm free. This the Gotland carvings confirm. The long cloak hanging freely from the shoulders is a stately garment. Its appearance is not in the least military, but it has a dignity which consorts well with the other civilian clothing of the Vikings. Where, as occasionally happens, Scandinavian leaders are shown in pictures from other lands during the Viking Age, they are wearing this impressive cloak over the long-sleeved knee-length jacket. This is how Cnut the Great appears on an English (illuminated) manuscript, which shows the king and his queen, beneath flying angels, placing a large cross of gold on the altar of the new minster at Winchester.

In the Oseberg tapestry are several women dressed alike in the long costumes which are also to be seen in various Swedish sources – carved stones from Gotland (Tjängvide for instance), and four small central Swedish silver figures. The textile expert, Agnes Geijer, in a painstaking analysis of the cloth fragments from the graves at Birka, has increased our knowledge of the clothing of well-to-do women in Viking times. Next to her skin the Viking woman of standing wore a fine chemise, sometimes pleated; and over this a sleeveless dress with straps which hung from two oval bronze brooches worn on the breast. The dress reached to the ground and even had a train. Over the dress was worn a sleeveless cape which, when thrown back, showed the whiteness of her arms, for which the Nordic woman was much admired. She must have made an impressive figure striding along in her flowing dress, adorned with necklaces and domed oval brooches from which hung on fine chains her scissors, a container for needles, knife, and keys. We shall be reminded of her appearance when we refer later to Ibn Fadlan's remarks about the women of the Rus folk. Her hair was worn in a big knot at the back of her neck, gathered into a hairnet or under a cap. Young girls were evidently permitted a less formal costume, as is shown on one side of the Oseberg wagon by the gay young girl wearing a short skirt and long boots.

Not infrequently men are depicted with pointed or round-topped hats. These were made of leather or cloth, and might be cut round the temples. Women too are sometimes shown with caps or cap-like head-dresses. Also from the Oseberg find are women's shoes sewn from tanned leather.

The Vikings loved splendour. In their graves, especially those of Birka, remnants of the most exquisitely decorated materials have been found. These include Chinese silk, embroidery in gold thread of extreme fineness and technical skill from Byzantium and the Orient, passementerie, heavy gold brocade, and plaited cords of the finest quality. The silks and many of the other materials were, of course, imported, but sometimes the brocade shows an unmistakably Nordic style. An example of the splendid equipment of a Viking warrior comes from a grave at Mammen in Central Jutland. With the dead man lay his silver-inlaid battle-axe, and under his head was a down pillow; only fragments of his cloak remained, but they showed it to have been adorned with free patterns in embroidery. His two bracelets or cuffs of wool, silk-covered and worked with gold thread were well preserved, and so too were a couple of very finely made, streamer-shaped, silk ribbons, the broad part of which showed delicate gold embroidery in an elaborate tendril pattern. These ribbons were probably the ornament called *hlað* in the sagas, which the Viking wore on his forehead. Even the toughest warriors enjoyed dressing in such finery; according to the saga Skarphedin, the most ruthless of all Njal's sons, wore his elegant silk *hlað* when he went to the Thing.

In this Jutland grave, as in about sixty of the Birka graves – and in Gotland finds too – are wool and silk ribbons made by the technique called 'tablet-weaving', an old method of manufacture in Scandinavia. In the grave of the Oseberg queen was found a ribbon loom, set up ready for work, and containing no fewer than fifty-two tablets. Another weaving technique, *sprang*, is evidenced in graves at Birka.

It is not easy to determine whether the finer textiles found in these graves were imported or home-produced. Silk, of course, came from abroad, but it is probable that a great deal of the elaborate material mentioned above was made by Norse experts. An example of an imported material is the extremely fine woollen fabric found at Oseberg and Birka, which resembles a worsted, and is so precisely woven as to suggest mass-production on a scale that could scarcely have been organized within Scandinavia. Agnes Geijer is inclined to think that this fine material is Frankish and to identify it with the famous 'Frisian cloth', called in Frankish texts *pallia fresonica*, which Charlemagne considered worthy to present to the Caliph Haroun Al Raschid in exchange for a white elephant.

Finally, in connexion with the Viking costume must be mentioned a *refill* or tapestry from the village of Skog in Northern Sweden, now preserved in Stockholm Museum. It belongs to the last years of the Viking period, and shows a number of figures, some human beings, others clearly gods, dressed in clothes which include wide baggy trousers of much the same kind as those in the Oseberg tapestry. This fashion, it seems, lasted right through the Viking Age, from the ninth century to the eleventh.

JEWELLERY

How did the Vikings adorn themselves and their women-folk? The man's only adornment, apart from the *hlað* mentioned above, was the bracelet, the braided or twisted ring of gold or silver so often mentioned in the sagas as the gift which a king or earl gave to his retainers or skalds. The women had more jewellery – gold and silver rings, like the man's but often bigger; used for the neck or perhaps the hair, as well as sets of brooches worn on the breast. The composition of these sets of dress-fastenings generally took a standardized form, with a pair of gilt-bronze brooches, recalling in their domed, elliptical shape the form of a tortoise-shell, flanking a third brooch of different type. Sometimes the central brooch might be round, but often it would be of the three-lobed 'trefoil' type, in bronze or silver. Comparative study shows that while one main element of the assembly was of Scandinavian origin, the other was derived from a foreign fashion. The 'tortoise-brooches' are native, developed from a well-known Scandinavian prototype. In early Viking times they were of simple shape, decorated with separate animal figures which were clearly drawn and easily distinguished. Later on they assumed a more elaborate form: over a smooth gilt bowl a second plate was added, and complex, rather degenerate, animal-ornament was imposed on a basic network of decorative framing. With the use of openwork and the generally more plastic treatment of the ornament (especially in the development of large bosses, which often bore animal heads or figures so prominent as to dominate the whole design) these late tortoise-brooches took on an almost baroque appearance.

The trefoil-brooch was not Scandinavian, but Frankish in origin, and began as an ornament for men. Frankish male garments used lots of straps – shoulder straps, belt, and sword straps. All these had oblong tags at their ends, decorated with leaf designs, especially of acanthus foliage. Where three of these strap ends met it was natural to combine them into a three-lobed complex which could then be used as decoration alone wherever three straps crossed; hence the three-lobed shoulder-brooch to be seen in Frankish miniatures. No doubt these were among the loot which the Vikings brought home from their raids. One such three-lobed gold trefoil-brooch, splendidly decorated, was found in a Norwegian hoard dating from the ninth century. This three-lobed type of brooch, then, embellished with characteristic Carolingian leaf-ornamentation of classical type, found its way to the North, but as the Viking warrior's costume did not particularly require it he gave the brooch to his wife. Thus the trefoil-brooch came to be worn by Scandinavian women. Before long its foliage decoration, so unusual in Norse design, was replaced by indigenous animal-ornament. Jewellery, too, can have a history all of its own.

Of course there were other types of decorative dress-fittings in the Viking Age. The 'equal-armed' bronze brooch had a similar origin to the three-lobed type, deriving from a combination of two metal strap ends. Probably the simple oblong brooch also developed from a strap end. A common type of the later Viking period is the round silver filigree brooch divided into four sections into which animal-motifs were fitted. The type of ornamentation, of course, indicates the age as well as the origin of these objects. Those with pure Carolingian plant-ornament or with animal-ornament characteristic of the British Isles are clearly imported: but the Viking silversmiths and goldsmiths were skilled craftsmen who are often found to have copied Frankish work; the products then show competence and a certain robust force, but do not achieve the finish and elegance of the foreign originals.

However, as early as the year 900, less than half-way through the Viking period, the Scandinavian goldsmiths and silversmiths came into their own. Their apprenticeship in design was over, and from then on they produced independent works in styles which were quite their own. A favourite type, especially in eastern Scandinavia, was the penannular brooch; another was the heavy silver bracelet either deeply-grooved or with the surface broken up into thick knobs or studs; a third was a spiral bracelet with impressed ornament and heavy, bevelled terminals. All these are probably of Baltic origin.

Certain types of silver ornaments are rarely found in Viking graves, but are common in those deposits that

archaeologists call 'silver hoards' or 'treasures' which are
particularly abundant on Gotland. These hoards were probably not votive offerings to the gods; accordingly there
would seem to have been two main motives for burying
them. The first is that the objects were buried because of
the common belief that they would be useful in the after-
life. A thirteenth century literary source, Snorri's *Ynglinga
Saga*, observes that what a man buried in the ground he
would enjoy in Valhalla. The second is that in time of war
or other misfortune people concealed their valuables in the
earth and did not survive to reclaim them. Each explanation
has some justification, though many scholars rely too much
on the second one when they plot the course of warfare.

Silver hoards from the ninth century are fairly rare, but
they become more numerous as the Viking Age develops.
They consist of three types of object: trinkets, 'broken
silver', and coins. Gold objects are very scarce, because
during the entire Viking period silver had replaced gold as
the primary metal of value. Silver production, especially
from the Arab mines, had ousted late-Roman gold.

The principal type of personal adornment found in the
older silver hoards is the spiral bracelet already mentioned,
with its characteristic terminals. In the later hoards, however, other types prevail: twisted or braided armlets and
neck-rings, round filigree brooches ornamented with spiral
and vine patterns (copies of Carolingian or perhaps English
originals) and long finely-made chains (showing the influence of textile techniques) ending in animal heads and
sometimes carrying amulets in the form of Thor's hammer.
It must be emphasized again that these objects are rarely
found in graves, a fact which suggests that definite laws or,
at least, traditions must have governed the choice of
objects fit and proper for burying with the dead.

'Broken silver', the second component of the hoards,
especially the later ones, was used for making payments by

weight for goods purchased. Sometimes the scales too were buried (they are also found in graves). They are small collapsible balances fitted with pans; and the weights are contained in round bronze boxes. The 'broken silver' itself consists of bits of rings and other bars and ingots, and coins which were therefore not used as currency. In many cases fragments of fine oriental metalwork show that when business required it the Viking would not hesitate to cut into pieces the most beautiful art treasures.

The third element in the hoards is coinage, mostly complete and undamaged. This is in general significant for the dating of such deposits. The coins which predominate are those of the east. Not only in the ninth century but throughout most of the tenth as well, the hoards contain masses of Arabic coins – *dirhems** coming in the main from the Samanide chieftains of Samarkand – but few Carolingian and Anglo-Saxon coins. Not until the large payments of danegeld by England at the end of the tenth century and the first half of the eleventh did Anglo-Saxon coins become plentiful. At the same period, German coins appeared from Saxony and the Rhineland, which confirms the fact that silver mining began in the Harz about the middle of the tenth century. Byzantine coins are rare throughout the entire Viking period. Arab coins were not imported into Scandinavia after the end of the tenth century. No doubt this is due to an Eastern 'silver crisis' which obviously affected the currency – fewer coins were issued and they were of debased metal. The region in which most of these foreign coins are found is Gotland, which shows that this large island was the main trading area of the Baltic and the whole of southern Scandinavia. A count made some years ago of the coins found on Gotland gave the following result: Arabic, 25,000; Anglo-Saxon, 18,000; German,

* With 'Kufic' inscriptions, named after the town Kufa, south-west of Baghdad.

30,000. For the whole of Denmark the corresponding figures were: 3,800, 4,000, 8,900; and for Norway they were smaller than for Denmark.

All this, of course, concerns foreign coins; but the Vikings also minted their own coins, both at home and abroad, and to this matter we shall return.

CHAPTER EIGHT

Transport

SHIPS

The ships of the Vikings were the supreme achievement of their technical skill, the pinnacle of their material culture; they were the foundation of their power, their delight, and their most treasured possession. What the temple was to the Greeks, the ship was to the Vikings: the complete and harmonious expression of a rare ability. Whether the black ship was on its 'cool keel', gliding peacefully away from land, or, like 'the goat of the sea', butting the waves with its stem, it was always the Vikings' favourite creation, made by his skilful hand and affectionately remembered in his poetry. It is appropriate that Norway in particular should have preserved for us several specimens of its vessels from the Viking Age, as, because of their extensive coastline, the Norwegians know the sea as do few other nations. An Icelandic poet from the Viking period, Egil Skallagrimsson, called the breakers that beat against the rugged, rocky Norwegian coast 'the island-studded belt round Norway'. Here, by the sea's edge, three great mounds were built in Viking times, each of which bequeathed a Viking ship to posterity. The three ships were found in the Oslo Fjord: at Tune on the eastern side, and at Gokstad and Oseberg on the western side. All three can be seen today in the Viking Ship Museum at Bygdø outside Oslo.

The Tune ship was excavated in 1867, in a huge grave-mound about 260 ft in diameter. The ship was lying

north-to-south, embedded in blue clay which had preserved
its timbers through the centuries. Athwart the stern was a
platform of poles, their ends penetrating into the clay beyond
the ship's bulwarks, and on this platform had been built a
burial-chamber of oak, covered by a flat roof. The chamber
had been robbed and ransacked in ancient times, but within
it the excavators found the remains of a man and a horse,
the latter apparently buried in a standing position. Little
else had survived: a wooden spade, some carved bits of
wood, fragments of clothing and weapons, and a few beads.
The ship itself, poorly preserved in the ground, was about
65 ft long, 14 ft in the beam, and about $4\frac{1}{2}$ ft deep from
its gunwale to the underside of the keel. It was made from
oak, with a rudder of pine. It had been placed in the
mound with its mast erect, but its eleven pairs of oars had
been removed before the burial ceremony. Shetelig describes this Tune ship as a good workmanlike vessel, devoid
of decoration; sitting low in the water, and very suitable
for navigating shallow water such as estuaries. It is dated
approximately to the end of the ninth century.

The Gokstad ship (Pl. 8), in a mound 162 ft wide and
16 ft high, was excavated in 1880. It was deeply buried in
blue clay, which had preserved it, with its bow towards the
sea. The mast had been cut off level with the roof of the
timbered burial-chamber which was built athwart the stern
of the vessel. This chamber, too, had been pillaged long
ago, as a large hole in the ship's side and in the wall of the
chamber showed. Within there had been buried a chieftain
lying, elegantly dressed and armed, in his bed. An examination of the skeleton showed him to have been a powerfully-
built man of middle-age, almost six feet tall. He was well
equipped for his journey: there were three rowing-boats and
five beds in the prow of the ship; amidships there was an
abundance of kitchen utensils, such as bronze and iron
cauldrons, plates, cups, candlesticks, barrels, and wooden

spades; and a wooden gaming board and a carved sledge were also included. In the burial-chamber there were fragments of woollen cloth and of silk enriched with gold threadwork, the remains of a leather purse, an axe, an iron belt-buckle, and strap-mounts of lead and gilded bronze. Outside the chamber were found the bones of a peacock, and near the ship the remains of eighteen slaughtered animals – twelve horses and six dogs. The burial dates from around the year 900.

The ship, which was composed entirely of oak, is well preserved; it is about 76 ft long, $17\frac{1}{2}$ ft wide, and nearly $6\frac{1}{2}$ ft deep from the gunwale to the bottom of the keel, and with equipment weighs a little over twenty tons net. A facsimile of the ship of nearly 32 registered tons, made in 1893, successfully crossed the Atlantic. The main components of the Gokstad ship are keel, stem, stern-post, ribs, and planking. Compared with the older vessels of the Scandinavian Iron Age, the Viking ships show several improvements in construction: the flat bottom plank is replaced by a true keel which serves as a backbone and is strong enough to resist the pressure of the water outside. The keel, stem, and stern-post are each made of a single piece of timber; of the sixteen rows of planking, nine are below the waterline, and the strakes are riveted together, each overlapping the one below, caulked with tarred rope, and lashed to the ribs by withies passing through cleats cut from the material of the strakes. This construction gave the vessel considerable elasticity in rough weather. Amidships was a heavy block of oak in which the mast was set, and on top of this block was yet another, shaped like a fish (hence the name 'mastfish'), with a hole in the middle, to support the erected mast.

Apart from mast and sail the ship was equipped with sixteen pairs of oars. As it stood in the mound where it was discovered, it bore along each gunwale thirty-two shields,

two for each oar-hole, hung in such a way that each shield
half covered the next. The shields were painted alternately
black and yellow, and formed a continuous line from bow
to stern. This display decorated the ship only in harbour,
not when it was under sail, and we shall return to this point
when we come to consider the original significance of the
ship-burial. The rudder was a single piece of oak, shaped
like the blade of a huge oar, about 11 ft long, fastened to
the starboard quarter of the vessel by a stout riveted cleat.
Through the rudder, through this cleat, and finally through
the ship's side and the rib, ran a hole for a thick rope of
osiers. In the rudder-neck the tiller was put in at a height to
suit the steersman on the rising poop. When the Norwegian
Captain Magnus Andersen sailed the facsimile of the Gokstad ship to America in 1893 he reported: 'This rudder
must be regarded as one of the conclusive proofs of our fore-
fathers' acumen and skill in shipbuilding and seamanship. The rudder is a work of genius . . . a man could steer
with this tiller in all kinds of weather without the least dis-
comfort.'

The ship's mast, estimated to have been about 40 ft high,
was made of pine. The sail was probably square, but further
details of its shape and colour are not given by the find. The
sagas, and other literary sources, tell of blue and red striped
sails, or of entirely red ones. The Gotland stones usually
depict chequered sails. In the bows of the Gokstad ship lay
its iron anchor completely rusted; and here too were the
pine oars: some 17 ft long, and some a little longer (up to
19¼ ft), their blades small and lancet-shaped. The oar-holes
were a little higher towards the prow and stern than they
were amidships. In neither the Gokstad nor the Oseberg
ship were there any traces of thwarts for the oarsmen, and
there was no chance, says Shetelig, to test the ship's qualities
under oars during the voyage of the facsimile, simply because no adequately trained rowers were available. It is

possible that the rowers used their own sea-chests, fastened in some way, as seats.

The gangway of the Gokstad ship also came to light: a narrow plank of spruce, some 24 ft long, with a hole at one end for securing it, and cut-out steps on its top-side. There were also found in the ship four strong planks, ending in carved animals' heads; these are thought to be the gables of a tent intended to be pitched on shore when the ship lay moored. The animals' heads were not intended only for decoration. They were also thought effective in putting to flight anything eerie which might come to attack those sleeping in the tent. No fewer than eight beds, or fragments of them, were provided for the Viking buried in the Gokstad ship, two of them with beautifully carved animals' heads to protect the sleeper. Presumably these two belonged with the tent. Fragments of blankets and eiderdowns came to light, too, of which the surviving colours were mainly black and yellow and, in a few cases, red. Both Shetelig and Captain Magnus Andersen testify to the remarkable attention to detail which distinguishes the Gokstad ship.

Finally we come to the Oseberg ship (Pl. 10), that celebrated revelation of the art and spirit of the Vikings. It was found in 1903, and excavated in the following year from a mound originally nearly 20 ft high and over 120 ft in diameter, made of peat which, with the subsoil of blue clay, acted as the preservative which kept the ship's wonderful wood carvings intact. This vessel, like the other two, faced north-south, the bow pointing south to the sea. Subsidence and pressure in the mound had somewhat damaged the ship, and grave-robbers had been busy in antiquity. The ship was moored to a large stone inside the mound, and the timbered grave-chamber in the stern contained the remains of two women. The skeleton of one of them, a young woman of twenty-five to thirty, was broken up: only a little of it was inside the chamber, rather more of it outside. The grave-robbers had evidently been particularly interested in removing her body. The other woman was older, sixty to seventy, and her skeleton showed signs of some such bone disease as arthritis. It is reasonable to conclude that the younger woman was the mistress, the noble lady (since it was her body the robbers had tried to remove), and the older one her servant. The Norwegian archaeologist, A. W. Brøgger, has advanced the attractive theory that the lady in the grave was Queen Asa, mother of King Halfdan the Black and grandmother of King Harald Finehair, on his father's side. This theory fits the dating of the Oseberg find, for the burial must have taken place some time in the second half of the ninth century. Examination of plant deposits indicates that the event occurred one August or September. The ship, however, was an old one for that time, for its ornamentation belongs on stylistic grounds to about 800, the very beginning of the Viking period. On this basis the Oseberg ship would be a hundred years older than those from Tune and Gokstad.

The two women had been given a splendid burial: beds, pillows, blankets, eiderdowns, several chests and barrels (one of which contained wild apples), four magnificent carved head-posts adorned with animal heads, the wall-hanging described in detail above, a couple of looms, and some iron 'rattles' probably intended, like the animal-headed posts, to frighten off evil spirits. The grave-robbers had broken in from the south, having dug out a 9-ft tunnel to the prow of the ship, cutting away its great spiral finial, they finally reached the burial-chamber, which they entered through a hole broken in its roof. In the bow of the ship lay many things of the greatest historical and artistic value: first of all a four-wheeled wooden cart or carriage with carved panels, and four sledges – three of them ornamented with magnificent carvings. Then there were two tents, three beds, a chair, a hand-loom, a round stave inscribed with runes,

two wooden barrels, a number of battens and oars, a large
baler, an anchor-stock, wooden tubs, gang-planks, and
numerous other things. Aft was found kitchen equipment:
an iron knife and axes with handles, wooden plates and
jugs, two iron cauldrons, one with a stand, and a hand-mill.
On a couple of oak planks was laid out an ox. Here and
there in the ship were found fruits, grain, and seed: two
kinds of apple, walnuts, hazelnuts, wheat, cress, and the
blue dye-plant known as woad.

The Oseberg ship is, for the most part, well preserved. It
is built throughout of oak, except for parts of the gunwale
which are of beech. The dimensions are about $71\frac{1}{2}$ ft long,
17 ft wide, and nearly 5 ft deep from gunwale to keel. Although in its design and construction it resembles the other
two ships, the Oseberg vessel is clearly less strongly built. It
contained fewer store-chambers for supplies; there was no
provision for closure of the oar-holes against heavy seas; and
the pine oars (fifteen pairs) were short (12 to 13 ft), elegant,
and decorated, and clearly newly-made for the funeral. The
mast and the rudder were new and not designed for practical
use. For these reasons Shetelig is inclined to believe that
the ship used for the Oseberg burial was an old vessel
which had been laid up, and that it was refitted for its last
journey. Even when this ship was new, however, it could
not have been intended for hard work or long journeys;
it was a luxury ship, designed as such. Its elegant lines and
superb, well-preserved ornamentation still charm everyone who comes to see it, as it stands in its wing in the Viking
Ship Museum near Oslo. No one has better described
it than Haakon Shetelig, the affectionate interpreter
of the Oseberg discoveries. He writes: 'The gunwales
run low above the water in a long straight line, to accommodate the oars at an even height, and then rise at each
end of the ship in a steep curve to more than sixteen feet
above the water-line, finishing in a slender free spiral.'

The lines of the Oseberg ship are inexpressibly fine and pure.

The prow is decorated on each side with elegant friezes which look like plant-scrolls but are not. They are in fact composed of true Scandinavian animal-ornament of the kind produced about 800, freely rhythmic yet indicative of academic discipline and training. The examples on the Oseberg prow convey a vivid impression of a traditional form of native art which was already nearly 300 years old at the beginning of the Viking period, and even so had not yet begun to degenerate. Elsewhere on the Oseberg ship we see another style of ornamentation, again based on animal forms, but of a different character. Its beasts are powerful, baroque creations made without concern for delicacy of line. The style is devoid of all elegance and relies for its effect upon bizarre presentation and grotesque humour. An innovation of the later Viking period, it was surely inspired by the Vikings' fresh, unconventional apprehension of the decorative classical lion-motifs of Carolingian France. These creatures seem to have attracted and amused the Vikings, who converted them into new types of tumbling, posturing comic beasts with broad faces and strong paws, the so-called 'gripping beasts'.

The prow of the Oseberg ship rises to a high spiral, ending in a snake's head. The top of the stern-post of the ship is missing, but presumably it showed the snake's tail. The whole ship, then, looked like a fabulous monster as it breasted the waves, its head and tail glistening, and its stout body filled with men.

Viewed in a nautical European perspective, the Viking ship represents the completion rather than the beginning of an evolutionary process. It marks the end of centuries of development of the clinker-built rowing-boat, which gradually transformed it into a craft equipped with keel, mast, and sail. Throughout the Viking period this 'longship' became steadily larger. The biggest vessels of Cnut the Great were probably twice as big as the Gokstad ship, but they remained the same in principle – vessels designed for battle as well as commerce. The Bayeux Tapestry, whose date coincides with the later Viking period, shows the same type of ship in use for all purposes. With the end of the Viking period this unity of function ceases and two separate types of ship were evolved: one built for speed and mobility in battle, the other for its carrying capacity as a trader; one for war and one for peace.

CARTS AND SLEDGES

The longships may have ruled the waves, but how did the Vikings get about on land? The best method of transport for the individual was – and had been for 2,000 years – the horse, and we have already noted the Viking's high regard and affection for his mount. But a horse alone does little to solve the problem of heavy transport. For this the Vikings had two traditional vehicles: the cart and the sledge. In the Oseberg ship was found the famous four-wheeled cart (Pl. 9) fitted with heavy wheels with a central hub and long shafts. The curved body of the vehicle is completely covered with carvings which are not only decorations but significant illustrations of myths and legends. Some perhaps will claim that this is a clear example of a sacred carriage richly decorated for religious use, and therefore no proof that four-wheeled carts were commonly employed as a means of transport in Viking Scandinavia, especially as the roads there cannot have been very serviceable. One answer to this argument is that, in fact, good paved roads already existed in Denmark in Roman times; and we must not be tempted to assume from Adam of Bremen's grim description of Jutland and

other northern territories that the north was a trackless
wilderness. Other evidence to this effect is found in the
Oseberg tapestry which depicts at least two varieties of four-
wheeled transport – one open and the other covered. Doubtless it was possible to drive four-wheeled carts and coaches,
protected by horsemen, across wide stretches of the Scandinavian lowlands. Yet another conformation of the existence of usable roads in the later Viking period is found in
the many Swedish rune-stones which, in paying tribute to
the man over whom they are raised, often mention that
among his good deeds was the making of a bridge; this
phrase 'to make a bridge' usually meant to lay a firm road
across swampy ground. There is good reason for agreeing
with Sune Lindqvist that this frequently implies the improvement or renewal of existing routes used by horsemen
and carriages. There is every reason to believe that carts and
carriages were extensively used in the north during the
summer, and in southern Scandinavia in spring and
autumn, too, when the snow was absent. But what about
the winter? The answer quite simply is that in winter transport was easier still, as the Vikings had their sledges. Among
the Oseberg relics were found three well-preserved, finely
carved wooden sledges with toboggan-shaped bases and
detachable bodies with carved animal heads and richly
decorated sides (Pl. 12).

In addition there was a less ornate fourth, a simple working sledge, also with a detachable body. The remains of a
sledge were also found in the Gokstad ship. It is evident that
in the long northern winter the extensive tracts of snow and
ice-covered lakes and rivers encouraged long journeys by
sledge or skis – for the Vikings used skis too. That, in winter,
the Vikings preferred to travel by land rather than by sea
is apparent from the sagas. For example, on his long journey
to Russia and back St Olaf travelled by land during the
winter; it was without doubt much easier.

CHAPTER NINE

Towns, Earthworks, and Camps

TOWNS

During the Viking period Scandinavian society gradually reached the stage of development at which towns were founded. There were two conflicting factors at work in the creation of the Viking towns: trade and piracy – the more flourishing the former, the more lucrative the latter. Accordingly towns were located well up narrow but navigable fjords and surrounded by defensive earthworks. There was always the danger that raiding enemies would suddenly attack, but the sea-going merchants were armed and knew how to use their weapons. Even so, things often went wrong; ships were plundered and towns burnt; but stronger than fear was the need for the trade on which their whole livelihood depended.

Along the North Sea and the Baltic coasts, like blind eyes, lie the vanished towns of the Vikings, the sites of Northern Europe's oldest trading centres, following the winding route from the mouth of the Rhine along the coast of Jutland right up to Lake Malar in the north. If you think of the traders of those times – wherever they came from or wherever they were bound – a picture of trading towns, once swarming with life, but now dead, springs to mind: the Frisian town of Dorestad; Hedeby in the south of Denmark; farther north, still in Denmark, Lindholm Høje, on the Lim Fjord; the Latvian Grobin; the Norse-Slav Wolin; the Estonian Truso; the Swedish Birka; and, in southern Norway,

Skiringssal. What do we know of these vanished towns? What traces of them remain?

Grobin has already been mentioned, and we have also dealt with Dorestad and its final destruction by natural forces, but let us now look at Hedeby.

Hedeby

It lay at the head of the narrow but navigable fjord, the Slie, which cuts deep into south Slesvig from the Baltic. Hedeby means 'the town at the heaths'. On three sides – north, west, and south – it was defended by a great semi-circular rampart, but to the east it was wide open to the waters of the cove of Haddeby Nor. The grass-grown remains of the defensive earthworks are still impressive, even though they are the less formidable for the decay of their former timber revetments. Within these defences the town covered some sixty acres, now fertile fields, and in circumference was the largest town in the North during the Viking period. There were two gates in the wall, south and north, and probably a third in the south-west. From 1900 until the outbreak of the Second World War with some interruptions, German archaeologists dug in and around Hedeby.

Their excavations showed that the semi-circular rampart was not at the outset as high and broad as it now appears. It grew in successive stages from a relatively low and simple rampart with a stockade and ditch to a defensive complex of extraordinary dimensions. On the other hand its circumference has apparently remained constant. Either the rampart when originally built enclosed space greater than the actual area of the town, with an eye to its expansion, or else it was not built until the town had already reached a certain size. The latter seems more likely.

In Viking times a rivulet ran through the town, cutting through the west wall and flowing into Haddeby Nor; the mouth of this stream is the site of the oldest part of the town. This modest stream was most important to the Viking town because it supplied drinking water. It has also proved valuable to the archaeologists, because successive deposits of rubbish on its bed – recognizable layers lying one over another – have provided a physical index to the relative chronology of the various phases of the town's occupation. The excavators were also able to observe the changing relationship between various of the town's wooden buildings and the river. At times the houses, whose sites were clearly to be seen, were built close to the stream, the banks of which were supported by wooden piles; in other phases the houses were built well back from the river, separated from it by an open space. In this low-lying part of Hedeby the inhabitants of nearly every house had dug a well fitted with a wooden pipe (of excellent cooper's work) which agrees with the Arab merchant Al-Tartushi's observations of the town's freshwater wells on his visit to it in the tenth century (See p. 42). The boggy ground at the edge of Haddeby Nor has preserved the lower foundations of the houses particularly well; and anyone who visited the site of the excavations where whole areas at a time were uncovered, must have left with the impression of a stubble-field in which the angel of death had carefully cut away with his scythe the upper ninetenths of all human habitations (Pl. 13). From these remains it has been established that the wooden houses included some that were stave-built (close vertical planking), others there were of framed construction with wattle-and-daub panels between the structural timbers, and others constructed like log huts. The houses had their gable-ends to the street, with barns and stables behind, and the hearths were in the centre of the floor. In the later, higher, western end of the town were found small wattle-and-daub buildings with 'sunken' floors dug into the ground, in which the fireplace occupied one corner.

Various crafts flourished in Hedeby. There are traces of iron-smelting, weaving, industries using bone and horn, bronze-casting, glass-making, minting of coins, and potteries. Sherds of imported Rhenish earthenware among the finds belong to the early ninth century. Very few farming implements were found. Inside the semi-circular rampart were two burial places, both in the western part of the town. One contained wooden coffins (lying east–west) but very few grave-goods. The other one, farther to the south, consisted of large wooden burial chambers, with a greater abundance of grave-goods, such as weapons and jewellery. A third, rather older, burial ground with cremation graves has recently been found close to the southern gate of the town. The animal bones found in many parts of the town were mainly food-remains, and they show that pigs and cows were the most plentiful and popular meat. Sheep and goats were also eaten, but very few horses and chickens, and no game at all. Dogs and cats had evidently been kept in the houses. Many varieties of plants and fruit were found: barley, wheat, hazelnuts, walnuts, apples, cherries, plums, sloes, elderberries, blackberries, raspberries, wild strawberries, and hops.

The cove, Haddeby Nor, provided a natural harbour for Hedeby. In 1953 divers found there a line of palisading, 480 ft long, which had apparently served as a harbour defence. South of this, about a hundred feet north-east of the estuary, and at a depth of about 9 ft the excavators came across the wreckage of a burnt clinker-built ship, made of oak and ash, about 48 ft long and 9 ft wide, a rather flat-bottomed coastal vessel, presumably of local construction; and in it were found the remains of a man whose face had been injured.

The question of the origin and age of Hedeby will be considered when we come to discuss its relationship with the adjacent earthwork, the famous Danevirke; but the town

clearly owed its existence to the trading-route between the
North Sea and the Baltic. It was a mercantile centre, sometimes in Danish, sometimes in German or Swedish possession.* The evidence for the final fate of Hedeby is provided
not only by literary but also by archaeological sources.
History testifies very plainly to the situation which arose in
the middle of the eleventh century, when King Swein
Estridsson of Denmark and King Harald Hardrada of Norway came to grips with each other. About 1050, while
Swein was engaged in the south with the German Emperor,
Harald seized the opportunity to fall upon Hedeby, plundering and burning it to the ground. As Swein, returning
from the south, approached the place, Harald's ships,
loaded with loot, made off. Swein pursued him and caught
up with him at Læso in the Kattegat, where Harald, to
lighten his vessels and escape, was forced to throw his rich
Hedeby plunder overboard – so that it floated on the wind-
swept Jutland sea, as the skald Thorleik the Fair says in his
song. Another skald, a Norwegian who was with King
Harald (quoted by Snorri), celebrated the fate of Hedeby in
jubilant song: 'Burnt in anger was Hedeby from end to
end. It was a doughty deed and one from which Swein will
smart. High rose the flames from the houses when, last night
before dawn, I stood on the stronghold's arm.' This 'arm' is
doubtless the northern extremity of the great semi-circular
rampart, where it runs into Haddeby Nor, and from where,
even today, one can command the best view of the whole
settlement.

During the excavations in the area of Hedeby near the
harbour, the top layer in many places proved to consist of
earth thick with charcoal and ash – evidence of the catastrophe by burning which brought the town's existence to an
end. On top of this layer there was no trace of refuse, and no

* There is reason to believe that it was the Swedes who constructed the
semi-circular wall, when they captured the town around 900.

other indication of human activity or survival. In the upper-
most deposits in the river-bed were discovered the burnt
remains of two men and a horse: these, like the ship in the
harbour, seem to be relics of the great fire of 1050 which destroyed the town of Hedeby for ever – or åt least almost for
ever. The earthworks of Hedeby will presumably last as long
as the earthworks of the Danevirke and it is noteworthy that
when, in the 1160s, King Valdemar reinforced the Danevirke with its strong red-brick wall, a hundred years had
elapsed since the razing of Hedeby. The town must have
had an attenuated life after 1050, for Adam of Bremen tells
the story of its plundering and burning by the Wends as
late as 1066.

In Scandinavian ecclesiastical history Hedeby is famous
as the scene of the first Christian mission to Denmark, where
the monk Ansgar was active between 826 and 829 as the
forerunner of the full introduction of Christianity to Denmark, which was to occur 150 years later. According to the
Arab trader who visited Hedeby in the middle of the tenth
century, the place was not quite without Christians, but the
religion did not really take root in Denmark until Harald
Bluetooth was converted. The oldest Christian church in
Denmark was undoubtedly Ansgar's, in or near Hedeby, but
all efforts to locate it have failed. It was doubtless built of
wood and, as we have seen, the lowest parts of timber
buildings were preserved in the swampy soil near the harbour; but nothing has been found there that might have
been Ansgar's church.

Slesvig

Near Hedeby, north of the Slie Fjord, lies the modern
town of Slesvig which cannot be proved by archaeological
evidence to have existed before the eleventh century. The
second element –vig is from the Latin vicus ('town') and was

embodied, in the time of the Vikings – and earlier as well –
in the names of many important trading centres in north-
west Germany, on the Channel coast, and in England:
among these are Brunswick, Wijk-bij-Duurstede (Dorestad),
Quentovic (Calais), Lundenwic (London), Eoferwic (York).
Slesvig, then, signifies 'the town at the Slie (fjord)', and
Hedeby 'the town at the heaths'; the latter corresponding
with the name *æt Hæþum* 'at the heaths', given to the place in
Alfred the Great's translation of Orosius (*c.* 900) by two
narrators, the Norwegian Ottar and the Anglo-Saxon
Wulfstan. Furthermore there is the important declaration
made a hundred years later by another Anglo-Saxon writer,
the chronicler Æthelweard, that the capital of the province
of Angel 'is in the Saxon language called Slesvig, but in
Danish, Hedeby'. Thus there is every reason to believe that
at the head of the Slie Fjord in the Viking Age lay the town
of Hedeby, and that it had two names, the Saxon Slesvig
and the Danish Hedeby. After the destruction of Hedeby in
1050, most of the survivors moved to the north of the fjord
and founded the present Slesvig, and the former name
'Hedeby' was gradually supplanted by 'Slesvig'.

Wolin

The next Viking town to be considered lay at the mouth of
the Oder in the Baltic, on the southern fringes of the Viking
'sphere of influence'. It is described by Adam of Bremen, in
the 1070s as 'the well-known town of Jumne, which affords
to the barbarians and Greeks [i.e. Greek Orthodox mer-
chants] in those parts a much used anchorage'. Adam continues:

As so many almost unbelievable tales have been told in praise
of this town, I think it is worth mentioning some matters of
interest: it is, for example, the largest town in Europe, inhabited
by Slavs and such other people as Greeks and barbarians.

Even visiting Saxons are permitted to live there on equal terms as long as they do not disclose they are Christians. But though the inhabitants are still bound by their heathen delusions, they are nevertheless more honourable and hospitable than any other people. There is an abundance of merchandise from the Nordic countries, and the town is well provided with all good and precious things.

Other writers who mention the town at the mouth of the Oder call it not Jumne but Jumneta (or, distorted : Vineta), Julin, or Wolin. Philologists have concluded that these are two names for the same place, comparable with Hedeby–Slesvig; on this basis Jumne or Jumneta is the Norse name for it, Julin or Wolin the Slav name – a conclusion all the more acceptable since the town probably had a mixed Slav–Scandinavian population. Archaeologists, on their side, have tried eagerly to locate the site or sites concerned. The Oder has three outlets: Peene in the west, Swine in the middle, and Dievenow in the east. On which of these three estuaries lay the town which Adam of Bremen mentioned so favourably? Answers to this question differ, but extensive excavations in and around the little modern town of Wolin on the Dievenow suggests that it may well have been there – let us then call the Viking town Wolin.

The most significant finds were located in the very middle of the town square at Wolin: thick layers of debris of which the lower strata date back to later Viking times. The remains of buildings and pottery have been dated with pretty fair accuracy; the various forms of house construction – stave, half-timber, log huts – represented on the site include Viking as well as post-Viking buildings (the latter from around 1200). There is a similar mixture of styles and techniques in the pottery, some of it Scandinavian and some Slav. The conclusion, then, is that here, where the present Wolin stands, on the eastern outlet of the river, the Vikings began to settle about the year 1000 and gradually became

assimilated into the existing population. There were doubtless good trading opportunities at such a place, though
Adam of Bremen's eulogies were probably a little exaggerated.

Another problem which has long occupied the interest of
historians is whether this Wolin, or Scandinavian Jumne,
is identical with the mythical 'Jomsborg' mentioned in
Danish historical writings of the twelfth century and in
Icelandic sagas of the thirteenth century (Sven Aggesen,
Saxo, the *Saga of the Jomsvikings*, and the *Knytlinga Saga*).
The Danish tradition is that when Harald Bluetooth was
banished from Denmark by his son Swein, he took refuge in
the land of the Wends, taught them the practice of piracy,
and established a base for these operations at Jomsborg.
Another version is that while at the height of his power in
Denmark he founded Jomsborg and gave it a Wendish
garrison, placing Danish chieftains in charge. The Icelandic
sagas are influenced by romantic ideas. According to them
Jomsborg was a purely Scandinavian military base, an
independent Viking colony, an ideal warrior community
run on Spartan principles, where no women were permitted,
and where great warriors and heroes were reared: figures
such as Palnatoki, Earl Sigvald, Bui the Stout, Vagn
Akason, Styrbjörn. Here was the famous citadel of the Joms-
Vikings, governed with harsh discipline; from its well-de-
signed artificial harbour, capable of accommodating 300
longships, the Joms-Vikings set out on those historic campaigns, which included Hjorungavag in Norway, Svöld
in Wendland or Denmark, and Fyrisvold in Sweden.
The splendour of their feats resounds through the ages
unaffected by the result of their battles – for the Joms-
Vikings seem to have been distinguished for suffering glorious defeats!

Behind the highly-coloured pictures the sagas present
there is certainly the historical fact that, throughout the

Viking period, from the time of King Godfred at the beginning of the ninth century to that of Jomsborg's destroyer,
Magnus the Good, just before the middle of the eleventh,
the Danes had vital interests along Germany's extensive
Baltic coasts, where the Slavs – Obotrites and Wends – lived.
There is a historical nemesis in the fact that Denmark,
when its lust for plundering had ceased, itself became
the victim of raids by the Wends who, in the twelfth century,
showed themselves so adept in the slowly acquired art of
piracy that it was not until the 1160s that the Danes and
Saxons managed to check them.

The question whether Wolin was in fact Jomsborg is not
at present settled. The solution of the problem would be
furthered if the town or its neighbourhood could produce
archaeological evidence of a Viking fort corresponding in
some degree to the account of the sagas, but no such evidence seems to be forthcoming. If the Viking relics discovered in Wolin had come to light outside the area where
Jomsborg was sought for, no one would have dreamt of connecting them with that stronghold.

Truso

Our next vanished Viking town is Truso. It is first mentioned by the traveller Wulfstan in the foreword to Alfred
the Great's version of Orosius's world history. Wulfstan's
account was re-discovered in early modern times – 1589 – by
the English geographer Richard Hakluyt, who was the first
to realize its significance; and since then it has been much
studied by both historians and geographers. As mentioned
earlier, Wulfstan describes his journey from Hedeby to
Truso; seven days and nights, he says, their vessel was constantly under sail; on their right was Wendland, on their
left Langeland, Lolland, Falster, and Skane – all belonging
to Denmark – then Bornholm, a sovereign state with its own

king, then Blekinge, More, Oland, and Gotland – all
Swedish. Wendland lay all the time to starboard, that is, as
far as the mouth of the Vistula. Then follows a somewhat
complicated account of Truso's position in the Vistula delta.
In their endeavours to locate the place scholars have come
to realize how little they could depend on Wulfstan's vague
description. Only the discovery of traces of a Viking colony
could give them something to go on, and in this connexion
German scholars have advanced the claims of the town of
Elbing, at the head of the Gulf of Danzig. No actual town
site has been uncovered there, but scattered deposits of
Viking weapons have been found and, more important, a
large and partly Scandinavian Viking Age cemetery has
come to light near Elbing railway station. Elbing's position
fits Wulfstan's remark that the Vistula formed the frontier
between Wendland in the west and Estland (Estonia) in the
east; and the name Truso may be connected with the half-
dried-out lake near Elbing, called Lake Drausen. If Truso
were indeed here, it must have had a mixture of populations
and excellent trading possibilities. The wide river Vistula
led towards the south-east, deep into the continent, and its
distant source was not far from the Dniester which flowed
into the Black Sea and provided a route to Byzantium.

While we are in the Baltic it is appropriate to mention a
commodity of the greatest importance in these regions many
centuries before the Vikings – amber. In the Bronze Age the
main source of supply was the west coast of Jutland, but by
the Iron Age the situation was entirely different. It is
significant that in early imperial times Pliny, when de-
scribing the quest of Roman traders for amber, does not
mention Jutland or other North Sea coastal areas, but
speaks only of the Baltic regions. The supplies of amber in
Jutland had become exhausted by the time of the Vikings, but
it was still plentiful in the Baltic. Truso must have been a
very convenient mart for amber trading.

Birka

The last of the vanished Viking towns, but certainly the most famous of them all, is Birka, the Swedish mercantile centre on the little island of Bjorko in Lake Malar in eastern Sweden. The island, like Hedeby, is well hidden from the open sea; to reach it one must first penetrate the Swedish archipelago, sail through the narrow strait where Stockholm now stands, and out into the wide expanse of eastern Lake Malar. And here, in the centre of the fairway, where the north-south and east-west sailing routes intersect, lies the island of Bjorko, lonely and secluded nowadays, but in Viking times seething with life and bustling with commerce. Birka lay on the north-western promontory of the island; and its fame as a market for furs and other Scandinavian wares attracted foreigners from many lands: Frisians, Anglo-Saxons, Germans, Balts, Greeks, and Orientals. That this is not just exaggeration and hearsay is evidenced by the rich finds in its many graves, in which Arab silver, Byzantine silks and brocades, Rhenish glass, Frisian cloth, and Frankish weapons have been found. Superb Scandinavian merchandise, too, has come to light in these ancient graves: first and foremost remnants of cloaks made of bear, fox, marten, otter, and beaver fur; and further such valuable commodities as reindeer antlers, walrus teeth, amber, and honey. Our sources of information about Birka are partly literary and partly archaeological. The latter evidence consists not only of grave-finds, but also of the remains of the town itself which can be seen to the present day. Some description of the scene would be appropriate. A visitor approaching the island of Bjorko from the south will first catch sight of a bare rock due south of the site of Birka, surmounted by a modern stone cross (of Irish design, oddly enough) erected in memory of St Ansgar's mission to

A. Danish sword-hilt

B. Simple iron sword

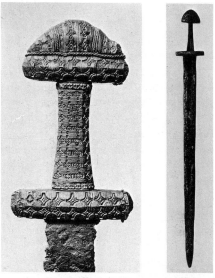

A

B

c. Ornamented Swedish sword-hilts

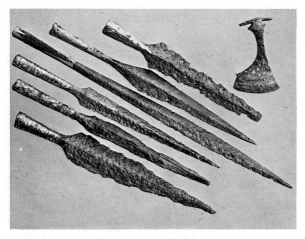

A. Swedish spear-heads and an axe-head

B. Ornamented Danish iron axe-head, inlaid with silver

2

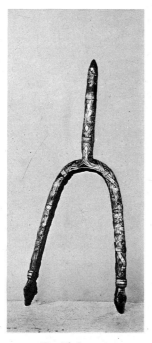

A. Danish iron spur,
inlaid with silver

B. Danish iron stirrup,
inlaid with silver

C. Richly ornamented Danish horse-collar

3

A. Bronze gilt heads on ornamented Danish harness

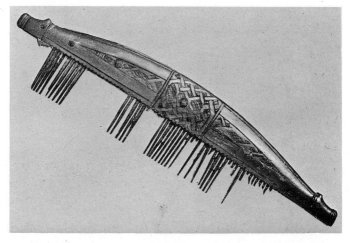

B. A horn comb from Hedeby in Slesvig

4

A. Glass imported into Sweden from the Rhineland

B. Danish gold brooch

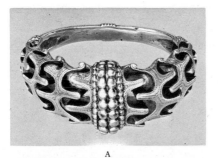

A

B

C

D

A. Danish silver ring

B. Gold jewellery from Hedeby

C. Danish silver brooch

D. Danish plaited silver necklace

A. Gold jewellery from Hornelund, Jutland

B. Silver brooch from Lindholm

C. Norwegian bronze brooch

B

C

7

The Gokstad ship, Norway

8

The Öseberg cart, Norway

Prow of the Oseberg ship

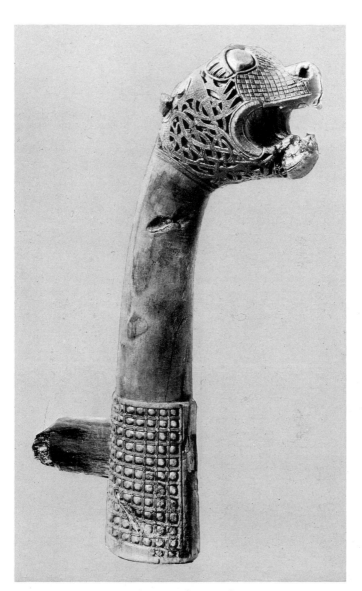

Wood-carving from Oseberg

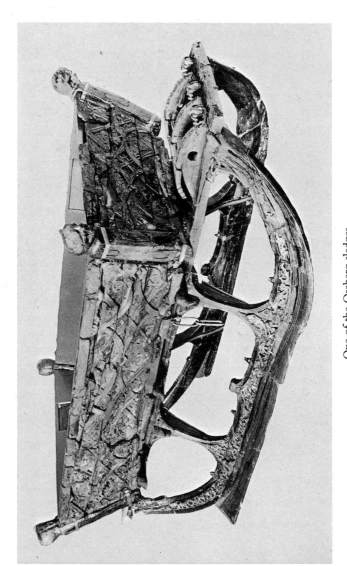

One of the Oseberg sledges

Birka in the ninth century.* On this rock was the fortress
and place of refuge of the town, surrounded by a rampart of
earth and stones 25ft to 50ft across, oval in plan and with
three gates: one facing north, one south, and one east towards the town. Outside the northern gate there have been
found relics of the garrison of the fortress. In a north-easterly
direction from this gate lies an area called the 'Black Earth'
and this is the actual site of the historic town of Birka.
Excavations here have not yielded, as at Hedeby, the lower
foundations of the houses, but only fragments of burnt clay
formed into two different pattern-types, from which it is
deduced that there were two kinds of houses in Birka, one
built of wattle-and-daub, and one of timber caulked with
clay. The soil on the site is mixed with charcoal, ashes, and
organic materials; in short it is a black occupation-earth,
and this dark area and its immediate surroundings cover an
area of thirty acres – or less than half that of Hedeby. The
defensive rampart of Birka, 22–39 ft wide and 6 ft high, is
considerably lower and weaker than that of Hedeby. Only
the northern part of this curving earthwork, stretching from
the fortress to the western harbour and protecting the town
on its landward side survives, a length of about 1,500 ft; it
may have been reinforced by a row of square wooden
towers. Birka possessed three harbours: an artificial one to
the west, which has completely disappeared, and two natural
harbours on the northern coast – Kugghamn in the west
(named after the Frisian type of vessel, the *kogge*), and Korshamn ('cross harbour') in the east. Still farther east, near
Salvik, there seems to have been a flat-bottomed harbour

* Sweden and Denmark share Ansgar, but Denmark claims precedence in him as he lived a few years in Hedeby before actually visiting
Birka. On the other hand, he was on two occasions – with an interval
of about twenty-five years between them – with the Swedes in Birka,
first in the reign of the benign King Björn and later during the reign
of the fiercer King Olaf.

for smaller boats. Salvik means 'the place of sale and trade', while Korshamn may be a corruption of an original 'Korn-hamn' – 'corn harbour'. One of the experts on Birka, the archaeologist Holger Arbman, has drawn attention to the latter possibility, and also to the likelihood that the great markets of Birka were for preference held in the winter when the finest furs would be available. He cites in support of this the fact that many of those buried in the Birka graves had crampons on their feet, and that in the 'Black Earth' have been found many ice axes and skates made of cow and horse bones.

Though Birka is smaller than Hedeby it has a far larger and finer collection of graves: thousands of them which have provided the famous collection now in the museum at Stockholm. No other ancient Scandinavian town has yielded so many and such diverse objects and relics as this. To the east of the defensive wall, on gently rolling open country, there are 1,600 burial mounds, large and small, huddled close together under pine and birch trees; this is Birka's biggest cemetery. There are several others, however: between the 'Black Earth' and the hilltop fort, for instance, there are a number of mounds; and in the area south and south-east of the fort 400 scattered barrows can still be counted. Farther east across the island are other isolated groups of graves. Some of the richest graves at Birka, large timber burial chambers, have been found not under mounds but beneath hollows produced by subsidence, the earth having sunk as the burial chamber rotted and collapsed. Two such burial places have been found inside the defensive wall of the town, one close to the north gate of the fort, the other south of Kugghamn. How long did Birka, the most thriving of all Swedish Viking towns, exist? Not as long as Hedeby, which perished in the catastrophe of 1050 already mentioned. Judging from the remains, Birka's decline began before 1000. It is not that Birka, like Hedeby, was destroyed

by fire, leaving a thick layer of ash to mark the town's end;
it is simply that there are virtually no finds from later than
the end of the tenth century. There are no examples from
Birka of the coins of the English King Æthelred II, common elsewhere in Sweden, in which the last substantial
amounts of danegeld were paid; and indeed, no coins minted
after the middle of the century have been found in the
graves. The latest datable find is a hoard of silver, discovered
in the 'Black Earth', in which no coin is later than 963 or
967. It has been assumed, though there is no certainty, that
Birka was destroyed by the Danish forces which set out to
conquer Sweden at the end of the tenth century but were
defeated by King Eric the Victorious at the great battle of
Fyrisvold described on the rune-stones. Whether this was so
or not, Birka drops out of history about 975; its function as
the centre of the Baltic trade was taken over by Gotland, and
the more local trade of Lake Malar was divided among
several other places on the lake: principally Sigtuna, half-
way between Birka and Uppsala.

Sigtuna

A few words about Sigtuna. The town was favourably
situated on the south coast of a peninsula in the broad part
of Lake Malar. Excavations there have revealed the remains
of houses, and have yielded material which, in the main, is
later than 1000. It is a 'long town' stretching about 600 yards
along the border of the lake, and about 200 yards inland.
It was Christianized early – perhaps right from its foundation – and had several churches. The earliest coins certainly
minted in Sweden were made at Sigtuna: Olaf Skotkonung's coins, copies from Anglo-Saxon designs, and certainly made by an Anglo-Saxon moneyer. They bear the
inscription SIDEI, which stands for SI (TUNE) DEI or 'God's
Sigtuna' – possibly a piece of propaganda, directed against

the neighbouring heathen in Old Uppsala. Olaf's son, King Önund Jacob, also had coins minted at Sigtuna. It is possible that coins were struck at Birka too, in its time, but there is no certainty of this. Two Swedish rune-stones of the first part of the eleventh century tell of a guild of Frisian craftsmen in Sigtuna, and Icelandic skaldic poems declare that King Magnus the Good and King Harald Hardrada stopped at Sigtuna on their way home from Russia. Adam of Bremen (c. 1070) describes the place as a large town (*civitas magna*), and records that it was the see of Sweden's first bishop, Adalward the Younger. It is likely, though not certain, that the earliest Sigtuna lay at Signhildsberg, about 2½ miles away from the present town, and that its layout followed an Anglo-Saxon plan. Excavations in Sigtuna have revealed, as at Birka, a thick dark-coloured occupation soil, a 'Black Earth' in which were found the remains of primitive houses with clay floors and wattle-and-daub walls, as well as larger log houses.

OTHER VIKING TOWNS

Apart from Sigtuna there are three existing Swedish towns which have origins back in the later Viking period: these are Skara in Vastergotland, Lund in Skane, and probably Talje, the modern Sodertalje, near Stockholm.

Denmark possesses one more lost town of the Viking Age: an abandoned site with a semi-circular defensive wall, at Brovold on the isle of Als, where Viking relics establish the age of the place. There are also, however, many modern towns which have their roots in Viking times, some of them also recorded as episcopal sees. In Jutland there are Slesvig, Ribe, Aarhus, Viborg, Aalborg; on Fyn, Odense; and on Zealand, Roskilde and Ringsted.

In Norway the modern towns of Oslo, Bergen, and Trondheim (Nidaros) can trace their origins back to the end of the Viking Age. There is also a lost town, the harbour called Skiringssal, mentioned by the trader, Ottar. Although its site has not been located, it is probable that it was somewhere near the so-called Kaupang farms in the south of Vestfold, where many Vikings' graves, including several ships, have been found containing imported objects of the ninth century – such as Irish and Anglo-Saxon metalware, and bits of finely-woven 'Frisian' cloth. The Norwegian archaeologist Charlotte Blindheim, who has been in charge of the more recent excavations (which have produced several interesting discoveries, such as the remains of a wharf, bollards, fragments of pottery and Rhenish glassware, an Anglo-Saxon and a Frankish coin, etc.) regards this settlement as an open (undefended) trading centre in a thriving district, in contact with several other trading centres including Hedeby and Birka. By means of the C^{14} method (a radioactive carbon test) all these finds have been dated to around the ninth century.

In conclusion we must mention the recent excavations of a trading settlement whose activity seems in the main to have been pre-Viking, dating in fact from the Merovingian period. Among the discoveries on the little island of Helgo in Lake Malar are gold amulets, fragments of glass, and a small gilded bronze representation of a face. There is also the top of an enamelled Irish crozier, a bronze Indian statue of Buddha, and several relics from the Viking period. These excavations were conducted by Mr W. Holmqvist.

Several causes acting together – or one if it were important enough – could lead to the foundation of a town in Viking times. The most common, no doubt, was trade, especially maritime trade, which would bring about the development of towns at harbours and centres of transport like Birka and Hedeby. Towns came into being in the interior too, at points

where the great land routes intersected and where legal
decisions on commercial matters were formulated: places
such as Viborg and Ringsted. Religious centres again,
whether pagan shrines or Christian churches and sees,
would have the effect of bringing large numbers of people
together as permanent residents; and so would a royal
centre. However, the most potent factor in the development
of the oldest towns was the existence of a local market where
merchants could buy and sell, and where the craftsmen
would find a ready and stable demand for their products.

EARTHWORKS

The Danevirke of South Slesvig

In the Frankish annals – *Annales Regni Francorum* – there is
described under the year 808 the action taken by the Danish
King Godfred after he had sacked and destroyed the north
German Baltic town of Reric. Godfred, says the chronicle,

carried the merchants off with him and sailed with his whole
army to the harbour called Sliesthorp. Here he stayed for some
days and ordered that his country's frontier with the land of
the Saxons should be fortified by a rampart, stretching from the
eastern bay called Ostersalt to the western ocean, protecting
the entire northern shore of the River Eider and having but a
single gate for carriage and horses to travel to and fro. After distributing this task among his chieftains he returned home.

This great earthwork across the neck of the Jutland
peninsula from the head of the Slie Fjord right across to the
west, was subsequently to be known (and still is) as the
Danevirke, and a good part of it is still visible (Pl. 14a).

This protective system of earthworks, securing Denmark
to the south, is the most extensive monument of the past to
be found in the Nordic countries. As the sketch-map on

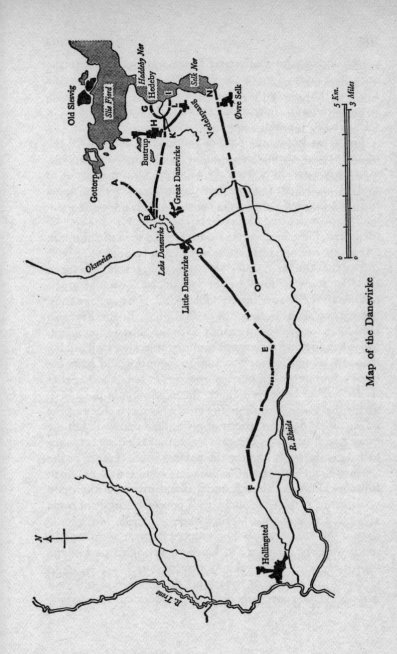

Map of the Danevirke

p. 167 shows, the Danevirke forms a barrier across the narrowest part of south Slesvig, from the head of the Slie Fjord in the east to the meadows by the Trene and Rheide rivers in the west. In addition to this there was the Østervold ('Eastern Rampart') across the Svansen peninsular.

The most important part of the main wall (A–F on the map) is the portion which stretches with some interruptions for nearly nine miles from the Gottorp area in the east to that of Hollingsted. One gets the impression that, apart from the isolated earthworks called Tyraborg (c) the main wall was constructed as a complete unit; and it may well be identified, therefore, with the wall referred to in the Frankish annals as reaching from sea to sea. It can be objected to this theory that the main wall does not, in fact, reach from sea to sea. The force of the objection is reduced if we add to the main wall the (now vanished) Østervold. Further, one must not expect such an account as that given in the Frankish chronicles to correspond exactly with the actual monument. Moreover, during spring and summer at least, a wall linking meadow to meadow and swamp to swamp would have the effect of an unbroken barrier from sea to sea. Another contradiction must also be noticed: the expression in the annals about the wall protecting 'the entire northern shore of the River Eider' does not strictly apply to the main wall. On the other hand, however, the gate for traffic is doubtless the so-called 'Kalegat' (D) where the ancient route (known as the 'Army Road' or the 'Ox Road') from south to north through Holstein, Slesvig, and Jutland intersects the main wall. From c to D the main wall covers a length of some 1,850 ft, and is about 18 ft high and 95 ft wide. The middle part of the main wall (D–E) continues for over $2\frac{3}{4}$ miles in a south-westerly direction, to Kurborg (E). This part of the wall is of very considerable dimensions, and, according to German archaeologists, was built during several different periods. It was strengthened by palisades and a shallow moat towards the south-east and its rear sloped down to an inner road well protected by the wall along its whole length. At some period this middle section of the main wall (D–E) was reinforced by a stone parapet 9 ft broad and 9 ft high: the celebrated 'granite boulder wall' with a facing of stones set in a zigzag pattern and bound with clay. In front of this parapet there was a U-shaped ditch. A further and final reinforcement of the middle section was supplied by a brick wall 6ft thick and 19–22 ft high, which was equipped with buttresses and probably with battlements and gallery as well. This addition, made in the 1160s by King Valdemar the Great, is still preserved in parts, and it is the only part of the Danevirke which can safely be dated from literary sources – i.e. by the writings of Sven Aggesen and Saxo and by the inscription on a lead tablet in Ringsted church in Zealand. In the final 1100 ft before the bend near Kurborg (E) the middle section again becomes comparatively low – 6–9 ft high – and no more than 65 ft wide. The western section of the main wall (E–F), which traverses the Hollingsted meadows, has the same dimensions. Examination by archaeologists of sections of this part of the main wall led to the conclusion that it was constructed at up to four different periods, and that here, too, there was a road along the inner side of the wall. This part of the main wall is called the 'Crooked Rampart', and here just south of Ellingsted, Søren Telling discovered, in 1959, an 800-yd-long double rampart enclosing a water pit.

Between the main wall of the Danevirke and the semi-circular defensive rampart of Hedeby runs a connecting earthwork (B–H), almost two miles long. It is about 15 ft high for most of the way, and its western end consists of two parallel walls. It traverses the low ground south of Bustrup and joins the semi-circular wall at the place where the rivulet cuts in. German archaeologists are of the opinion that this connecting wall was built at three different periods, and that from the very first it was protected on the south side by a moat.

Hedeby's defensive semi-circle of earthwork (G–I) is over three-quarters of a mile in length, while its height varies between 12 and 25 ft (Pl. 14b). Near its northern gate, according to German experts, there is evidence of no fewer than nine periods of construction, but this figure is perhaps an overestimate. Outside its south-western stretch there was an advanced earthwork as well, of which only slight traces remain. North of Hedeby lies the 'Højborg', a steep hill with a flat top on which there are a number of shallow burial mounds surrounded by a low wall; this whole system, however, seems to date from before the Viking period. About $1\frac{1}{4}$ miles south and south-west of Hedeby there used to run, from the head of the Selk cove to the meadows by the river Rheide, a completely straight wall (N–O) about $3\frac{3}{4}$ miles in length and 6 ft high, with a V-shaped moat to the south; it is called the 'Kovirke' but has now almost disappeared. Stretching across the peninsula of Svansen from the Slie Fjord to the Vindeby cove, was the Østervold, some two miles long; but this too has almost wholly vanished.

The Danevirke as a whole is an impressive feat of engineering, covering 350 years of Danish history, from its beginning in Viking times to the addition of King Valdemar's brick wall in the 1160s – a most fitting memorial of days gone by. Long stretches of these broad earthworks still remain as a testimony to Denmark's ancient history and activity, but during the Second World War – and especially in the spring of 1945 – several sections of the Danevirke were badly damaged during German preparations against an anticipated attack by British forces. Admittedly most of this damage has been made good, but it will never be possible to repair the demolition by the Germans of large parts of the Kovirke (N–O) to make way for their airfields.

The scientific investigation and dating of the different parts of the Danevirke has been going on now for almost a century. It has led to much discussion, but the various points of view cannot be enlarged upon here. Instead we shall give only a summary of the probable course of development.

King Godfred's wall, mentioned in the Frankish annals of 808, can apparently be identified with the main wall (A–F) of the Danevirke. The location of the harbour of Sliesthorp which, according to the annals, was used by Godfred, is uncertain, but as it must have been protected by his new wall it was probably somewhere on the north side of the Slie, near the present Gottorp or Slesvig. Shortly afterwards, in the ninth century, there grew up the trading centre of Hedeby–Slesvig at the cove Haddeby Nor. Around the year 900 this place fell into Swedish hands and was protected by a semi-circular earthwork later connected with the main wall of the Danevirke.* After the collapse of Swedish power the main wall was reinforced by the 'granite wall' and at the end of the tenth century the Kovirke was built. In 1050 Hedeby was destroyed and most of the surviving inhabitants moved to Slesvig on the north side of the Slie Fjord; soon afterwards the name of Hedeby was lost. This outline of development is full of uncertainty. In particular the problem of Sliesthorp presents difficulties. It should be kept in mind that the absence of archaeological evidence from before the eleventh century in modern Slesvig is hardly conclusive evidence for doubting the existence of the town in Viking times; yet the absence is undeniably striking.

OTHER EARTHWORKS

Elsewhere in the three Viking countries there are no other extensive systems of defence comparable to the Danevirke.

* This, of course, presupposes that this section of Danevirke was also in Swedish hands.

One would not expect it to be otherwise, for defences of this elaborate kind, built of earth, stone, and timber, were only required at the place where Viking territory met that of considerable and hostile foreign powers. The Danevirke was to protect the north's only port of entry against Frankish and Saxon powers coming from the south. The construction of similar defences in the other northern countries was quite superfluous, not because the Vikings were at peace with each other – far from it – but because militarily they were maritime powers and for preference campaigned by sea. There are, then, no other Danevirkes in Scandinavia. There are, of course, many smaller earthworks scattered everywhere, but these are generally attributed to tribal conflicts in pre-Viking times.

It might be expected that in the Viking colonies in England and France earthworks would be used as protection against attacks by the natives, but there is no certain example for us to point to. It is very difficult to fix the date of any earthwork unless datable objects are found within it or literary evidence certainly referring to it exists. There are in England many 'burhs' and 'camps' and 'dykes' associated philologically with Danes but so far we have no positive knowledge of their origin – though perhaps future research will bring fresh evidence to light. This is more or less the case in northern France too; but attention must be drawn in this connexion to the Dano–Swedish excavations in 1951–2 of the remarkable earthwork which cuts off the northern end of the Cotentin Peninsula in Normandy and is apparently directed against attack from the south. In its east-west course to sea it takes in two small harbours, and was apparently built by sea warriors to guard against their southern foes. It is named 'Hague Dike' – that is the rampart (*dik*) which cuts off the tongue of land (*hagi*) – a pure Old Norse place-name. This fortification may very well have been constructed by the Vikings in the ninth or tenth

century. The excavations have proved its military character: on top of the earthwork, for example, were found extensive traces of fire, indicating that long trenches were filled
with a fiercely burning fire as a means of defence. No datable objects have yet been discovered, and Hague Dike so
far remains undated. Perhaps the C^{14} method will bring
results.*

MILITARY CAMPS

In a special category must be placed the one kind of Viking
monument so far found only in Denmark: the military
fortress. Of these, four have so far come to light on Danish
soil – one in Zealand, one in Fyn, and two in Jutland. The
earliest to be found, and the only one fully excavated
(between 1934 and 1941), is Trelleborg on Zealand (Pl.
15A).

Trelleborg

Trelleborg was excavated by Dr Poul Nørlund, who in
1948 published a detailed account of his work. It is situated
in western Zealand, two and a half miles west of the town of
Slagelse, between this town and sea (the Store Baelt). The
actual site is on a headland formed by two rivers as they
join to run into the Store Baelt north of Korsor. Here, in the
later part of the Viking period, the fortress was built,
apparently on top of an old heathen place of sacrifice comprising sacrificial pits and remains of houses. The work

* C^{14} tests, recently carried out on some Hague Dike charcoal material,
point to the Hallstatt period, 800–900 B.C. Yet the place-names show
a Viking settlement. It is probable, therefore, that this very old rampart was re-used in Viking times.

seems to have been very thoroughly carried out: the site
was levelled and filled in, and all was built according to
carefully made plans by experienced engineers working
with mathematical precision. The fortress consisted of two
sections: a main and an outer enclosure.

The main part of the fortress is circular in plan, surrounded by a strong rampart which still exists. On its landward side – south and east – it is further protected by a wide,
deep, U-shaped ditch. In the rampart there were four gates
at the four main compass points. These were linked by two
streets, constructed with wood and crossing at right angles
at the centre of the site, thus dividing the circular area into
four quadrants. In each of these there stood four houses of
equal size, arranged in squares, making sixteen in all. In
plan, these buildings – with curving long-walls and straight
ends – resemble ships with their bows cut off. Each of the
houses is divided into three sections, the centre one being
the largest (58 ft long). Although the timber from which all
these buildings were made has vanished, the plan of the
houses can be traced from the remaining post-holes in the
ground. As a rule the houses had doors in both gable walls,
with corresponding doors between the three inner rooms.
The large centre room also had side doors diagonally placed
in each of the long sides of the house. The end rooms sometimes had cellar-like pits underneath them, perhaps for
stores, rubbish, or even prisoners. The floor of the centre
room was of planks or clay, with a fireplace in the centre –
flanked, it is assumed, by wide settles on which the Vikings
used to sit or lie. In the roof there was, presumably, a venti-
lation hole (Old Norse *ljóri*). Besides the sixteen houses there
were a number of small detached ones: guard houses at two
of the gates, officers' houses in the centre of two of the
squares, and a boat-shaped house of smaller dimensions to
the north of the north-eastern square. There appears also to
have been a street or footpath running inside the whole

length of the circular rampart. This ring-wall round the
main camp was strengthened and retained on both sides by
palisades, and reinforced internally by lacing with transverse and longitudinal timbers. Its four gates, defended by
palisades covering heavy stone packing, probably had
wooden roofs which would have given the effect of tunnels.
Two folding doors barred entry from the outside: iron rings
and massive keys were found near the gates. The outer surface of the ring-wall facing the land was faced with thick
clay held together by stout sticks and branches; and where
it lay towards the swampy areas to the north, west, and
south-west, the wall rested on a foundation of stones and
piling, and was well protected higher up by vertical palisades.

The outer defence-work served as a reinforcement on the
landward side: its southernmost section is curved, concen-
trically with the shape of the main fortress, but to the north
the enclosed area is rectangular, widening to the east;
throughout, the defensive earthwork consists of a low rampart and a shallow ditch. Within the curved section were set
radially thirteen long-houses of the same elliptical plan as
the sixteen in the main fortress, though of smaller size. Near
the main eastern gate (in the rectangular part of the outer
work) were two similar houses set parallel to each other; and
farther east in the same square was the stronghold's cemetery (comprising about 150 graves), probably a continuation of the ancient burial ground which had belonged to the
sacrificial place existing before Trelleborg was built. Dr
Nørlund surmises convincingly from the two parallel houses
that the engineers originally intended to build a set of house-
squares in the outer camp, but that, in view of its curved
shape, they altered their plans and built instead the radially-
set series of houses which has been revealed. The principal
approach both to main and outer camps was from the south.
We are justified in calling the men who built Trelleborg

engineers, so mathematically precise was their method of
planning. Their standard unit of measurement was a modi-
fication of the Roman foot; that is, 29.33 cm. compared with
the Roman 29·57 cm. On this scale the houses of the squares
are 100 ft long, the houses in the outer work 90 ft long, the
circular rampart 60 ft wide. The small houses in the middle
of the two of the squares are 30 by 15 ft. The radius from the
centre of the main enclosed area to the inner side of its circular rampart is 234 ft, the distance between the ditches of
the two enclosures is for some distance also 234 ft, and the
distance between the centre of the main enclosure and the
nearer gables of the houses in the outer work is exactly
double this: 468 ft. The engineers began by marking the
centre of the fortress and from it striking the circles of
the ramparts and ditches. The same central datum is also the
point of intersection of the two transverse axes, cutting each
other at right angles, which divide the area of the main
fortress into its four quadrants, linking the gates and continuing outwards through them. The constructors' exacti-
tude is everywhere apparent. Dr Nørlund points out that the
curved sides of the long-houses are always symmetrical about
central axes and that their construction was based on ellipses. Two houses at right-angles to each other had the same
focus, and to construct the four ellipses of a house-square the
engineer only had to fix four focuses constituting the corners
of a square whose side was about 36·45 m. or 124 Roman
feet. The construction of the whole house system within the
circular earthwork of the main fortress is consequently based
upon squares.

Trelleborg is splendidly situated in wide meadows backing
on to the higher land. The holes in the ground which, in
ancient times held timbers, have been clearly marked by the
excavators with cement; ramparts and ditches have been
cleared and partly reconstructed, so that the visitor nowadays gets a graphic impression of what a Viking base

looked like, particularly if he has enough imagination to picture the former appearance of the square groups of elliptical houses.

The Trelleborg cemetery reveals, as we would expect in a military garrison, that most of those buried there were youngish men – between twenty and forty years old. There were also a number of women, but few children or old people. Grave goods were very scarce, but there was no specific evidence of Christian practices.

Inhumation-graves orientated east-west were not unknown in Denmark before the advent of Christianity. Three mass graves were found at Trelleborg, the largest containing ten bodies (Pl. 15B). The objects from the graves included few weapons, although one notable find was a silver-inlaid battle-axe with a very broad edge but narrow blade. There were a quantity of tools such as scythe-blades, and coulters, ornaments, earthenware, and objects used in spinning and weaving. From these discoveries it is possible to give an approximate date to Trelleborg, within the period from the later part of the tenth century to the first part of the eleventh, say 975–1050. The camp did not have a very long life, therefore, but it evidently existed at the time when Swein Forkbeard conquered England and when Cnut the Great fought the 'battle of the three Kings' at the River Helge in 1026.

It stands to reason that Trelleborg was primarily a military and naval base: it had the classic location for this purpose, providing easy access to the sea and yet protected against attacks and sheltered from storms. It is presumed that vessels were towed up the river to the camp, and that each of the boat-shaped houses afforded quarters for a ship's crew. The contents of graves (coulters, scythe-blades, etc.) suggest that the garrison were able to keep themselves supplied with certain commodities, so that foraging raids upon adjacent farms need not have been too frequent. The building of the Trelleborg houses must have made heavy demands upon the near-by forests.

It has been suggested by some scholars that each house at Trelleborg had as its roof a ship turned upside down, and that in this way the camp provided winter quarters for the fleet, but this thesis is scarcely tenable. Another supposition – acceptable as long as Trelleborg was the only such camp known – was that here, at long last, was the elusive and perhaps fabulous Jomsborg, for the ground plan did indeed conform to the legends about Jomsborg. However, this theory was completely shattered when four Trelleborg-type camps were unearthed in Denmark alone, and was invalidated also by the fact that (as the graves proved) there had been women in the camp, whereas women were prohibited from entering Jomsborg. One thing is certain: Trelleborg betokens a powerful organization; only a king would have had the means and power to carry out such a large project. That Trelleborg (and its equals in Denmark) should have been built by enemy invaders is very unlikely; it is not supported by the archaeological evidence, and still less by the historical records, which show that Danish power was at its height during this period. Dr Nørlund contends, with great justification, that Trelleborg seems to point to Swein Forkbeard's and Cnut the Great's powerful military force, their *hirð* or housecarls. Such conquering monarchs as these would be likely to use effective garrisons to maintain peace in the homeland. Trelleborg must have provided accommodation for about 1,200 men. How and when it ceased to be a base is not known: there are certainly no signs of destruction by fire.

Aggersborg

The next military fortress of the Trelleborg type is at Aggersborg in north Jutland, and it was partly excavated by

C. G. Schultz between 1945 and 1949. It is situated almost in the centre of Denmark's largest fjord system, the Lim Fjord, a long fairway which cuts across north Jutland from sea to sea and was as in early Viking times the starting-point of many raids on England. The location of this fortress is in its own way as significant as that of Trelleborg. Lying between the Aggersborg estate on the coast and the church and churchyard on top of the hill, it occupies sloping ground commanding an extensive view of the fjord. Nothing of the old camp is visible on the ground, which is now just ordinary cultivated land, but anyone who knows what he is looking for can just about trace the vague outlines of the circular wall which surrounded the camp. It was similar in layout to Trelleborg, about the same age, but much bigger. A conjecture can be made about the date of its destruction. In 1086 the rebellious peasants of north Jutland rose against the King, St Cnut, and sacked his stronghold.* The monk Ælnoth gives a vivid description of the destruction of the king's stronghold – could this have been Aggersborg?

The site has not been completely excavated, but enough has been done to establish the shape and size of the fortress. There was no outer annexe as at Trelleborg. It consisted simply of one large circular area; but within its rampart there were no fewer than forty-eight houses in twelve squares – compared with sixteen houses in four squares at Trelleborg. Moreover, the houses are 110 Roman feet long – that is one-tenth longer than those found at Trelleborg. The two axial roads across the camp had on each side a shorter upper and lower road. The inside radius of the Aggersborg camp was 407 Roman feet (cf. Trelleborg's 234), its extreme diameter no less than 960 ft. It has a central square 72 ft by 72 ft, and there seem to have been wooden towers over its gates. The encircling rampart was timbered inside and out –

* The revolt ended with the killing of the king in St Albans church at Odense in the same year.

more strongly on the outside – and was presumably topped with a timber parapet and doubtless strengthened with transverse timbers. The houses at Aggersborg had walls with a less pronounced curve than those at Trelleborg, but their gable ends were much broader. The excavator reached the conclusion that the walls were not constructed of close-fitting upright planks, but of heavy upright structural members with a filling of wattle-and-daub between them, and that the gable-ends of the houses were built of horizontal planks.

A most interesting discovery was that the fortress had been built on the site of an earlier settlement; a village with much smaller boat-shaped houses built on the same general pattern as those of the later stronghold. The village also included many outbuildings laid out east–west, without fire-places. Large post-holes at the ends of these buildings must have held supports for a horizontal member, probably the roof-ridge. Scattered finds on the site indicate that this village must have been there a couple of centuries before the military camp was constructed in the middle of the eleventh century; so that the boat-shaped type of house was evidently a much-used design throughout the Viking period – in Denmark certainly, and probably throughout the North. It is likely, indeed, that the design originated from the primitive shelter made by dragging a boat ashore and upending it across standing posts, either to repair or to store it. This explanation is more likely than the somewhat far-fetched theory that the early builders had made the technical discovery that a curved wall resists the wind better than a flat one! Later discoveries in Denmark have definitely confirmed that these 'boat-shaped houses' were known before the Viking period.

Fyrkat

The third Viking camp of the Trelleborg type was found in north-east Jutland at the head of the narrow Mariager–

Hobro Fjord a few miles south-west of the modern town of Hobro. It is called Fyrkat, a comparatively modern name which has been explained by the excavator of the camp, C. G. Schultz,* as follows: the word *kat* (English 'cat') is a seventeenth century term used in the art of fortification for a work built on top of a bastion or rampart, and when, during the Renaissance, there was nothing visible of this old fortress except the ruins of four walls between four collapsed gateways, it was known as *de fire katte* – the four *kats*. Fyrkat, not yet fully excavated, closely resembles Trelleborg, although it has no outer annexe. It stands on a low promontory, and it is fair to suppose that vessels could have been towed up the little river Onsild from the fjord. The site, once more, is militarily correct – providing free access to the sea and natural protection. The encircling rampart was about 10 ft high: a solid wooden affair filled with earth, reinforced internally with timbers, and doubtless crowned with a parapet. Its four gates were, like those at Trelleborg, elaborate timber-lined tunnels; and within the circle of the camp were sixteen houses arranged in four squares. The boat-shaped houses were rather shorter (96 ft) than those at Trelleborg; they had double clay-built walls, and were equipped with tambours. The axial streets of Fyrkat were of wooden construction, and so was the road round the inside of the circular wall.

In the post-holes of one of the gateways the remains of the heavy oak timbers which supported the gate still survived. Various objects have been found on the site – fragments of a gold filigree brooch, a pair of silver bracelets, a silver finger-ring, an iron axe, a couple of whetstones, some vessels made of soap-stone – and from these finds the camp has been dated, like Trelleborg, to about the end of the tenth century. Fyrkat appears to have been destroyed by fire during a

* An architect as well as an archaeologist, and fully familiar with Trelleborg and Aggersborg.

south-westerly storm, but it is not known when. It may well be that it was sacked and burnt in 1086 during the rising of peasants which brought about the fall of Aggersborg; but we do not know. Quite close to and north-east of the camp lay its cemetery.

Odense

Finally we come to the fourth and, for the time being at any rate, the last of these Viking camps in Denmark. This one was situated right in the middle of the present town of Odense, the capital of Fyn, on a hill called Nonnebjerg. The existence of this camp was demonstrated partly by the discovery by the artist Ernst Hansen of an old map of Odense on which it was mentioned and partly by trial excavations on the spot – sufficient being uncovered to confirm the existence here of a fortress of the type now familiar. Further discoveries of various silver hoards of the Viking Age in the same vicinity have made it possible to date the Nonnebjerg fortification to the end of the tenth century, contemporary with Trelleborg and Fyrkat. It is a reasonable conjecture that this fortress, which lay quite close to the church where King Cnut met his death in 1086, was destroyed on that occasion. Nonnebjerg, like the other three military sites, was located in the usual way at the head of a long fjord, in this case that of Odense.

Perhaps the future will bring to light more of these circular Viking strongholds in Denmark, and so prove that Swein Forkbeard and Cnut the Great secured the loyalty of their home country by means of a network of bases manned by their housecarls and mercenaries. These camps are strategically placed for communication by land and water, and could serve an army no less than a fleet.

FOREIGN INFLUENCE IN MILITARY WORKS

Where did the Vikings learn the science of constructing such fortresses? The question is far from easy to answer. To some extent this mastery of the science of fortification might be said to have a native Scandinavian origin, as even before Viking times the northerners could build circular places of refuge of earth and stone, as, for example, the fifth-century fort at Ismantorp, on Oland, Sweden, with its nine gates and its houses radially placed on the inner area. Yet this primitive work affords no real comparison with the Viking feats of engineering; nor do the circular defensible works of a later date found in north-west Germany and in England help us in our inquiry. What we need for comparison are duplicates of Trelleborg in other countries, not merely more or less primitive planned forts. Even if such were found we should still have to determine whether they preceded the Danish examples or were imitations of the Danish prototype. The Anglo-Saxons, for instance, had no more particularly a native technical or traditional basis for constructing a Trelleborg than had the Danes, and a Trelleborg in England would appear just as foreign a phenomenon as are the Danish ones in Denmark. If we inquire which of the two peoples – the Anglo-Saxons or the Danes – would have been more likely, around the year 1000, to learn the science of engineering from a foreign source, the answer must be the Danes – because of the wider horizons given them by their Viking campaigns. Engineering as skilled as that revealed at Trelleborg was not native: it must have originated either in Roman tradition, via the western Roman Empire; or in Byzantium, whence it could have reached Denmark along the routes through Russia; or else in the Near East, derived, perhaps, from the Arab Empire, and spread along the eastern or the western ways (Russia or Spain), to Denmark.

If, however, we assume that military engineering of this sort began in Rome, and penetrated north through the country of the Franks, we at once run into a problem: the Roman camps and fortresses were invariably rectangular, not circular; the Frankish forts too, were never circular. The unit of measurement, the Roman foot, is the only link between the Trelleborg and the Roman camps, but this has no significance considering the radically different building designs of the two types. That the basis of the engineering of Trelleborg derives from Byzantium seems much more likely, but before enlarging on this I must mention the opinion which sees resemblances between Trelleborg and the Arab and Oriental (Persian–Sassanid) circular forts, towns, and holy places; resemblances and comparisons which are much too vague, tenuous, and far-fetched.

The Byzantine world, as we know, was not very remote from the Scandinavian countries, especially Sweden. Without repeating what has been said earlier on this matter, I refer to the salient points of the connexion. At the end of the tenth century the Greek Emperor in Constantinople engaged Vikings as mercenaries in his household guard. The contact between Byzantium and the North was a lively one at this time; about half-way between the Greek and the Scandinavian worlds lay the important Norse town of Kiev. Some archaeologists have compared the huge earth, wood, and stone ramparts of Hedeby with the famous semi-circular wall which shielded Constantinople from attack by land. It is not unlikely that the highly developed mathematical skill revealed in the construction of the four Danish Trelleborg-type fortresses was brought to the north from Byzantium: perhaps by Byzantine engineers who had been taken prisoner and who applied the science they had practised in stone to similar engineering projects in timber. However, this imported skill did not last long in the North. It could be employed only in the service of a powerful employer: that is

TOWNS, EARTHWORKS, AND CAMPS

to say, a strong king, for no common chieftain would be able to take the task of building himself these imposing military bases. For that reason alone it seems quite likely that no other Trelleborgs will be found in Denmark. The four we know of would amply suffice for the security of the kingdom, though perhaps a further one in the south of Jutland would be warranted. The Danish writer Palle Lauring has ventured the suggestion that a fifth stronghold – now vanished – once existed at Egernborg near Eckenförde. There would also seem to have been scope for one in Skåne.

If a Trelleborg-type camp should ever be found in England it seems highly probable that it would owe its existence to Danish influence.

Though scholars are on the whole agreed that Trelleborg, Fyrkat, and Nonnebjerg were built in the late tenth century, there is some doubt about Aggersborg. The supposition most favoured is that it dates from about the middle of the eleventh century, the reigns of Kings Hardacnut (1035–42), Magnus the Good (1042–7), and Swein Estridsson (1047–76). It is relevant here to point out a clear Byzantine influence on Danish coins minted in this period, an influence which began with Hardacnut and was increased in the reigns of his two successors. Coins from Lund, for example, show Swein Estridsson in the style of a Byzantine Emperor: at full length, holding sceptre and orb. This phenomenon is generally explained by the fact that the Varangians (and not least Harald Hardrada) brought back a lot of Byzantine coins from their journeys, coins which were then copied by local moneyers. Should it prove correct that Aggersborg was built as late as the middle of the eleventh century, we can point to the fact that at this very period Byzantine influence was affecting another field of Danish design, that of coins.

CHAPTER TEN

Coins and Weights and Measures

COINS

During the greater part of the Viking period a coin, as such, was quite worthless to the ordinary man; only as a piece of precious metal did it represent a certain value dependent on its weight. This is proved by the many hoards of silver containing coins cut into pieces of certain weights or adapted for use as jewellery or amulets by the addition of loops or holes. Although the Vikings had very little use for coins, it was during their period that the first Scandinavian coins were struck. The coin-making can be divided into two periods: one in the middle and latter part of the ninth century, the other around 960–80. The model for coins of both these groups was the Emperor Charlemagne's Dorestad coinage, dating from the early ninth century, before the destruction of that town. The obverse of this well-known and much used Dorestad silver coinage was inscribed:

CARO   DOR

and the reverse

LUS   STAT

These dies were copied more or less exactly by the earliest Scandinavian moneyers. Where they actually carried out their work is not certainly known; some say Birka in Sweden, others Jumne in Wendland and Hedeby in Denmark. Hedeby is perhaps the likeliest, being so close to Dorestad. This oldest Nordic coinage shows how a coin type

can continue – through copying – long after the disappearance
of the place where it was first struck. The Dorestad coinage
was well known and valued on the great trade-routes between Friesland and the North, and after the destruction of
Dorestad in the 830s the Northmen tried to copy it. However,
in their ignorance the Scandinavian die-cutters misunder-
stood the legends of the prototypes and these became so
blundered as to be unrecognizable and were quickly replaced by entirely new motifs, such as human masks,
quadrupeds ('harts'), birds, ships, etc. Coins of the second
period, dating from the later tenth century, are as a rule
light and thin, sometimes struck or embossed on one side
only: hence the name 'half-bracteates'.

The first Danish Viking king to have struck his own coins
abroad was once thought to be Halfdan Lodbroksson in
London in 872; but modern scholars doubt this. Other
Danish kings, Cnut and Siefred, struck a coinage at Quentovic on the Continent at the end of the ninth century, and
Norman princes did the same at Rouen from the 930s. From
about 900 to the middle of the tenth century the Danish and
Norwegian kings of Northumberland produced coins
bearing their own names – Sitric, Regnald, Anlaf, Eric (no
doubt Eric Blood-Axe, Harald Finehair's son).

It is interesting to study these Anglo–Scandinavian coins
more closely. Some of them bear martial designs – sword,
banner, or bow and arrow – others Christian symbols and
legends – crosses, the hand of God, the monogram of
Charlemagne, or letters like D(omi)-N(u)s D(eu)s REX
('Lord God the King') or MIRABILIA FECIT ('He accomplished miracles'). There are other coins, decorated with
birds, or a type of triangular design or hammer; of these it is
difficult to say whether they were pagan or Christian. The
bird may be Odin's raven or the dove of the Holy Spirit; the
triangular designs may be three shields or a symbol of the
Trinity; the hammer may be Thor's celebrated weapon or

the pallium or Tau cross. One would not consider the last
two were it not for coins from ecclesiastical centres such as
St Peter's, York, and St Martin's, Lincoln, which carry the
same hammer-like design. This group of coins illustrates the
conflict between paganism and Christianity among the
Danish and Norwegian emigrants at a time when both
homelands were still heathen. The largest hoard of Viking
silver coins in England was deposited at Cuerdale in Lancashire, shortly after 900. The Viking kings, Cnut and Siefred, mentioned above, introduced the Anglo-Saxon penny
to Northumberland at the end of the ninth century; and a
hundred years later the Norwegians did the same in Ireland,
through Sigtrygg Silkybeard of Dublin.

In general the Anglo-Saxon coinage system formed the
basis for the first independent regular minting in Scandinavia other than the imitated Dorestad coinage. This native
production began about the same time in all three countries:
in Denmark about 1000, under Swein Forkbeard (988–
1014); in Sweden under Olaf Skotkonung (994–1022); and
in Norway under St Olaf (1016–30). It is only during the
last third of the Viking period, therefore, that the Northmen
produced their own native currencies.

The first Danish (also the first Scandinavian) coinage
with a king's portrait is a very rare silver one bearing a bust
of Swein Forkbeard holding his sceptre vertically before his
face; he has a fierce aspect, though one must not expect an
exact likeness. The coin legend is 'Swein, King of the
Danes', the title formulated half in Latin (*Rex*) and half in
inaccurate Anglo-Saxon (*Addener*). The reverse of the coin
bears a cross with the Latin word *crux* and an Anglo-Saxon
legend running 'Godwine (moneyer) of the Danes'. The
mint is not named on this, the oldest, Scandinavian royal
coinage. Cnut the Great's coins, on the other hand, frequently give their mint names: Lund in Skane; Roskilde,
Ringsted, and Slagelse in Zealand; Odense in Fyn; and

Ribe, Viborg, and Ørbæk in Jutland. Later coins mention several other places in Jutland – Hedeby, Aarhus, Randers, and Aalborg. It was customary to name not only the mint, but also the moneyer, so that we now know the names of several hundreds of these *monetarii*. What their status was, however, is not known: whether they were civil servants in the king's employment, or persons licensed to make coins. On Cnut's coins, in addition to the royal portrait, there occur several Christian symbols – the Lamb of God with the Gospel book, God's hand, and the dove of the Holy Ghost, the three of these simplified in the sign of the Trinity; the three shields; a cross bearing the magic Latin inscription *Lux, Lex, Pax, Rex* (light, law, peace, king). Occasionally too, heathen symbols appear, such as the six-footed dragon guarding the treasure, or the man's mask for warding off evil, or a distorted classical (Carolingian) temple gable. As mentioned above, a distinct Byzantine influence is noticeable in the coins of Cnut's successors, Hardacnut, Magnus the Good, and Swein Estridsson (the period 1035–75): here we can see such motifs as the full-length portrait of the king with orb and sceptre, or two angels, or an angel presenting a banner to the king, or Christ enthroned.

In the last quarter of the eleventh century Danish coinage became fully stabilized: the royal monopoly of making coins seems to have been confirmed; the number of mints was reduced to five – Lund and Tumatorp in Skane, Roskilde and Slagelse in Zealand, and Viborg in Jutland; and the number of coin types to two – the King and the Holy Bishop – both of which weighed 0·9 gm. The east Danish penny maintained its quality, but in Jutland it deteriorated during the reign of St Cnut (1080–7), and was not only underweight but also debased with copper. (This may well have been the result of Cnut's rearmament programme when he planned to conquer England). This deterioration continued under Cnut's successor Olaf Hunger (1087–95), and it was probably German influence which produced coins of the same weight as before but on a larger and thinner planchet and, therefore, more crudely stamped. At the same time and also due to German influence, the bishops began striking coins; but by this time the Viking period was over.

The currency situation in Sweden during Viking times was rather complicated. To begin with, in the ninth century, there was the Dorestad coinage; this may well have originated in Birka, and in that case it represents an isolated development in Swedish numismatic history. Native Swedish coins appear under King Olaf Skotkonung (994–1022) and King Önund Jacob (1022–50), and coins of both these kings were modelled from Anglo-Saxon exemplars. They were minted at Sigtuna, and most of the moneyers are also known from their work in England, where they had made coins for Æthelred II and Cnut the Great, particularly in Lincoln. It is reasonable to surmise that a group or colony of moneyers was brought across from Lincoln to Sweden by King Olaf Skotkonung in order to produce the native Swedish product. One of King Önund Jacob's coins, minted by Thormod in Sigtuna, is remarkable in carrying the legend 'Cnut, King of the Swedes'. This Cnut can be none other than Cnut the Great. The implications of the legend are uncertain: perhaps it has no great significance. At the death of Önund Jacob in the middle of the eleventh century, minting in Sweden was temporarily suspended, and it was not resumed for more than a hundred years. The reason for this can only be the powerful heathen reaction which occurred in the turbulent latter half of the eleventh century when, after the banishment of the bishop of Sigtuna, Christianity was forced on the defensive, almost to the point of dissolution, for a long time.

Greater continuity of coinage can be seen in Norway. It has been much debated whether Norwegian minting first began under Olaf Tryggvason or under St Olaf; probably it was under the latter. The Norwegians, too, followed Anglo-Saxon models, the pennies of Æthelred II. Their coin legends give the royal title 'King of Norway', the moneyers' names are all Anglo-Saxon: no Norwegian mints are named. Harald Hardrada (who was killed in 1066) played a great part in the development of the Norwegian coinage from the middle of the century. He brought great wealth back with him from Byzantium, and must have been largely responsible for the Byzantine influence on Danish and Norwegian coin types. He frequently used the symbol of the Trinity on his pennies, but it seems that he had no scruples in striking two coinages; one of fine silver, the other debased and containing half, or less than half, silver. The latter was certainly not accepted outside his own domains. This situation was improved to some degree by King Olaf Kyrri (1066–93), whose coins, though only half the weight of the old ones, were at least made of fine silver. In the second half of the century, Norwegian mints begin to be named – at Nidarnes, Hamar, and Kaupangr (in Trondelag) – and shortly after Hardrada's death coins begin to appear with legends in runes and in the Norwegian language, doubtless a nationalist reaction against those in Latin and Anglo-Saxon.

WEIGHTS AND MEASURES

We now turn to the Viking system of weights and measures. As we know from archaeological finds, their weights (made of lead, bronze, or iron) were almost spherical and often had stamped characters on the flat base. Elegant small collapsible scales in round bronze containers have also been found. Extensive research has been conducted into the Viking systems of weights and measures, especially by Swedish and Norwegian scholars, in whose countries most

of these finds have been made. Foremost among them are
the Norwegian, A. W. Brøgger, and the Swede, T. J. Arne.
Although final answers have not yet been achieved, much
has already been established. In the later Viking period and
the Middle Ages there was a widespread system based on
this formula:

1 *mörk*—8 *aurar*—24 *ertogar*—240 *penningar*

These units developed at different times, the later being
the *mörk* 'mark', whose name probably derives from the
mark on the bar of the steel-yard. It appears in literature for
the first time as a unit of weight in a treaty between the
English King Alfred and the Danish (East Anglian) King
Guthrum at the end of the ninth century. It seems to have
spread from Scandinavia to England, and towards the close
of the Viking period it also reached western Europe and
Germany. It has been suggested that this mark, with its
equivalent of eight *aurar*, constituted an arithmetical unit
related to the Carolingian *libra* (the pound with its 12 *unciae*)
in the proportions of two to three; and that the mark bore
a relationship to silver, as the *libra* did to gold, which
facilitated the transition from reckoning in gold to reckoning
in silver.

The oldest element in the system is the *eyrir* (plural *aurar*)
(derived from the Latin *aureus* ['of gold'], as applied to the
Roman *solidus*). It originated in the days of the Roman
emperors and was, as the name implies, based on gold and
not silver. Examination of Scandinavian gold hoards of the
migration period has revealed gold rings which are mul-
tiples of a gold *eyrir* weighing about 26.4 gm.: a correspondence resembling the relationship of the *uncia* to the Roman
pound or *libra*. As the Viking period advanced, the *eyrir* was
reduced in weight to 24.5 gm., corresponding approximately to about 3 *ertogar* of 8 gm. each.

The third component in the system was the *ertog*, which is

Excavations at Hedeby

13

A. Part of the main earthwork of the Danevirke

B. Part of the walls of Hedeby

14

A. The military camp at Trelleborg in Denmark

B. A common grave at Trelleborg

B. Runic stone at Turinge in Sweden

A. Runic stone at Högby in Sweden

16

A. Runic stone at Sparlösa in Sweden

B. Runic stone at Rok in Sweden

17

A. Runic stones at Jelling in Denmark

B. Picture of Christ on the great runic stone at Jelling

18

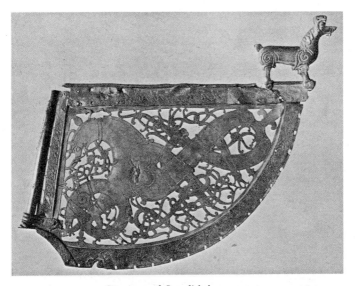

A. Ornamental Swedish bronze vane

B. Carvings on the Ramsund rock in Sweden

19

B. English silver bowl found at Fejø in Denmark

A. Irish bronze ornament imported into Norway

Carolingian gold ornament found in Norway

A

A. Carved and painted
tomb-stone from Lärbro on
the isle of Gotland

B. Runic stone from Dynna
in Norway

B

22

A. A Norwegian
Viking head, from
the Oseberg cart

B. A Swedish Viking
head: the top
of a bone stick from
Sigtuna

A. A Danish Viking head: the head of a bronze pin

B. Bronze statuette of the god Frey

from a later period than the *eyrir*. The derivation of the word is doubtful, but Marstrander suggests it may be a compound of Latin (*denarius*) *argenteus* 'of silver' and a Germanic word for weight. The *ertog* was based on silver (the basic precious metal of the Vikings) as the *eyrir* on gold. Brøgger believes that the model for the *ertog* as a unit of weight was the Emperor Valentinian's silver coin called the *tremissis* (one-third of a *solidus*) which became the basis also of the Anglo-Saxon pennyweight.

The fourth and last element in the Viking system of weights, the *penningar*, coincided with the silver coin of the same name which was (or should have been) of the same weight. The existence of under-weight coins led to the practice of differentiating between weighed *penningar* and counted *penningar*.

T. J. Arne, after examining Viking scales and weights found in Sweden, has arrived at a unit of weight averaging a little over 4 gm. He relates this, keeping in mind the possibility of losses in weight of his specimens due to various causes, to the Sassanid drachm, a unit equal to 4.25 gm., and suggests, somewhat doubtfully, a connexion between the two systems.

Very little is known of Viking linear and cubic measures. It was noted in an earlier chapter that the construction of Trelleborg fort in Denmark was based upon a measure roughly equivalent to the Roman foot (about 29.5 cm.); but that is about all we know. No yardstick of any sort has been found. As to measures of volume, the Viking trader no doubt knew the accepted rules when buying or selling – the accepted sizes of the pot, the mug, or the bushel – but for reasons best known to himself he did not deem it necessary to enlighten others, and, in consequence, we do not know.

CHAPTER ELEVEN

Runic Inscriptions

It is through their runic inscriptions that the Vikings speak to us with their own voices and in their own language. They are our most important direct sources, though as such they are regrettably brief and very frequently stereotyped in form. Yet they do tell us something, if only in snatches, about the modes of expression, beliefs, and social conditions of the time.

ORIGINS AND PURPOSE

At the beginning of the Viking period runes had already been known in the North for many centuries. Without elaborating on the numerous theories of the origin of the runes, we will only mention the one interpretation which seems the most likely. This is that the oldest Germanic runic alphabet, consisting of twenty-four characters and now called the *futhark*, was created by the Germanic peoples themselves somewhere about the year 200 or soon after, under direct or indirect Roman influence, based on one or more of the southern European alphabets. These twenty-four characters – the 'longer rune-row', as it is called, to distinguish it from the later sixteen-letter alphabet used in the Viking period – have characteristic angular shapes, which suggest they derive from the technique of wood-carving.

Throughout the ages there must have been something of a

mystery about each newly-created script, for it could only be used and interpreted by the select few. The runes were thought by the Germanic peoples, and the Northerners too, to possess occult powers, powers which could be turned to advantage. These powers were not invented by the rune-masters who carved the letters in stone or wood : they existed already in the runes themselves, and could be released only by the initiated. This concept is reflected in the Norse myth of Odin, wisest of the gods : even he is not credited with inventing the runes but rather with finding them and releasing from them their magical powers.

A further confirmation of this attitude is provided by the practice, common in the centuries immediately preceding the Viking Age, of putting short runic inscriptions – of more or less magic content – on arms, jewels, and implements : often a short but significant phrase, at times only the owner's name ; and sometimes only on the back of the object, where it would not be exposed to general view but where the spell could work in secret. On a scabbard chape, for instance, there is engraved 'May Márr [the name of the sword] spare nobody'. These runes would invest the sword with irresistible potency. And on another chape : 'I Alla own the sword Márr', a formula designed to increase the weapon's value to its owner. Such hidden magic runes can also be found on the back of a woman's brooch or on the underside of a shield boss. A similar belief in rune magic is shown by the carving of the entire runic alphabet on a stone which formed the side of a fourth-century grave at Kylver in Gotland; the dead alone were to benefit by its power. Another runic inscription, cut on the underside of a slab covering a grave of about a century before the Viking Age at Eggjum in Sogn, (Norway), declares that neither stone nor runes have ever been exposed to the sun's light and that the runes were not carved with an iron knife. In other words : both stone and runes are dedicated in secret to the

dead man and to none other. This, the longest of all the early
inscriptions, commands further that the stone must never
be brought out into the light of day. In these early times,
then, the Germanic runes were not used for literary or
practical everyday purposes. There is no doubt they were,
first and foremost, sacred, magic symbols which the initi-
iated could employ for good or evil.

But in the period immediately before the Viking Age
runes were already developing into something else; they
were being used in commemorative inscriptions. In the pre-
Viking period inscriptions of this kind are found in Sweden
and Norway, though not in Denmark. At Möjebro, in
Uppland, for instance, there is a stone bearing a picture of a
horseman above a runic text. The rune-stone from Tune, in
Ostfold (Norway), was undoubtedly raised as a memorial.
In these cases rune magic or sorcery are out of the question.
In Denmark no rune-stones of the pre-Viking period are
known, either hidden in graves or raised as memorials.
The practice of setting up inscribed monuments probably
came to Norway from western Germany in the late Roman
period, by the sea route from the mouth of the Rhine
round Denmark; from Norway the practice may have
travelled to Sweden by the ancient route from Trondelag
to Jamtland and so to Uppland and other central Swedish
provinces.

This double use of runes, for hidden magic and open
commemoration, continued into the Viking period. The
two uses were not always differentiated. A stone erected
primarily as a memorial might bear in addition a magic
formula, either an open curse upon anyone who might
deface or remove the monument, or a group of secret words,
perhaps involving numerical magic, incomprehensible to
modern runologists. There can be no doubt that number-
magic was used by Scandinavian rune-masters – though
some philologists have so exaggerated its importance as to

promote strong reaction against their interpretations on the part of more cautious scholars.

THE 'FUTHARK'

At the time of the transition from pre-Viking to Viking times the twenty-four signs of the older rune-row were replaced by a shorter set of sixteen, the 'later *futhark*'. Why this transformation occurred is a debatable question. With the relatively small number of runic inscriptions available, it is difficult to trace the continuity and identify transitional forms. The change was clearly a simplification of the runic system, and the reasons for this reform may have been purely practical; but the use of fewer runic signs for the same number of phonetic values must mean that a single rune now covers several related sounds – a factor which in itself presents the modern interpreter of the later inscriptions with a number of difficulties.

Three different rune-rows can be traced in these later inscriptions: first, the Danish, or 'ordinary' runes, which are encountered throughout Denmark (including Skane), western (later the whole of) Sweden, and Norway; second, the Swedish–Norwegian runes of eastern Sweden, southern and western Norway, which also appear in the Norwegian colonies of the west, especially the Isle of Man; and, thirdly the so-called Halsinge runes, a sort of cryptic or cursive script, prevalent in north Sweden, produced by omitting the stem of each rune form.

DISTRIBUTION

In Denmark most rune-stones belong to the period 950–1050, and they are fairly evenly distributed throughout the country, though with special concentrations in south-west Skane and east Jutland (e.g., Randers, Aarhus, Slesvig). The island of Bornholm has, as a late group of its own, some rune-stones of the eleventh century. In Norway there is a concentration of them in the region of Jaeren, south of Stavanger, and Ostland has some specially interesting decorated examples. The Isle of Man, a Norwegian colony, has runic crosses of the tenth and eleventh centuries. In Sweden, rune-stones occur throughout the south and the middle of the country; the province in which they are most abundant is Uppland, which has a total of about 1,000 stones. This Uppland group belongs mainly to the eleventh century and is distinguished by its abundance of ornamentation. Of all the Scandinavian countries Sweden can claim by far the most rune-stones, some 2,500 in all.

HISTORICAL VALUE

What do the rune-stones reveal? First of all, they tell a little about leading personalities in the aristocratic circles of the community: the kings, chieftains, and warriors. The man who erected the stone often gives his own name and always, of course, that of the man in whose memory the stone was raised; the latter is sometimes briefly characterized. Now and then the rune-master's name is given, and not infrequently a stone records that it was raised in memory of someone who fell in battle in a foreign land, on a raid to the east or west, or within Scandinavia itself. Occasionally the social position of the dead man is recorded, his position

in the *hirð* or in the heathen priesthood. Less often a rune-
stone mentions peaceable occupations, such as road-making
or bridge-building. The inscription may express a wish of
some kind, that the stone will remain long in its place, that
the dead man may enjoy his grave, that the god Thor will
sanctify the runes, or that the Christian God will help the
soul of the dead man. Many of the late Viking rune-stones
show Christian influence.

It is useful, at this point, to illustrate these themes in detail
from runic inscriptions of the Viking Age – to let the stones
speak for themselves.

REFERENCES TO KINGS AND PRINCES

The most important references in this category are to the
Danish royal house of Jelling. The two Jelling stones (Pl. 18)
have already been mentioned, one set up by King Gorm
for his wife Queen Thyri, calling her *Danmarkar bót*, the
second erected by Harald Bluetooth in commemoration of
his parents, King Gorm and Queen Thyri. The latter is the
most impressive runic stone in the whole of Scandinavia, including in its inscription a summary of Harald's own
achievements as king – the pompous final statement that he
was 'the Harald who conquered all Denmark and Norway
and Christianized the Danes'. There are three Jutland
stones in this category, one from Sønder Vissing, one from
Læborg, and one from Bække, all of which refer, as it seems,
to King Harald and his mother Queen Thyri. The Swedish
royal house in Hedeby is commemorated in a pair of rune-
stones from this locality, both raised by Queen Asfrid and
dedicated to Sigtryg, her son, by King Gnupa. Two other
stones from Hedeby probably refer to Swein Forkbeard:
one erected by Swein's housecarl Thorolf over his comrade

Eric, a most distinguished warrior who 'met his death
while men sat around [besieged] Hedeby'; the other put up
by King Swein himself and inscribed: 'King Swein raised
this stone in memory of his housecarl, Skardi, who had
roamed the west but now has met his death at Hedeby.'

REFERENCES TO CHIEFS AND NOBLES

A Danish rune-stone from Snoldelev is carved with various
pagan symbols – swastika, sun-wheel, and tricorn – and its
inscription says: 'The stone of Gunnvald, son of Hroald,
þulr in Salløv'. A *þulr* probably occupied a religious post, but
the wording is so terse that we cannot determine whether
Gunnvald or his father Hroald was the *þulr*.

Two Danish chieftains were both married to a Ragnhild,
presumably one and the same woman. The first was
Gunnulf, from Zealand, 'a baying man' (that is a pagan
priest and sorcerer); the second was a chieftain and priest
from Fyn called Alli Sölvi. The first to die was Gunnulf; his
rune-stone (at Tryggevælde in Zealand) says:

Ragnhild, Ulf's sister, raised this stone and constructed this
mound, placing stones in the outline of a ship, in memory of
her husband Gunnulf, a baying man, the son of Narfi. Few men
nowadays are better born than he. A *rati**** be he who destroys
this stone or drags it from here.

Next, Alli died, having several sons by Ragnhild; and his
stone (at Glavendrup on Fyn) declares:

Ragnhild raised this stone in memory of Alli Sölvi, priest of the
vé most worthy *þegn* of the *lið*† The sons of Alli made this monument in memory of their father, and his wife in memory of her

* What the word *rati* meant can only be surmised: an outlawed spirit
perhaps.

† *Vé* means 'holy shrines'. *Þegn* means 'chief'; *lið*, 'housecarls' (*hirð*).

husband. Soti Carved these runes in memory of his lord; may Thor consecrate them. A *rati* be he who destroys this stone or drags it for another.

Dragging a stone for another can be interpreted as using it to commemorate some other dead man, a form of thrift which is evidenced by stones thus used at Tillitse in Lolland, and Alstad in Norway. Another stone, at Ronninge in Fyn, also refers to the carver Soti, whom it describes as 'son of Asgaut with the red shield'.

The inscriptions frequently emphasized the honourable lineage of the person they commemorate: 'a highly born chieftain', 'a warrior of very good descent', 'a chieftain of noble lineage', 'a most noble warrior', 'a woman of noble birth', 'a man of noble birth', and so on. Still better, of course, is the stone which embodies the family tree or a portion of it, as the north Swedish stone from Malsta does, proclaiming: 'Freymund raised this stone in memory of Fe-Gylfi, the son of Bresi; and Bresi was the son of Lini, and Lini the son of Aun, and Aun the son of Ofeig, and Ofeig the son of Thori.'

REFERENCES TO VIKING LIFE

Two qualities especially appreciated by the Vikings were hospitality and generosity; and both these are sometimes specifically referred to on memorial stones. The runic stone from Sovestad in Skane declares: 'Tonna raised this stone in memory of her husband Bram and [i.e. together with] Asgaut his son. He was the best among the land-owners and the most generous with food.' Bram was evidently a land-owner who kept a good table.

Another merit much valued by the Vikings was a land-owner's readiness to employ his men on such public utilities as making roads across marshes, filling up swampy patches, and building bridges across rivers. It seems probable that it was the clerics who persuaded noblemen to act in this way, because it is most often Christian runic inscriptions which praise a man for 'bridge-making', as this kind of public-spirited action was called. A classic example is provided in Uppland, where Jarlabanki, a great landowner, refers to himself on several rune-stones, two of which are still standing on the road through the village (Taby) where he lived, and where he filled in swamps and made paths. These two stones testify that 'Jarlabanki raised these stones in his own honour, while he was still alive, and made this bridge for the good of his soul. He was the sole owner of Taby. May God help his soul'. It may well have been in his mind that these beneficent actions would assist his passage through purgatory. Three other similar stones are still in the vicinity. Farther north in Sweden, on the small island Froso (Frey's island) in Lake Stor, Jamtland, mentioned earlier, lived another great Christian landowner, Austmann Gudfastarson, who commemorated himself on a stone inscribed: 'Austmann, the son of Gudfast, had this stone raised and this bridge made, and he made Jamtland Christian. Asbjörn made the bridge, Trion and Stein carved the runes.' The Kallstorp stone in Skane says: 'Thorkel, son of Thord, made this bridge after his brother Vragi' – the word 'after' probably signifying that by building the bridge he wished to benefit his brother in the next world. Similarly, a rock inscription at Sodertalje, near Stockholm reads: 'Holmfast had the ground cleared and a bridge built in memory of his father Geir, who lived in Nasby. May God help his soul. Holmfast had the ground cleared in memory [also] of his good mother Ingigard.'

There are rune-stones of this type in Denmark too. One which now stands in Fjenneslev Church on Zealand reads: 'Sazur raised the stone and made the bridge'; and in a swamp near-by there is actually a little bridge crossing a rivulet, and to this day this bridge bears the name 'Sassebro' (Sazur's bridge).

In Norway only one example of this type exists, but it is one of the few which, like the Kallstorp stone already mentioned, declares that the bridge was made to benefit the soul of the dead. This is the high, pointed, carved stone, belonging to the mid eleventh century, which originally stood at Dynna in Hadeland, and is now in Oslo. The carvings show God the Father and the star of Bethlehem, and below, on horses, the Three Wise Men; the inscription says: 'Gunnvör Thririk's daughter made the bridge after Astrid her daughter. She was the most skilful maiden in Hadeland.' This good deed performed by a woman landowner for her dead daughter is one of many reminders that women enjoyed a high degree of freedom and respect among the Vikings.

One more Norwegian carved stone, this too erected by a woman, deserves to be mentioned. This is the splendid stone (now also in Oslo) from Alstad in Ringerike, which tells of a well-to-do family estate and a freeborn bride's journey to her bridegroom. The actual inscription reads: 'Jörun raised this stone in memory of Öl-Arni who took her hand in marriage and took her away from Ringerike from Ve to Ølvestad. Ögmund's stone commemorates this occasion.' The stone is a work of art on which there are elegant pictures of a hunt, with horses, hounds, and falcons. No wonder Ögmund wanted his name on it. There is, however, a later and a very significant additional inscription at the foot of the stone: 'Igli raised this stone in memory of Thorald his son, who met his death in —.' This is a clear case of pilfering of someone else's magnificent memorial, a bold action by Igli; but as the stone was not protected by a curse upon defacers and thieves he was evidently willing to take the risk. Another example of the same kind (Danish this

time) is the rune-stone from Tillitse, Lolland, which reads:
'Askel the son of Sulki had this stone raised in his own
honour. While stone lives, this memorial which Askel made
will always stand. May Christ and St Michael help his soul.'
Elsewhere on the stone, however, there is a further inscription: 'Toki carved the runes in memory of his step-mother,
Thora, a woman of good family.'

REFERENCES TO WARRIORS

One would expect a common theme of Viking runic inscriptions to be the commemoration of the prowess of
warriors killed on raids to the west or east, but nearly all the
ones which do so are Swedish, and belong to the later part
of the Viking period. There are, however, some memorial
stones set up over slain Vikings of Norway and Denmark, for
instance the Stangeland stone from Jaeren, South of
Stavanger in Norway, refers to Steinthori 'who fell in Denmark' and in Denmark there is the Kolind stone in Jutland
in memory of Tofi 'who met his death in the East', and the
Uppakra (Skane) stone to Toki 'who met his death out in
the West'. These are rarities, however, and it is central and
eastern Sweden which provide large numbers of this type of
stone, telling of the great Viking raids to the West and
especially to the East.

Of the Western raids there is a commemoration in the
stone at Grinda in Sodermanland, raised by two sons 'in
memory of a brave father. Gudve went west to England,
and received a share of the *geld*. Fortresses in Germany he
bravely stormed.' Danegeld is mentioned again on the stone
at Orkesta in Uppland: 'But Ulf received danegeld three
times in England. The first was that which Tosti gave. Then
gave Thorkel. Then gave Cnut.' These men were undoubt-

edly the famous historical personalities, Thorkel the Tall and
Cnut the Great. Another rune-stone in Uppland is dedicated
to 'Geiri who was a member of the housecarls in the west',
the celebrated *hirð* of Cnut the Great. Another Swedish
Viking with a similar name is mentioned on the Harlingtorp
stone in Vastergotland: 'Tola raised this stone in memory
of his son Geir, a very good man. He died on the western
road during a Viking raid.'

Most of the Swedish Viking stones, however, naturally
refer to campaigns in the east rather than the west; and
Uppland and the other eastern provinces of Sweden are
prolific in stones of the tenth and eleventh centuries, when
such famous rune-masters and artists as Asmund Karason,
Lifstein, Balli, and Øpi inscribed and decorated an immense
number of memorial stones for brave Vikings who had
perished in the east. *Austrleið, austrferð, austrveg* were general
terms for many places in the 'greater Sweden' of the east,
but many individual eastern countries and places are
specifically mentioned on the Swedish stones: 'Semgall' is a
part of Latvia, 'Domesnes' is in Courland, 'Virland' in
Estonia (all three in the Baltic); 'Holmgard' is Novgorod,
'Gardariki' Russia, 'Grikkjaland' either Greece or more
often Byzantium; 'Serkland' (which means 'Silk land')
comprises the territories south and south-west of the Caspian
Sea. 'Jerusalem', finally, is just what it says. Let us quote
some of these Swedish voices from the Eastern road.

Both sides of a rock at Ed in Uppland have runes by the
Viking Rögnvald. One side says: 'Rögnvald had runes
carved for Fastvi, his mother, Onæm's daughter. She died in
Ed. May God help her soul.' The other says: 'Rögnvald had
runes carved; in Byzantium he was commander of the *lið*.'
The Byzantine *lið* may be the Emperor's bodyguard, the
Varangian Guard, of Constantinople; if so, Rögnvald held a
very important position indeed. Two inscriptions are found
on a large stone at Högby in Ostergotland (Pl. 16A): the

first says: 'Thorgerd set up this stone in memory of Ozur his uncle, who died in the east, among the Greeks'; on the second we are told more of this Ozur and his brothers: 'Gulli the Good had five sons. The brave Asmund fell at Fyris. Ozur died in the east, among the Greeks. Halfdan was slain in a duel. Kari died at home. Dead too is Bui.' Thus could a Viking family lose all its menfolk. The stone at Angeby in Uppland records that Björn fell in Virland (in Estonia), and that Asmund (Karason) carved the runes. The Broby stone in Uppland tells of a Viking, Eystein, who went to Jerusalem and died in Greece (perhaps Byzantium). A stone of special interest is that from Sjusta, in Uppland, which declares of the warrior Spjallbodi: 'he met his death in Holmgard [Novgorod] in the church of St Olaf. Øpi carved the runes.' An inscription from Turinge in Sodermanland (Pl. 16B) first relates in prose that the stone is a memorial to the warrior Thorstein, erected by his sons Ketil and Björn, his brother Önund, his housecarls, and his wife Ketillaug; and then breaks into a poem of praise of both brothers – the dead Thorstein and the still-living Önund – thus:

Ketil and Björn erected this stone in memory of Thorstein, their father, and Önund of his brother, and the housecarls of their equal, and Ketillaug of her husband. These brothers were the best of men both in their homeland and away at the wars. They looked after their housecarls. He fell fighting in the east, in Russia. He was in the forefront of battle, the best of countrymen.

Finally we quote the rune-stone from Gripsholm castle: 'Tola had this stone raised for his son Harald, Yngvar's brother. They went boldly away in search of distant gold, and in the east they gave to the eagles – they died in the south – in Serkland.' To give (food) to the eagle means to kill in battle. In such words a Scandinavian land commemorates her fierce sons.

The Yngvar referred to on this last stone is a remarkable
figure, part real and part fictitious, from the later part of the
Swedish Viking Age: Yngvar the Far-Travelled appears in a
late Icelandic saga as a Swedish royal prince who went with
many companions on a difficult and disastrous campaign
to Serkland in the distant East. In fact no fewer than
twenty-five rune-stones from eastern Sweden, dating, it
seems, from the mid eleventh century, refer to Yngvar (and
his four brothers). Yngvar himself was killed on this great
enterprise, and the Swedish Yngvar stones, set up as
memorials to his many high-born compatriots, commemorate the raid in such phrases as: 'He fell on the eastern road
with Yngvar. May God help his soul', or 'He met his death
in Yngvar's troop', or 'He journeyed east with Yngvar'.

A number of Swedish Viking stones refer to a single great
event: the celebrated battle on Fyris plain near Uppsala,
where the Swedish king, Eric the Victorious, defeated his
dangerous and turbulent nephew Styrbjörn who, with a
force including Danish warriors and Jomsborg Vikings, was
attempting to gain the throne. There are two of these stones
in Skane, one from Hallestad, one from Sjorup. They commemorate Toki ('He did not flee at Uppsala') and Asbjörn
('He did not flee at Uppsala, but fought as long as he had
weapon'). Another such stone is the one mentioned above
from Högby celebrating, among five brothers, the brave
Asmund, Gulli's son, who also 'fell at Fyris'.

REFERENCES TO PEACEFUL PURSUITS

Scandinavian rune-stones seldom mention peaceful activities, except for the occasional references, already noted, to
road-making or bridge-building. Yet there is one, now badly
defaced, from Mervalla in Sodermanland, which records

that 'Sigrid had this stone raised in memory of her husband Swein. He often sailed to Semgall [Latvia] with his
fine ship round Domesnes [Courland].' This Swein was
apparently a peaceful thrifty trader, who followed a regular
route across the Baltic.

Not infrequently the texts of rune-stones are cast in
metrical form. The phrases, pithy yet splendid, are strongly
rhythmical. Here, as a matter of interest, are the texts of two
of the rune-stones mentioned above. The Turinge stone (see
p. 16B) says:

> *Brœðr váru þeir – bestra manna – á landi ok –*
> *í liði úti – Heldu sína – húskarla vel – Hann fell í*
> *orrostu – austr í Görðum – liðs foringi –*
> *landmanna bestr.*

The Gripsholm stone (see p. 206) says:

> *þeir foru drengila – fiarri at gulli – ok austarla –*
> *erni gáfu – Dóu sunnarla – í Serklandi.*

To this splendour of language the rune-stones often added
an ornamental and colourful splendour of appearance. The
eleventh-century rune-masters of Uppland developed a
whole decorative tradition of curling scrolls and animals.
One recurrent motif, intended to ward off evil spirits as well
as to decorate, is the large human mask with braided beard
and round eyes. Ships are used solely for ornamental effect.
Significant symbols as well as illustrations of Christian or
pagan myths occur on stones of all three Scandinavian
countries: at Dynna in Norway (Pl. 22B), Jelling in Denmark (Pl. 18B), Sparlösa (Pl. 17A), Altuna, Hunnestad in
Sweden, and on the carved stones from Gotland. The
Ramsund rock in Sodermanland depicts the myth of
Sigurd, Killer of Fafni. From traces of paint which have
occasionally been found on rune-stones it may be concluded

that colour was used to emphasize both text and ornament. Yellow, red, and blue are the favourite colours.

Not all extant rune-stones can be deciphered; some use cryptic runes or obscure wording which may never be certainly interpreted. The classic example is the famous stone of Rok in Ostergotland (Pl. 17B) containing the longest runic inscription in Scandinavia – about 800 characters – which begins: 'In memory of Væmod these runes are cut. But Varin carved them, the father in memory of his doomed son.' This mammoth inscription, full of cryptic runes, number magic, and puzzling and inscrutable passages, has given rise to a large and controversial literature among specialists, one of whom has claimed a connexion between it and the fortress of Trelleborg in Zealand.

RUNE-STONES OUTSIDE SCANDINAVIA

Are there any Viking rune-stones outside the North? The question is really a double one: (a) Did the Vikings erect stones over their families in the lands they colonized? and (b) Did they set up stones to their fallen dead on raids into foreign countries? To both these questions the answer is yes.

Examples of the first kind are the richly decorated Anglo-Danish stone crosses found in northern England, many with runic inscriptions and animal patterns of Scandinavian type. There are also the Norwego-Celtic runic crosses on the Isle of Man (some of them the work of the rune-master, Gaut). The latter have been described by the Norwegian scholar Haakon Shetelig as 'Christian memorials inspired by Celtic culture, but Norwegian in their language and runes and showing conspicuously the survival of pagan traditions.' These Manx grave-stones are often decorated with a great

Celtic cross in relief, filled with Celtic interlace, but frequently surrounded by figures illustrating Nordic pagan myths, such as those of Odin and the wolf Fenri, Sigurd, killer of Fafni, etc.; also their decorative pattern is sometimes of Norse type. A similar example is the fragmentary stone cross found in the churchyard of Killaloe in Ireland, with a Norwegian runic inscription, 'Thorgrim erected this cross'.

Rune-stones raised over a fallen comrade by Vikings on a foreign raid or journey are rare, but they do exist. In the Guildhall Museum, London, is a rune-stone, apparently once forming the side of a coffin, decorated with the figure of a lion in early eleventh-century style, and bearing an incomplete runic inscription: 'Ginni had this stone laid and Toki . . . .' The remainder of the text, containing the name of the buried person, was probably on another side of the coffin, which has now disappeared. The stone, probably Danish, was found in 1852, and at that time showed clear traces of blue colouring. Another stone, Swedish in origin and rather insignificant in appearance, was found on the island of Berezanj in the Dnieper Delta (it is now in Odessa). There the Swedish Viking, Grani, lost his comrade Karl, and recorded it thus on the stone: 'Grani made this grave for his comrade Karl.' In this connexion mention must be made, too, of the celebrated classical marble lion which now stands at the entrance to Venice's old naval arsenal, where it was brought long ago by Venetians who found it in the Greek harbour of Piraeus. This lion is not a memorial, at any rate not a Scandinavian one, but it is undeniably a Scandinavian (Swedish) runic monument, as its left shoulder still bears the indistinct remains of a runic scroll or ribbon of the same kind as those on Uppland rune-stones of the tenth and eleventh centuries. The inscription unfortunately is so weathered that it is no longer decipherable – it would have been interesting to know what a Swedish Viking wished to confide to a Greek lion.

Finally, before we leave the Viking rune-stones, let us return to Sweden for a look at the stone from Skarpaker in Sodermanland. The whole of its broad front side is taken up by a richly luxuriant Christian ring-cross, the arms and top of which, however, are entwined with pagan decorations, while the foot of the cross is planted as a mast in a ship, the old heathen Viking ship. In the surrounding runic scroll, which bears a heathen animal's head, is carved: 'Gunnar raised this stone in memory of Lydbjörn his son' – and then partly in Halsinge runes: 'the earth shall fall asunder and high heaven.' In other words: *ragnarök* (see p. 272). Were these two, father and son, pagan or Christian? No one can tell – but this they knew: all things shall perish.

CHAPTER TWELVE

Art

DECORATIVE ART

In the three centuries of the Viking period the Nordic countries developed a rich and varied decorative art whose essential component was a native and traditional development of animal-ornament. In the period from 800 to 1100, however, it was stimulated by outside influences from the many lands, both in the east and west, with which the Vikings made contact. There were three principal spheres of art in western Europe able to influence the North: the Irish, the Anglo-Saxon, and the Frankish (Carolingian–Ottonian). In addition to these there was some influence – though of no great significance – from the Orient which reached the North either directly because of the connexions between Russia and Sweden, or indirectly via western Europe. Animal motifs, however, were always predominant during the Viking era; ornament based on plant-forms played only a secondary role.

The Pre-Viking Period

Before considering the development of the decorative art of the Vikings, in each of the ninth, tenth, and eleventh centuries, we shall look briefly at its progress during the pre-Viking period. All the Germanic peoples shared a preference for animal-ornament in their forms of decoration. They are not alone in this: so too, indeed, did other races such as the

Irish and the Scythians. The Germanic peoples of the south
were never entirely dominated by this fashion, but the
northern tribes practised it intensely and constantly for half
a millennium. As early as *c.* 700, animal-ornament was de-
clining among the Continental Germanic peoples, but in
Scandinavia it continued to flourish throughout the entire
eighth century. By the beginning of the Viking era the
Scandinavian artist was at the height of his skill, having
achieved an extreme refinement in the practice of his art.
This had reached its highest stage of development: therefore
all possibilities open to the artist had been exhausted. The
animal drawing – intricate, capricious, and refined – is now
far removed from its prototype of the sixth and seventh centuries. Its elaboration is now on a par with that in many of
the most extreme works of the contemporary Irish masters.
At the same time, however, the identities of the motifs have
been preserved, they have not been disintegrated as had
been the fashion in the earliest phase of Teutonic animal-
ornament. Each beast can be followed through – just as in
Irish art – despite all its curves and twists. Much delibera-
tion has gone into the invention of all sorts of fantastic
variations of animal heads and feet. But the means the artist
uses to give the pattern refinement and elegance – dividing
the beast's limbs and giving elaborate decorative emphasis
to its joints – are dangerous. Since no art-style on earth has
the power to stop its own development, they lead to the
degeneration of animal-ornament into facile linear patterns
based in turn merely on the exaggeration of such conven-
tions. Such a development, however charming, leads,
inevitably, to decline. Throughout the eighth century the
style reveals its inner weakness. Only an injection of new
force could save it from collapse. Such was the artistic
situation in Scandinavia at the end of the eighth century.
Now to the Viking Age.

Of the three spheres of Western European art with which

we have seen the Vikings to have been in contact, the following characteristics must be noted. The Irish possessed a fully
developed independent animal style as old as the Germanic
style, but they had not allowed their designs, however intricate, to degenerate. Anglo-Saxon decorative art employed
in the south of England an animal-style influenced by the
Irish, and in the north a particularly fruitful motif borrowed
from Syrian craftsmen who had immigrated to northern
England – namely regularly curving ornament, vine-scroll
with animals – either leaping, climbing, or flying – decora-
tively disposed within it. In adopting this Syrian design the
Anglo-Saxons gradually stressed the animals more than the
vine; and, in the eighth and ninth centuries, new patterns of
this kind became a popular form of decoration on stone
crosses and other monuments in the north of England. The
third influence was Frankish. Merovingian artists of the
eighth century used half-Oriental, half-barbaric animal
motifs; while the Carolingians adopted classical-type
naturalistic animal ornament (lions, bears, etc.) with leaf
ornament (particularly acanthus), a group of motifs continuing into the Ottonian period.

Let us now look at the further progress of Scandinavian
decorative art during the Viking period, century by century.

The Ninth Century

The century began with just such an infusion of new the-
matic material as was needed to save Scandinavian animal-
ornament from decadence. The new motif was, in fact, a new
animal. During the ninth century it appeared everywhere in
the decorative art of the North, occurring with the richest
and most surprising variations and nuances in the Norwegian wood-carvings of the great Oseberg find. It may be
asked how a single animal motif could, within a century,

transform the decorative traditions of three countries. Yet
that is precisely what happened. The invention which
achieved this result is called the 'gripping beast'. This
'gripping beast' was a fantastic, composite creature, a
mixture of bear, lion, dog, and goodness knows what; a
fierce little troll full of vigour and animation. It was never
still: its paws were always clutching either itself, a neighbouring animal, or the edges or corners of the frame. Its
head was large, its eyes so round and solemn as almost to
suggest that it wore spectacles; the forehead was bald, and
there was a long tuft of hair at the back of the head. Its body
was often elongated to a thin thread. This fantastic invention
seems to have captured the Viking imagination immensely,
for it dominated their decorative art in the ninth century.
The restless energy and mobility of the 'gripping beast',
expressed in its ever-clutching limbs, invested it with endless
possibilities from the designer's point of view as he drew its
image inside frames or cages of various shapes; and its
wildness and virility were evidently qualities which keenly
appealed to the Vikings. The 'gripping beast', then, was a
versatile and regenerating force in transforming the traditional Scandinavian animal-art. It is important to stress the
fact that it was a new beast which could not have developed
from the old forms: this is shown by the fact that on ninth-
century bronze ornaments from Gotland the new animal
is placed in its own special frames, side by side – but never
intermixed – with the old familiar designs.

Where did this remarkable beast come from? What seems
a feasible answer to this question was offered in 1880 by the
Danish scholar Sophus Müller, and subsequently endorsed
by the Norwegian Haakon Shetelig and others. It is that the
animal is a composite figure due to the impact upon Viking
artists of the realistic Carolingian renderings of lions and
other creatures. The ferocity and power of these beasts took
the fancy of the Northerners, who liked animals, and they

proceeded to stylize the motif in their own way. Shetelig has pointed out that the characteristic frames or cages in which the 'gripping beasts' are presented are also found in Carolingian art. Although, as we noted above, the Gotland bronzes show that to begin with the new animal motif was isolated from the old one, the Oseberg material indicates that by the middle of the ninth century it had penetrated and fused with the old, to produce by the end of the century a new style, named by archaeologists after a place called Borre near Oslo Fjord, where examples were first found. This 'Borre animal' retains from the old tradition the elongated animal body, though somewhat coarser; and from the 'gripping beast' it has borrowed the clutching paws and the mask-like head. What is significant about the new style is its uninhibited vigour, sometimes even a roughness of surface; the earlier refinement is abandoned in favour of a robust and barbaric expression. Thus did the 'gripping beast' play havoc with the decorative fauna of Nordic art.

Viking artists were rather unresponsive to plants and flowers as a basis of decoration; not yet aware of their beauties, they went for animals almost every time. Nevertheless they do appear to have seen possibilities in the Carolingian handling of classical plant forms, especially the acanthus. The three-lobed golden brooch from Hon in Norway, brought home by a Norwegian Viking, was a masterpiece of Carolingian goldsmith's work – and it was completely covered with luxuriant acanthus (Pl. 21). Such revelations as this induced Viking metal-workers to try their hand at similar decorations on three-lobed and oblong brooches, but with little success. Their stiff and clumsy copies of floral motifs soon gave way again to their old favourites, the animals. They did better in their efforts to copy the Carolingian vine-pattern designs in filigree, usually silver; but here too, the animals intruded.

The Tenth Century

The Borre style continued in the tenth century, but a new
influence had the effect that the dominant motif became a
ribbon-shaped animal figure, harmoniously drawn in the
shape of an S, often symmetrically crossing another beast of
the same shape. The head with the tuft at the back (now
dog-like) is displayed in profile. The origin of this new influence is disputed, but I have no doubt that the 'Jelling
animal', named after the little silver goblet found at Jelling
in Jutland on which it appears, is of Irish inspiration. Most
probably the 'Jelling style' arose from the long and intimate
association of the Norwegians with Ireland. I cannot accept
the theory, sometimes advanced, that this style is a revival of
eighth-century Scandinavian art, to which it bears no resemblance. This Jelling style, with its ribbon-shaped animal,
must not be confused with the ornamentation found on the
Greater Jelling Stone (Pl. 18B) mentioned earlier, the
splendid monument which King Harald Bluetooth raised
in Jelling over his parents. This famous rune-stone is three-
sided; most of the inscription is carved on its largest side
between horizontal lines as in a manuscript; one side bears a
figure of Christ, and one a large animal – a fine ornamental
'lion', its mane and tail adorned with leaves, and a snake
coiled about its body and throat. This great Jelling lion, related to beasts on Swedish rune-stones of around 1000, is
evidently inspired by English art (as are the floral motifs on
the same stone). 'The great animal' festooned with interlaced ornament derives from Anglo-Saxon art, from the
'Anglian beasts' of the stone crosses of northern England.

The Eleventh Century

The great lion of Jelling seems to have established the
predominant design for decorative art throughout the

remainder of the Viking period. It appears again and again
in various sizes: on rune-stones in eastern Sweden; in wood
on a stave-church in western Norway (Urnes); in bone, on
carved treasure chests; in metal, on Swedish and Norwegian bronze weather-vanes (Pl. 19A) and on personal
adornments of silver and bronze. It is a leading motif of
eleventh-century Scandinavian art. During this century the
Viking artists seem more sympathetic than before to plant-
ornament, as the beautiful Norwegian rune-stones of the
'Ringerike group' reveal. On these the motifs are acanthus
and bunches of long leaves rolled up at the points and
arranged overall in an oddly bristling or whirling pattern.
There is scarcely any doubt that this design shows influence
from southern-English art, as it is seen in the illuminated
manuscripts of the Winchester School. Elsewhere in Scandinavia, too, there are to be found English influences upon
Viking art in the eleventh century, a circumstance probably
due (as Holmqvist suggests) to the extensive English ecclesiastical activity in Scandinavia at that time. The last remains of pagan Scandinavian animal-ornament, before it
was decisively replaced by the flora and fauna of Romanesque art, can be seen in the 'great lion', with its network of
lines and vines, carved on the late east-Swedish rune-stones,
or on the beautiful wooden door frame now set in the little
stave-church at Urnes in western Norway. With this we
take our leave of Viking decorative art.

PICTORIAL ART

Apart from decorative art the Viking period also produced a
fine figure art – of which we have several examples, large
and small. The themes of these were largely taken from
myths and heroic tales, and sometimes even from recent

history. The following examples are derived partly from the
three Northern countries, partly from their foreign colonies.

An important group is constituted by the large carved and
painted memorial stones from Gotland. One of them, the
Lillbjärs stone, depicts a large rider, no doubt the deceased,
riding to Valhalla: a fine, severe representation in which
the proud motion of the horses is particularly well depicted.
The Lärbro stone (Pl. 22A) is a typical example of those
grave-stones of Gotland nobles. At the base is the dead
warrior's longship, its armed crew manning the rails and
holding the ropes, and its steersman, higher up in the stern,
handling the long steering oar. The square sail is taut as the
high-stemmed vessel breasts the foaming waves which, as
one sees better on other stones of this type, are skilfully
formed by elegant spirals. Many of the Gotlandic carved
stones of the Viking period depict this most treasured possession of the Viking as, in brilliant sunshine, it glides over
the waves; it is as typical of these later stones as is the circular ornamentation on top of the older, pre-Viking, Gotlandic stones. The ship on the Lärbro stone has, in fact,
nothing to do with the actions depicted on the three upper
sections of the stone. The top section, a great semi-circular
field, shows a battle in progress; the sky is swarming with
eagles and men. On the right a warrior is pitching off his
horse, and on the left, in a building, two sword-bearing men
seem to be pledging an oath together. The middle section
shows Odin's eight-legged horse, Sleipni, across which the
body of a man is lying; and to the left walk three men each
holding before him a sword pointing down towards the
ground. The third section displays a proud rider (the deceased evidently) followed by his men, arriving at the gates
of Valhalla where he is welcomed by a man with a drinking
horn. The purport of the Lärbro picture-stone, therefore, is
to show, first of all, at the foot, the customary emblem of
nobility, the longship; and above it the dead hero's end on

the battlefield (where Odin is aiding him) and his final arrival at Valhalla.

Other Gotlandic picture-stones portray mythical scenes and episodes, such as those we know from the *Edda*, and other Old Norse literary sources: Odin riding Sleipni; Thor fishing for the Midgard serpent with a bull's head for bait; Völund's (Weland, as he is known to English literature) smithy, and Völund himself in his feathered skin; Loki and his wife Sigyn. Not all these picture-stones, however, can be interpreted, partly because some of the myths they portray are not known to us from other sources, and partly because we cannot tell whether real scenes and exploits from the dead man's glorious life are being shown.

Another group of picture-stones are the crosses, already mentioned, of the Isle of Man, on which Celtic and Norwegian pagan and Christian influences are combined.

There are, here and there in Scandinavia, other survivals of their pictorial art, engraved on stone, cut in wood, and woven in textiles. Some of these have already been referred to, but the following may be named here. At Ramsundsberg in Sodermanland, Sweden (Pl. 19B) the heroic story of the slaying of Fafni is depicted, in a naïve, but most lucid way, within an oval ribbon – which at the same time represents the dragon Fafni and contains the runes. From left to right we see the dead smith, Regin, his decapitated head lying among his blacksmith's tools (hammer, tongs, anvil, bellows); the hero Sigurd cooking Fafni's heart and putting his finger in his mouth (turning at the same time to the birds in the tree, for he now understands their language); Sigurd's horse tethered to the tree, with the two birds at the top; and, finally, the great deed itself – Sigurd thrusting his sword through the body of the dragon. The Alstad and Dynna (Pl. 22B) stones in south Norway show respectively a chieftain hawking, and the Three Wise Men. The Altuna rune-stone in Uppland, Sweden, the Hørdum stone in north

Jutland, the cross-fragment at Gosforth in Cumberland, all
illustrate (though in different styles) Thor's fantastic attempt
to fish up the Midgard serpent itself. There are also the carvings on the famous carriage from Oseberg, bearing two
versions of the tale of Gunnar in the snake pit, and the
Oseberg tapestry, with its coloured pictures of horsemen,
warriors, carts, and weapons, and Odin's holy tree with men
sacrificed by hanging dangling from the branches.

We know from Scandinavian literary sources that it was
the Viking custom to paint figures on shields and to decorate
the great hall with tapestries and paintings. There is similar
evidence of great wood carvings as well, e.g. Adam of
Bremen's famous account of the three statues of gods in the
heathen temple of Old Uppsala. Statuettes of silver, bronze,
and amber (some of them certainly figures of gods, Frey, for
example) may well be small reproductions, used as amulets,
of a now lost sculpture of great dimensions.

The favourite themes for pictorial art among the Vikings –
whether in painting, carving, or weaving – seem to have been
taken from the myths and heroic tales. Especially popular
were such incidents as Odin's fight with the wolf, Fenri, and
with the giant, Thjazi; Thor's feats against the giants and
his fishing of the Midgard Serpent; the cremation of Baldr;
Gefjon ploughing with her oxen; the tale of Weland;
Sigurd slayer of Fafni; Gunnar in the snake pit. And there
remain many representations we cannot interpret. No doubt
certain stylized forms became significant and well-known
symbols of particular stories: a man surrounded by serpents
stands for Gunnar; a man spearing a dragon, Sigurd; a
man fishing with a bull's head as a bait, Thor, etc.

Did the Vikings ever depict contemporary or recent
events? Is it conceivable, for instance, that the splendid
scenes on the Gotlandic stones represent the feats of the
dead man? This is not an easy question to answer. Some
scholars declare that such action would be completely alien

to the Norse mind. It seems to me, although I can produce
no proof, that it is not an impossible idea. I wrote a little
earlier that the themes of Viking pictorial art included recent
history. I had in mind the Bayeux Tapestry made in the
latter part of the eleventh century to commemorate the
glories of the Norman Conquest of 1066. Of course Norman
women were not Viking women, yet Normandy had been a
Viking colony created only 150 years before the Norman
Conquest. Therefore it may be suggested that since the idea
of celebrating contemporary achievements in art was
accepted in Normandy around 1070, it may not have been
wholly foreign to the Vikings in their homelands at the
same time. However, it must be admitted that the parallel
is not a close one. The Bayeux Tapestry is an expression of a
foreign feudal system very different from the Norse way of
life. A Norman duke was a monarch more absolute than a
Viking king. In Normandy the people were suppressed by a
despotic duke who created round him a complaisant and
obedient court. Scandinavian traditions in Normandy had
been intermingled with alien feudal customs, so we had
better pursue no further the hypothesis provoked by the
Bayeux Tapestry. Yet if we turn from one Viking art to
another – from pictorial art to skaldic verse – we observe a
remarkable phenomenon. It was very acceptable to an earl
or chief to be praised by the skald for his glorious exploits;
and it seems but a short step from this practice to that of
painting or carving the exploits of someone recently dead, or
even still alive, on a gravestone or on the wall of the great
hall.

CHAPTER THIRTEEN

The Viking Way of Life

ADAM OF BREMEN'S ACCOUNT

Something can be said of the conditions of life and social organization of the Vikings in their homeland, though contemporary sources are particularly scanty and, moreover, not always reliable. We referred earlier to the description of the Scandinavian peoples and countries given by Adam of Bremen at the end of the Viking period, about 1075, in which he describes the three countries in detail, in the order Denmark, Sweden, Norway.

Of the Danes he tells us that they amass much gold by piracy, that their Vikings pay tax to the Danish King for the privilege of pillaging the barbarians living around the Norwegian Sea (i.e. the Kattegat and the Skagerrak), but that they often abuse this privilege and turn treacherously upon their own countrymen. 'As soon as one has caught his neighbour, he sells him ruthlessly as a slave, to either friend or stranger.' Danish laws and customs, adds Adam, contain much which conflicts with justice and reason; he gives as examples:

If women have been unchaste they are sold off at once, but if men are found guilty of treason or any other crime, they prefer to be beheaded rather than flogged. No form of punishment other than the axe or slavery, is known to them. Even when a man is condemned it is honourable for him to remain cheerful as the Danes detest tears and lamentations and all other expressions of grief, which we consider wholesome, to such a degree that no one weeps for his sins or for the death of his loved ones.

The Swedes are characterized by Adam of Bremen in terms which bring to mind the rather stereotyped praises lavished upon the Germanic peoples in classical literature from Tacitus onwards; the similarity is clear when he deals with their noble frugality and generous hospitality, though this should not be taken as implying that the latter quality was not in fact present. This is how Adam expresses himself in his rather tortuous prose:

The Swedes lack nothing except the arrogance which we love or, rather, adore. The empty vanity of this world – gold, silver, splendid chargers, beaver or marten pelts, all things which we admire to the extent of madness – means nothing to them. It is only for women that they show no moderation; every man, each according to his means, has two, three, or more wives at a time; the wealthy and the noble have numerous wives. The sons of all these unions are accepted as legitimate. The death penalty, however, is invoked if one has intercourse with a neighbour's wife, or rapes a virgin, or plunders a neighbour's property, or does him an injury. All Northern people are noted for their hospitality, but the Swedes exceed all. They consider it shameful to refuse travellers shelter and food, and there is keen competition among them for the privilege of entertaining a stranger. They show him every courtesy, and, for as long as he wants to stay, he is introduced into the homes of all the host's friends. These good traits there are in their customs.

The Swedes are made up from several tribes, distinguished by their strength and their weapons; they fight as well on horseback as they do at sea, and have the warlike skill to keep other Northern people in check. They are ruled by kings of ancient lineage, but the monarch's power is limited by the will of the people; what they decide in unity, the king must ratify, unless he proposes a course of action better than theirs, when they sometimes accept it, though reluctantly.

This is their mode of political equality in peacetime – in war they are completely obedient to the king or to a leader appointed by him because of his skill. If they find themselves in dire trouble in battle they call upon one of their many gods, and if victory is secured they give him precedence in their thanksgiving.

We have already referred to Adam of Bremen's observations about the piratical practices of the Norwegians. And he further comments on these people:

> They manage to live off their livestock, using the milk for food and their wool for clothing. Consequently their country breeds many brave warriors who attack more often than they are themselves attacked, for they have not been softened by rich harvests. They live peacefully with the Swedes, but are sometimes raided by the Danes (not without retaliation) who are as poor as they are. ... They (the Norwegians) are a most frugal people, they greatly appreciate simplicity and moderation in food as well as habits. ... Their good habits are marred only, as I have heard tell, by the greed of their priests. In many parts of both Norway and Sweden, herdsmen are highly esteemed, living as patriarchs and by the work of their own hands.

Thanks to the archaeologists, we now know that, by Adam of Bremen's time, the three Nordic peoples had been living in their present countries for more than 10,000 years – a long period of time during which they were reinforced by only one immigration of population of any size, an Indo-European one from the south and south-east soon after 2000 B.C. A good deal is known of the development of their material culture and industry during the Stone, Bronze, and Iron Ages. Although it is only during the Viking period that the three Nordic peoples first come under the spotlight of history, and so appear to the historian as new phenomena, they are archaeologically an ancient race; indeed, we have enough archaeological knowledge to correct even a contemporary source as, for instance, master Adam himself, when he declares that agriculture was unknown in Norway. Archaeological evidence proves, in fact, that Norwegians had practised agriculture for many centuries, although it is equally true that their main activities, especially in the north, were cattle-breeding, hunting, and fishing.

Of the fertility and suitability for cultivation of the Scandinavian countries, Adam gives a number of different assessments. Norway, he says, is quite impossible (*sterilissima omnium regionum*). The soil of Jutland is barren (*ager sterilis*); but the islands of southern Denmark are fertile (*frugibus opulentas*), and so are Skane, Fyn, and the adjacent islands (*opulentia frugibus, frugibus plenae*), Sweden is extremely fertile (*fertilissima*), but even more so, apparently, is Zealand, which is widely acclaimed for its productivity (*opulentia frugum celeberrima*). In speaking of Jutland's barren soil, Adam says:

Apart from the areas of land near rivers, practically all the region looks a desert, a salt land, and a vast waste. Germany as a whole is covered with terrifying dense forests, but Jutland is even worse. People shun its land because of the poor crops it yields, and its waters because of the hordes of pirates. Hardly anywhere is it cultivated or even habitable – except along the fjords where there are considerable towns.

These comments are distinguished by Adam's usual rhetorical exaggerations, yet there is, no doubt, much truth in his picture of Jutland – whose 'vast waste' is, of course, its great heaths. Adam is in general very conscious of the great stretches of wild countryside scattered over Scandinavia; and he notes that sea-routes are to be preferred, in so far as they are safe from pirates. The difficulties of travel in the wilder regions during Viking times is graphically described in the *Austrfararvísur*, a poem which Sighvat Thordarson, the Icelandic skald of St Olaf, wrote after returning from a journey on the king's behalf to the Swedish chieftain, Rögnvald, somewhere in the Malar district. His route lay

through the forest of Ed, on the borders of southern Norway
and central Sweden: 'Hard it was for men to penetrate the
Ed forest', and the poem continues, 'it was not for pleasure
that I, in sombre mood, struggled the thirteen miles*
through the forest from Ed; God knows we suffered. Of the
king's men all had blistered feet – I had sores on both mine.'

Apart from the Danevirke in south Slesvig there were no
fixed man-made boundaries between the Scandinavian
countries, and the natural frontiers were formed by the sea
and wilderness. Towards the close of the Viking period,
however, during Adam of Bremen's time, the Swedish king,
Emund, and the Danish king, Swein, agreed to define the
boundaries between their two countries. The line of demarcation ran from the northern end of the province of Halland
(not far from the present Gothenburg), north of Skane,
along the southern border of Smaland, to the Baltic near
Karlskrona. At that time Halland, Skane, and Blekinge
belonged to Denmark, and Oland to Sweden. The frontier
was defined by a commission of six Swedes and six Danes,
who set up six demarcation stones. Gotland was an independent country at this time, and the province of Bohuslan
was Norwegian. The River Gota was Sweden's narrow link
with the Kattegat; throughout the Middle Ages the three
Nordic countries met at the mouth of the Gota river, and it
was here – we learn from Icelandic literary sources contemporary with or a little later than the end of the Viking
Age – that the Scandinavian kings met on ceremonial
occasions, either on the Brann islands, off the estuary's
southern branch, or on the Dana island (Danaholm) in the
river itself. A whole series of such meetings is recorded. In
the *Older Lawbook* of Vastergotland – a medieval Swedish
source – a conference of three kings on Danaholm is mentioned. This island was divided into three: 'One section is
owned by the Uppsala king, one by the Danish king, and the

* This equals eighty-five English miles.

third belongs to the king of Norway. When the meeting took place, the Danish king held the Uppsala king's bridle and the Norwegian king held his stirrup.' Apparently the Swedish king held highest rank, though we must not overlook that this source is Swedish!

OCCUPATIONS

The Scandinavians of the Viking period had, as we have seen, many thousands of years' experience behind them. Their principal peaceful activities were partly the ancient ones of hunting and fishing, and partly the more recent ones of agriculture, cattle breeding, and, finally, trading. All five of these occupations were often simultaneously pursued in southern Scandinavia.

The most important agricultural implement was the plough, of which the Vikings knew several varieties. There were two old types of *arðr*, the crook-*arðr* and the bow-*arðr*, and also the more effective plough fitted with mould-board, front wheel, and ploughshare made either from wood reinforced with iron, or entirely of iron. Some of the fields were flat and wide, others narrow and steep. We do not know directly which particular regions of Scandinavia were cultivated during Viking times; but from the evidence which we have of agriculture during the Iron Age (i.e. before Viking times) and during the later Middle Ages (i.e. after the Vikings) it is possible at least to point out the districts the Viking peasants preferred to till. In Sweden this was a broad strip, running from modern Gothenburg towards the northeast between the two great lakes to the Malar district and the Uppsala plain. Towards the Baltic the region east of Lake Vatter was well-suited for ploughing, as well as extensive areas of Gotland. In Norway, which in later Viking

times stretched as far as the River Gota, the most fertile
regions seem to have been in Bohuslan and Vik, farther
north in the valleys of the Østland, south-west in Rogaland,
and still farther north, in the Trondelag. In Denmark the
plough was widely used in Skane and Halland, west and
north Zealand, on Fyn and its surrounding islands, and in
north Jutland – mainly the regions of Himmerland and
Vendsyssel. These areas, roughly defined with the help of
Iron Age archaeology and medieval history, differ quite
widely (especially in regard to Norway and Jutland) from
Adam of Bremen's Latin account.

For the Nordic peoples as for many others, the practice of
agriculture was closely connected with fertility beliefs and
rites. The evidence of this is very old. For example, it is to be
found in Bronze Age rock carvings in southern Sweden,
dating from about 1000 B.C., in which the figures of the
ploughman and his oxen are given a strong 'phallic' emphasis as they cut the first three furrows in the field, driving
the ploughshare into the fertile womb of mother earth.
Here is evidence from 2,000 years before the Viking period.
In our own times, 1,000 years after the Vikings, there are
old-fashioned Swedish peasants who participate in ancient
ceremonies at the beginning of the spring ploughing, and
practise rites devised long ago to bring fertility to their fields.
At this time of the year, for instance, a Swedish farmer and
his wife eat and drink in the company of their plough horses
and the plough, out in the fields; for it is vitally important
at this fateful period of seed-sowing that all concerned in the
process should come together in comradeship, to make contact with last year's bounty and stand together against evil
forces. The lady of the house brings out into the field drink,
cake, and pork carefully put by after the solstice feast at
Christmas. The cake will very likely be fashioned in the
shape of the sun-wheel. The ploughman and his beasts must
all have a piece of it; the rest is crumbled into the seed

trough, so that fragments of the cake, along with the new seed, will be ploughed into the freshly turned soil. The farmer brings three drinks: one for the ploughman, one to throw over the horses, and the third for the plough. Then the ploughing can begin. Thus, from long before the Viking Age to long after it, the association of agriculture and religious magic has persisted.

Other agricultural implements of the Vikings were the sickle for the corn harvest, the scythe for the haying, a sharp knife for cutting branches and leaves for cattle-fodder, the spade, and the hoe. All these tools have been found in Norwegian and Swedish graves. From settlement sites have come fragments of the corn itself, or impressions of it in clay. Investigations in Denmark suggest that, in comparison with Roman Age finds, rye was a more important crop during the Viking period, while the proportion of barley and oats remained more or less unchanged. The barley was of the usual Scandinavian type in olden days. In southern Scandinavia the breeding of cattle was no less important than agriculture, and in northern Scandinavia far more so. Adam of Bremen is indeed justified in saying that as we get into the far north agriculture ceases to exist.

The domestic animals of the Vikings were the horse, ox, sheep, goat, and pig, and also the dog and the cat. In the lower mountain regions of eastern Norway the peculiar method of cattle-raising still in use in modern times is the *seter* system. This entails driving cattle, sheep, and goats up into the higher pastures (*seter*) in the summer and letting them run wild until autumn. Was this the practice of Viking Age Norway too? A comprehensive study of the Norwegian archaeological evidence has shown that from the beginning of the migration period (the fifth and sixth centuries) people began to take over the lower mountain regions of east Norway (the modern *seter* ranges) as hunting grounds, and that in Merovingian times (the seventh and eighth centuries) farming and hunting areas were extended widely into the mountains. The oldest known burials in the *seters* date from this time. In Viking times this development continued and reached its peak. As far as Norway is concerned, therefore, the basic activities of the inhabited mountain regions were the breeding of cattle on the *seters*, hunting, and the production of iron.

Finally, the fifth of the Viking methods of gaining a livelihood: commerce. The two principal commodities exported to southern Europe, furs and slaves, are frequently mentioned in literary sources. There is Ottar's report to King Alfred on the fur trader (p. 41 given above) there are many accounts of the slave trade. The life of Rimbert recounts how, on a visit to Hedeby, the saintly traveller gave away his horse to ransom a poor slave woman. Adam of Bremen makes frequent references to the slave trade; Arab accounts of the Rus make it plain that slaves were one of their most important (if not the most important) trading commodities. The late *Laxdæla Saga* (which, it is true, mirrors conditions in the post-Viking period) makes direct reference to the slave trade. Most of the slaves seem to have been women, presumably members of the thrall class. The Rus acquired their stocks of this human commodity by raids on their Slav neighbours.

HOUSES

There was no single pattern of house in Viking Scandinavia. On the contrary, there were several types; some derived from old building traditions, some marking responses to climatic conditions and other natural circumstances such as the availability of building materials, and so on. Countries which are well-wooded naturally encourage the building of

timber houses, the actual type varying according to the type
of forest (deciduous or coniferous), while treeless regions en-
force use of stone, clay, and turf. Where forests exist on a
moderate scale the tendency is towards varied types of
houses, and here external influences – through trade contacts, etc. – play an important part.

Remains of Viking houses exist in Sweden, though they
are few and widely scattered. The site of a house some 58 ft
long and about 22–25 ft wide has been excavated at Levide
on Gotland. The roof was carried on free-standing inner
posts, and the walls were made of logs with wattle-and-daub
in-filling. Viking houses of this kind have been found on the
Aland islands also. Related to it is a site at the 'Triangle'
in Sigtuna of a small square house with walls of close-set
wands (set into a wooden ground-sill) through which
wattlewood was woven horizontally to hold a rendering of
clay daub. At Glia near Stockholm the remains of a small
out-house without a fireplace has been excavated, but unfortunately it is not possible to say to which type the house
belonged – its walls could have been either of wattle-and-
daub with or without a sill, or of some more robust form of
timberwork. Another discovery – probably from the Viking
period – this time near Onbacken in Halsingland shows a
large rectangular house made from close-set tree trunks
faced externally with turf; but here again there is uncertainty as to the type represented. In Lake Tingstäde on
Gotland there stands a peculiar wooden fort, possibly from
the Viking era, named the 'Bulwark', with primitive timber
structures partly recalling framed log-houses (see below)
and partly those with corners formed by overlapping of the
horizontal wall-timbers. Viking-Age corner-timbering has
also been found at Sigtuna. These and other discoveries have
established the wide range of Swedish Viking buildings. As
one would expect in a well forested country, there were, in
addition to the wattle-and-daub house, several methods of

building in wood: walls of horizontal logs jointed at the
overlapping corners; framed log-houses in which horizontal planking is emplaced between upright structural
timbers; and finally 'stave-houses' with walls formed of
vertically-set staves or planks. In the pre-Viking period the
Swedes knew the Early Iron Age 'long-house' of the Danes
and Norwegians – a building, with two rows of free-standing
load-bearing posts and with thick earth walls which
sheltered both human beings and animals. They existed on
Oland and Gotland in the migration period. But during the
Viking period the typical Swedish farm probably comprised
several separate small buildings. This illustrates man's dependence on the building materials at hand, for such small
units lend themselves well to construction mainly in timber
whereas stone, clay, turf, and posts are adaptable to the
building of such forms as the long-house and the great hall.
Variations of both types of houses were known in Sweden
during Viking times. In towns, such as Sigtuna, closely-
packed small timber houses were used.

Although archaeological discoveries tell us even less about
Danish building construction than about Swedish, certain
suppositions can reasonably be accepted. For instance, if the
traditional Jutlandic long-house, mentioned above, of the
Iron Age was common in Norway and its western colonies,
it is unlikely to have gone out of use in Denmark. Remains
of such houses must be found sooner or later. There are remains of wholly timber-built houses in Denmark too: the
large buildings inside the military camp at Trelleborg. The
houses at Fyrkat and Aggersborg, on the other hand, show
wattle-and-daub on the long sides and horizontal planking
on the gable ends. The very substantial houses in these
fortresses were of course designed for garrison life, but there is
also some evidence available about ordinary dwellings.
Under Aggersborg was found a village in which the houses
resembled those in the camps – with long curved sides – but

on a much smaller scale; and these houses also had small half dug out out-buildings. On Lindholm Høje near Aalborg, rectangular long-houses and stables have been found. An example of rather crude and palisade-like construction is given by the grave chamber of the northern mound at Jelling, and remains of a stave building have been established under St Maria Minor in Lund, Skane. Finally, in Hedeby, excavations have disclosed several types of small town-house: wattle-and-daub houses; stave buildings with vertical planks of triangular section, the broader edge of each upright being rabbeted to house the adjacent narrow edge of the next; and houses whose walls were double, that is to say, made of two layers of planking made fast to each side of the structural upright posts.

Apparently the Danish peasant's dwelling developed, during the late Viking period, from a single long-house, shared by man and cattle, into several buildings – either two parallel ones or two or three forming an angle. In this way a barn and other storehouses were added to the long-houses as independent smaller units. Thus the farm gradually became a couple of buildings, so that even the square, four-element plan was known by the later Viking Age – as has been shown by the excavations at Lindholm Høje in north Jutland.

In Norway, the Danish 'long-house', built east-west on the lines already described, appeared in the south-west (Rogaland and Lista) in the migration period. Viking Age sites have been found at Langset and Nygard in Gudbrandsdal. We find here large rectangular buildings, some 55 ft by 23 ft, and some 80 ft by 55 ft, in which a stone sill was the basis for wooden walls packed with clay, and the roof was supported on free-standing inner posts. They were presumably the farm-houses of chieftains. A similar farm lay-out has been identified at Øvre Dal, but this cannot be definitely dated to the Viking period. All these houses in the well-forested country of eastern Norway were presumably either of stave-construction or of horizontal logs jointed and over-lapped at the corners. Incidentally, corner-timbering, al-though in a primitive form, is also illustrated in the burial chamber in the Gokstad ship (about 900).

Viking houses outside Scandinavia are much rarer in the east than the west. Some small corner-timbered buildings were found in Russia during the excavations at Old Ladoga (Aldeigjuborg); a farm-house at Novgorod has signs of a related technique, as have some burial chambers in the Ukraine. In the west, Viking houses are known not from England, Normandy, or even Ireland, but from some on the Scottish islands, the Faroes, Iceland, and Greenland. In these areas the climate is wet and windy and there are no forests. The builders therefore had to use materials other than wood. Of these, the first was stone. In the Orkneys and Shetlands they used natural flat stones or flags, admirably suited for dry-stone walls. In the Hebrides the choice was field-stones or blocks of lava, in Greenland, natural flags. Another material used in these regions was turf. The wide grazing lands of the Atlantic islands produce good building turf, some of it solid, durable, and well padded with earth, and some thin and tough, rather like a carpet. Timber appears to some extent, for, although the islands were tree-less, the sea yielded a supply of drift-wood heavy enough for building. It is seldom possible to find sites datable to the Viking Age on the Hebrides, Orkneys, Shetlands, and Faroes; one must usually draw inferences from the building practices of later times. The usual belief is that the Viking long-house was brought from western Scandinavia to these islands, where it continued for centuries. The stone-built long-house of Jarlshof, Shetland, was continually added to throughout the Viking period.

We are better informed about Iceland, where large sites have been located and dated to the later Viking period.

Examples are the ruins at Hofstaðir, near Myvatn, in the north of the island (once believed to be those of a pagan temple), and the site at Skallakot in Thjorsardalur, not far from Hekla in the south. Hofstaðir was an immense long-house, 117 ft long, built north-south with thick and slightly curved turf walls, and a fireplace in the centre. At its northern end was a small separate room, divided from the hall, with a door to the open air. The hall itself had a door at the northern end of the eastward wall. At Skallakot, too, there was a large long-house, 84 ft long, with walls built entirely of turf to a width of more than 7 ft, and again so curved that the house was almost oval in shape. Here too there was a hearth for the *langeldar* in the middle of the floor. The excavator, Aage Roussell, points out that cattle had not been kept in this long-house, so presumably here the Vikings had out-houses or cattle folds. He further says: 'One long central room, the *skáli* (hall), served as living-room, dining-room, and bedroom; the cooking was done at one end of it, perhaps behind a wooden partition.' In this long room were found two rows of stone-set holes in which had been sunk the posts which carried the roof. The *langpallar* (side-aisles) had floors set at a higher level than that of the central part and were divided by short rows of stones into sleeping compartments. The *skáli* could accommodate a large number of people for feasts, but it was low and dark and full of smoke. This one-room dwelling does not correspond with the descriptions given in the sagas (which clearly apply only to the Middle Ages), but it fits very well the conditions of the old-fashioned recent houses of the Orkneys, Hebrides, and the Shetlands. The truth must be, Roussell concludes (and rightly, I think), that in Iceland the notion soon developed of extending the plan of the long-house by adding rooms to the *skáli* – lobby, *eldhús* (kitchen), scullery, and bathroom, thus creating a new pattern altogether: the medieval long-house with annexes. It was not until later, in the fourteenth century, that the so-called 'passage-house' with rooms built on either side of a corridor, came into existence.

Poul Nørlund's excavations in Greenland have unearthed house sites of the late Viking period and Middle Ages; the farm of Eric the Red himself has been excavated – at Brattahlid in the 'Eastern Settlement', and this shows that the earliest house-plan in Greenland was the long-house with a single room – the *skáli*: later, various additions were built within the space available. Apart from Brattahlid there is the great hall at Hvalsey, also in the Eastern Settlement, Eric the Red's *skáli* was some 50 ft long and 16 ft wide, with solid turf walls over 10 ft thick; a stone conduit carried water through from the back wall and out through the front. The Hvalsey *skáli* was 46 ft by 13ft. In Greenland, as in Iceland, various small outbuildings gradually came to be added, and finally, in the Middle Ages, this pattern was superseded by the 'passage-house' which afforded so much better protection against the cold. The 'passage-house' may well have originated in Greenland, but not until the Viking period had come to its close. From this house the latest type, the large 'central house' with all its rooms concentrated into one big block, developed in Greenland in the course of the Middle Ages. It is odd that most of our knowledge about Norse houses in late Viking times and the Middle Ages should be derived from distant Greenland.

One question which may well occur to anyone who tries to visualize the Viking at home is: did his house have any windows? We do not know for certain; neither archaeology nor literature provide any certain clues. It is generally assumed that windows did not appear in Scandinavia until the Middle Ages, and that until glass was invented, pigs' bladders and foetus membranes served as 'panes'. The north-west Scandinavian long-house with its thick walls built of stone, earth, and turf had no windows of any kind

and even today there are completely windowless houses of
the same sort in the Hebrides. Windows no doubt began in
wooden houses, and to start with were probably narrow
peep-holes protected by inside shutters. It is possible that the
Vikings had something of this kind in their wooden houses,
but of this we have no evidence.

SOCIAL STRUCTURE

Let us look next at the social organization of the Vikings;
the division of their society into classes, the importance of
the family, the status of women, the powers of the king, the
code of law. We may set out from the famous Old Icelandic
poem (influenced perhaps by Celtic ideas) called *Rígspula*
(the Song of Rig). It recounts the origins of the social classes
in a story with the threefold repetitions of the folk tale, the
incidents divided by lists of names. According to the prose
introduction to the poem, Rig is identical with the god
Heimdal. He is wandering far and wide. First he comes to a
cottage with a door ajar and a fire on the floor, where live a
worn and ragged couple, Ai (great-grandfather) and Edda
(great-grandmother), who give what food they can: 'unclean bread, lumpy and thick and full of husks', but with a
bowl of soup and boiled veal. He gives them advice and gets
into bed with them, stays for three days and nights, and nine
months later Edda bears a son, Thræl (thrall), of whom it is
said 'the skin on his hands was wrinkled, his knuckles were
swollen, his nails short, his face ugly, his fingers coarse, his
back bent, and his heels long', but he was a hard worker.
Next there comes to the farm a girl called Thir (drudge):
'her legs were crooked, her feet dirty, her arms sunburnt, her
nose pendulous'. These two produce children, a whole flock
of them, girls and boys, a family of slaves, all of whose

names are given. They do the hardest chores, tend the pigs
and goats, manure the fields, lay fences, dig peat.

Again Rig is wandering. He comes to a hall with its door
closed, he enters; there is a fire on the floor where sits Afi
(grandfather) and Amma (grandmother), both at work. He,
with hair covering his forehead and a well-cared-for beard, in
a tight jacket, is skilfully making a loom; she, with a smock
on her shoulders, a kerchief about her neck, and a linen
cloth on her hair, is turning the distaff and spinning the
thread. Rig gives them advice and gets into bed with them
and departs after three days. In nine months' time Amma
produces a child, a son called Karl (peasant), red and fresh
and bright-eyed. He loves his work: breaking-in oxen,
making ploughs and timber houses, raising barns, building
carts, and following the plough. Along comes a bride for
him 'with the keys of the house, wearing a goat-skin jacket'.
They have many children whose names are listed in the
song, and these become the peasant stock.

And again Rig is wandering. He comes to a hall facing
south; its door, decorated with rings, is open. He enters:

There sat a couple on the floor strewn with rushes, looking at
each other, their fingers busy – Fadir (father) and Modir
(mother). And the big farmer twisted a bowstring, bent an
elmbow, made arrows; while the mistress looked at her arms,
smoothed her clothes, tightened her sleeves. On her breast was
a brooch, her shift was blue, her cap straight, her train long.
Her breast was fair, her brow fairer, and her neck whiter than
new-fallen snow.

Rig gives them advice.

Modir took a patterned cloth of bright linen and covered the
table; then she took fine white wheaten bread and covered the
cloth. She carried in full bowls embellished with silver, put on
the table pork and game-birds. There was wine in the jug; the
silver mug was heavy. They drank and talked, the day was
waning.

Rig gets into bed with them, stays three days and nights, and in nine months' time Modir produces a son Jarl (earl) and wraps him in silks. 'Blond was his hair, his cheeks bright, his eyes piercing as a young serpent's.' Jarl grows up: makes bows, rides horses, hunts with the hounds, is a fine swordsman and swimmer. Rig meets him, teaches him runes, gives him his own name and bids him take possession of his ancient estates. Immediately Jarl goes to war; he spurs his horse, strikes with his sword, raises warfare, stains the land with blood, slays his enemies. He then owns eighteen farms, and gives rich gifts of gold and horses to his friends. He marries Erna, the daughter of Hersi: beautiful, fair, and wise, her hands are slender. They have children (whose names are duly given), the sons as doughty as their father, especially the youngest, Kon ('king'). He learns to read runes of fortune and life, and discusses the runic mysteries with his father. Soon he can blunt his enemies' weapons, calm the waves, save men, quell flames, dispel grief. He has the strength and capacity of eight men. He knows the language of the birds, and one day in the forest as he stands over a bird he has shot, a crow perched in a tree urges him to attempt greater deeds of daring and valour ... and at this the song of Rig breaks off. The rest is lost.

This colourful poem distinguishes the three social groups of the Viking period – the thrall, the peasant, the earl. The names given in the song are entertaining: the serf boys for instance, are: Cattle-man, Foolish, Clumsy, Grumpy, Howler, Ugly, Clot, Fat, Sluggard, Grey, Lout, Longshanks. The serf girls are Clot, Clumsy, Fat-legs, Talkative, Cinder-nose, Quarreller, Torn-skirt, Crane-legs. The peasant's sons have more dignified names: Freeman, Warrior, Brave, Broad, Smith, Settler; and the girls: Quick, Bride, Wife, Woman, Weaver, Ornament, Modest. And of Earl's sons we are told that Bur ('son') was the eldest, and that the others were Child, Young, Noble, Heir, Lineage, Offspring,

Son, Lad, Kin, and Kon, the youngest; they all practised sports. And the Song finishes, forgetting to give the names of the Earl's daughters.

In this vivid language the three classes of the Viking community are described. In the highest class, the king, chosen by the chiefs, is *primus inter pares*, the first among his equals. We know this situation from Tacitus's description of the Germanic peoples about A.D. 100. There we learn that the power of the king was limited by the assembly of the people, that is to say, of the free men. It was difficult, virtually impossible, for the king to take a decision in opposition to the assembly of chieftains, who were his equals in all but name. In early Viking times, when the North was divided into many loosely associated clans, a chief became king simply by the nomination of a group of other chiefs. In later Viking times, when the monarchy had become a more powerful instrument, inheritance rather than nomination became the rule. Significant of the way of thought of the early Viking period is the answer given by Danish Vikings in the late tenth century to a messenger from the Franks. The messenger, standing on the bank of the River Eure in France, hailed the Viking ships and demanded, 'What is the name of your master?' 'None,' was the reply, 'we are all equals.'

After the king, but close to him in rank, were the *jarlar* (earls), owners sufficiently wealthy in land and goods to have a company of housecarls, to own ships and to assert their importance. Of their aristocratic way of life we have heard in the *Rigspula*. For them, the family and the hereditary estates, which passed to the eldest son, were the centre of this existence, as the significant names of Earl's sons in *Rigspula* show.

The solid backbone of the Viking people was the peasant class – smallholders but free men. In *Rigspula* the first of the peasant's sons is called 'Freeman', the next 'Warrior', and

only farther down the list come such names as 'Smith' or
'Settler'. In the two superior social classes, earls and
peasants, women enjoyed high esteem and full freedom, as
Norse literature abundantly testifies.

Lastly the thralls, the bondmen, necessary to the community but little heeded by it. Of the thrall's condition of
life, degree of dependence, rights, or rather lack of them,
we know little, but it is clear that he was little more than a
slave. Killing a thrall was not a major crime.

Our knowledge of the legal systems of Viking society is
scanty: for the contemporary primary sources are almost entirely missing. Something may be inferred from the legal
texts and literature of the early (post-Viking) Middle Ages,
but such inferences must be regarded with caution. We have
extensive knowledge only of the position in Iceland. What
can be positively asserted about all the Nordic countries,
however, is that Viking law was based upon the proceedings
of the institution called the Thing – the assembly of free
men.

In Viking times Denmark was divided into a couple of
hundred districts (Old Norse *heruð*) each with its own Thing.
The Thing was a gathering of free men of age and quality to
bear arms who met to put the law into effect, pronounce
judgements, and discuss matters of interest within the community. The law was a customary one, handed down orally
from one generation to the next; and it was therefore the
responsibility of the older members of the Thing to remember and uphold it, their memory supported by the
alliterative formulae in which it was couched. The punishments for murder or acts of violence were based on a scale of
compensatory payments (*mannbœtr*); the full penalty was
exacted for killing a man or for chopping off his nose; half
for poking out an eye; a quarter for an ear; etc. Judgement
was delivered by the members of the Thing, but the enforce-
ment of the penalty was sometimes a difficult matter. In a

feud between a strong family and a weaker one, for example, the injured member of the weaker side, although adjudged the victim of aggression, must himself secure payment of compensation and this he might find difficult to do. This was an essential weakness in the legal system.

The first element of the word *heraδ* is perhaps Old Norse *herr* ('army'), and the word may originate in a military obligation to furnish a quota of warriors or ships in wartime. In the later Viking period the major decisions of the country – choice of king, declaration of war, or fundamental problems of justice – were reached at the great regional assemblies called the *Landþing*, held at Viborg in Jutland, Ringsted in Zealand, and Lund in Skane.

Complicated disputes were often decided by duels (*hólmganga*) fought under elaborate traditional rules, or by *járnburðr* (ordeal by fire) : an admission that the case was to be decided by the law of superior force or by the judgement of the gods. Stealing was a dangerous crime to indulge in, for the penalty was hanging – not from any moral point of view but rather because of the assumption that the culprit, evidently being (by the nature of his offence) a poor man, could pay the penalty only with his life. The most dreaded punishment was banishment, and those who refused to accept the decision of the local Thing and whose case therefore came before the higher court of the *Landþing* risked this dire fate. It was impossible to exist for long as an outlaw from the community, isolated, deprived of legal rights, rejected by one's fellows; there were only two ways out, fleeing the country, and death.

The man who respected and obeyed the unwritten Viking traditions, and the laws laid down from time immemorial, had nothing to fear. If he enjoyed 'good luck' he could expect to enjoy a prosperous and varied life. In the summer an earl or chieftain could organize and lead a Viking raid, or join with others in a similar and profitable enterprise, returning in the winter laden with loot. Or he might become a trader on his own account. When he was home he had his estate to look after, might serve as a judge at the Thing, and, as a priest, make himself responsible for seeing that the forms of public worship were properly observed.

Conditions similar to those in Denmark prevailed also in Sweden: a closely integrated community based on hereditary possession of land, governed by traditional laws and observances as laid down at the Things; joint responsibility for the provision of men and ships in war-time; and a monarchical power subject always to the consent of the people. Of the latter principle Ansgar's biography tells us, indeed, that major issues were decided, in council at Birka, by the will of the people rather than by royal decree. We shall deal later with two fundamental concepts of Viking behaviour: luck and honour.

It is from Sweden that we have some interesting information about duels as a method of resolving disputes of honour between individuals or families. The oldest extant fragment of Swedish law reveals the pride and touchiness of the Vikings, and the brutality of their belief in the right of the strongest. This fragment declares that if anyone abuses his neighbour saying 'You are not a man's equal nor have you a man's heart', or 'I'm as good a man as you', then the disputants must be summoned together at a place where three roads meet. If the man who has offered the insult turns up, but the other man does not, then the latter must be considered to deserve the epithets applied to him; his honour is tarnished, he is no longer allowed to take an oath or to bear witness. If, however, the aggrieved man turns up but not his accuser, then the former cries out three times, 'Coward!' and makes a mark on the ground. The accuser loses face for not substantiating his claims. If the two men meet and fight it out and the aggressor meets his doom, all is well: crime in words is the worst possible offence, and a loose tongue brought about his death. It is apparent that the duel was misused, as it was to be much later in France and Germany.

In Norway, again, the same pattern of social life existed: local Things for each *bygð* or district, and regional ones of higher status for coping with major problems under the guidance of chiefs and experienced old men; here, as in Denmark, the individual, with the support of his family, tried to get compensation for injury (*mannbœtr*). In Norway, too, primary sources of information on legal organization in the Viking Age are missing, and we have to rely on inferences drawn from the later medieval law-codes, those of the *Frostuþing* and the *Gulaþing* which, according to the sagas, were drawn up by Hakon the Good for Trondelag and Vestland respectively. From these we may conclude that in Norway, as in Denmark, it was the duty of each district to raise a *leiðangr*, a levy of men and ships for the common defence in national emergency. As in Denmark and Sweden the power of the monarch was limited by the sovereign will of the people as expressed at the Things. It would be wrong, however, to underestimate the royal status among the Vikings. The King's corps of housecarls, the *hirð*, which had originally been little more than a private bodyguard, became in the course of time a powerful armed force capable of serving as the *élite* nucleus of a greater army.

Iceland had no king. Its legal organization was naturally based on west Norwegian practice, on the rules and principles reflected in the later *Gulaþing* law. A constitution based on Things was accepted over the entire island from 930. Every summer the common Thing, the Althing, was held, the law-speaker announcing the law, but the real power exercised by the priest-chieftains, the *goðar*. Subsequently the island was divided into quarters (*fjórðungar*), three with three local Things, the other with four. As the *goðar* were both priests and temporal chiefs it would be proper to describe the Icelandic free state as an oligarchy, a kingless union of chieftains.

VIKING ANTHROPOLOGY

Although anthropology has provided us with some indications as to the human type the Viking belonged to, the skeletons from settlement sites and graves which have been examined and measured do not provide satisfactory data, partly because the remains are so scanty, and partly because they are difficult to date accurately. In this respect Denmark is better off than Norway or Sweden, though only about fifty of the Danish skeletons subjected to anthropological tests come from graves certainly dated in the Viking period. In Norway, about sixty remains have been tested, but scarcely more than half these can be quite safely dated as Viking. In Sweden the material is both scarce and widely scattered. Some of the skeletons measured from the churchyard in Skeljastaðir in Iceland are without a doubt from the Middle Ages.

The Danish skeletons, for the most part, have long (dolichocephalic) crania of the kind usually called Nordic: a slender, gracefully shaped cranium, the face low and slightly slanting, low eye sockets. The height of the men seems to have been around 5 ft 8 ins. (170 cm.). An examination of material from Trelleborg disclosed much wear on the crown of the teeth, but very small incidence of caries (less than 1 per cent). The Swedish material is too insignificant to permit any general conclusions, but it appears that the Swedish Vikings were taller than the west Norse ones – a difference which can still be seen in Scandinavians today, and which confirms Arabic statements about the exceptional height of the Rus. Of the Norwegian male skulls, more than three-quarters were long, about one-sixth medium, and very few (about one-fourteenth) were short ones. Of the female, about a half were long, one-third medium, and one-tenth short. On these figures it seems that Norwegian Viking women showed less tendency to long (dolichocephalic) skulls and a greater tendency to shorter (mesocephalic) skulls than their men. Bold scholars might try and explain this difference by the supposition that the Norwegians obtained many of their women from raids upon the Celtic countries such as Ireland; but in my opinion the Norwegian material (the dating of which, in any case, is dubious) is far too scanty to afford statistically significant results.

All one can say for certain of these fifty-five male and thirty-five female Norwegian crania is that they belong to the Nordic type. The Icelandic material reveals a shorter cranium than the Danish and Norwegian, which the Icelandic scholar Jón Steffensen attributes to the influence of the Irish.* According to the *Landnámabók*, 84 per cent of the Icelandic colonizers came from Norway, 3 per cent from Sweden, and about 12 per cent from the British Isles. From these proportions one would expect a greater conformity between the Norwegian and Icelandic cranium material than there is, and Steffensen therefore is disposed to believe that the Irish element among Iceland's earliest inhabitants was much larger than the figures given by the *Landnámabók*. The Icelandic material, however, cannot wholly be assigned to the Viking period, and it is surely too small to allow any substantial statistical use. On the basis of the available evidence, the average height of the Icelanders appears to have been 5 ft 8 ins. (170–1 cm.). One curious deduction from the examination of the female shin-bones was that the Icelandic women must have sat a great deal in a squatting

---

* The part played by Celts in the first colonization of Iceland seems to be estimated more highly by Icelandic than by Norwegian historians.

position. There are signs of tuberculosis, but the teeth again are sound and healthy, although the crowns are worn down – probably, according to Steffensen, by the grit in their dried fish and dried meat.

APPEARANCE

What did the Vikings look like? What would we not give for a contemporary portrait of Olaf Tryggvason or Harald Bluetooth or Eric the Victorious? All we have are occasional wood and bone carvings of heads, represented in such a way as to suggest they are portraits. There are three heads in the round on the Norwegian Oseberg cart (see Pl. 23A) and a little bone man's head from Sigtuna in Sweden (Pl. 23B). Of course, many other Viking carvings of human heads exist, but these are either magic masks to ward off evil spirits, or are used as themes in pieces of decoration, and can therefore scarcely be regarded as attempts at portraiture. Two of the Oseberg heads (the bearded ones) seem to me conscious expressions of an artistic purpose. They impress me as being more than naturalistic representations, and although the artist used models for his work – old chieftains in a benign mood – he seems to have wished to give something more than a mere likeness. I do not hesitate to use the word 'expressionism' to describe these two carvings. The third head on the Oseberg carriage is of a totally different kind, the realistic presentation of a greedy, savage, and ruthless man. The fourth head – that from Sigtuna – is equally realistic; but whereas the Oseberg Viking looks a rough plebeian, the Sigtuna portrait is that of a man of high birth, an earl, with a finely shaped head, a short beard on his strong jutting chin, his hair well groomed, and his fine profile continued in his conical helmet. Thus might

Styrbjörn or Thorkel the Tall have looked. These four heads seem to reveal the presence of notable artistic talent among the Vikings; we can only regret that no more samples have survived.

BEHAVIOUR AND THE 'HÁVAMÁL'

Of Viking manners, behaviour, habits of thought, and experiences we know very little from contemporary sources, but some of the later literature, such as the Eddic poems and the sagas, throws an oblique light upon their mentality. It is always a problem, of course, to determine how far this sort of testimony can safely be applied to a period two or three hundred years before the literature was actually written down; but where the sagas and poems are permeated with pagan beliefs and attitudes they are surely admissible in this sense. It is a commonly accepted view that the celebrated poem *Hávamál*, 'The Sayings of the High One' (that is, Odin), embodies the wisdom and experience of the later Vikings of Norway and Iceland. The *Hávamál* contains aphorisms, advice, and admonitions – sometimes cynical, sometimes matter-of-fact, sometimes ironical or sarcastic, sometimes earnest and sincere – which, combined, reveal a daily life which we may believe reflects the reality of the Viking Age. Here are some samples of it:

Let the man who opens a door be on the lookout for an enemy behind it.

When a guest arrives chilled to the very knees from his journey through the mountains, he needs fire, food, and dry clothes.

A man must be reticent, thoughtful, and bold in battle; cheerful and active until death.

A coward thinks he will live for ever if he avoids his enemies, but old age no man escapes even if he survives the spears.

A visitor must leave in time, not outstay his welcome; even a friend becomes odious if he bides too long in the house of his host.

A man should never move an inch from his weapons when out in the fields, for he never knows when he will need his spear.

To one's friend one must be a friend and to his friend; but to one's enemy's friend no man should be a friend.

Young I was long ago; I wandered alone and lost my way, but I found wealth in a companion. In man is man's delight.

A man must be moderately wise, never too wise. The man whose mind is most free of care does not know his fate in advance.

A man who wishes to take another's life and goods must get up early. A wolf that lies in its lair never gets meat, nor a sleeping man victory.

Beer is not so good for men as it is said to be; the more a man drinks the less control he has of his thoughts.

If you do not trust a man and yet want him to do you good, speak him fair; but think him false and give him treachery in return for his lies.

A lame man can ride a horse; a man without hands can be a shepherd; a deaf man can kill; it is better to be blind than to be burned on the funeral pyre. A dead man is of no use to anyone.

Cattle die, kinsmen die, I myself shall die, but there is one thing which I know never dies: the reputation we leave behind at our death.

In other words take life as it comes; learn from your experiences; it is better to be alive than dead; do not be naïve; look out for treachery; cherish a friendship and do not practise deceit; do not bore or irritate a friend by trading upon his hospitality; outwit your enemy, if you can, with false words.

The word seems to have meant much to the Vikings; they were influenced by its potency and feared its permanence. The last quotation above from the *Hávamál* is really a reminder that a man should do his best to deserve a good

obituary notice. Some modern people attach too much importance to this last sentence and give it an ethical importance, whereas it is quite simply a reminder that the spoken
word can be either a tribute to a man's memory or a con-
demnation of it. The Vikings were susceptible to satirical
verses (*níðvísur*), and there was a carefully worked out system
whereby the insults of such verses could be wiped out or
rendered ineffective by duels.

The foregoing quotations from the *Hávamál* are all taken
from the first and most unified part of the poem. The later
part is more a collection of fragments, some of them mirror-
ing personal experience. The misogynist speaks:

No one should trust the words of a girl or a married woman, for
their hearts have been shaped on a turning wheel and they are
inconstant by nature.

There are abundant injunctions against excess, in drink
or in love, and pleas for the cultivation of friendship,
reason, and moderation:

Be cautious but not over-cautious; be most cautious with beer
and with another man's wife. Beware too, that thieves do not
fool you.

No man is so good as to be free from all evil; nor so bad as to
be worth nothing.

Never confide your troubles to a bad man; he will never repay
with good your open-heartedness.

Never quarrel with a fool. A wise man will often refrain from
fighting, whereas a fool will fight without cause or reason.

Do not break an alliance with a friend; your heart will grieve if
you lose the friend in whom you can confide.

The *Hávamál* even goes into homely detail, such as advis-
ing men to get up in the night to relieve nature, or to make a
good meal in the morning if they are setting out on a long
journey across mountains and fjords. However, to connect

Odin with the matter-of-fact advice given in the *Hávamál* can only be regarded as a stroke of genius on the part of a later editor. Odin was the least matter-of-fact of gods.

FOOD

The sagas say a good deal about food and drink; but their evidence belongs to the time of the saga-writers, the thirteenth and fourteenth centuries, rather than the Viking period. It is fair to surmise that the Viking's daily diet included wholemeal bread made of rye; oat and barley porridge; fish (especially herrings); the meat of sheep, lamb, goat, horse, ox, calf, and pig; cheese, butter, and cream; and, for drink, beer, mead, and (among the wealthy) wine. Whale meat, seal meat, and the meat of the polar bear were important foods particularly in Norway and Iceland. Boiled meat seems to have been preferred to roasted: the *Rígspula* recounts that even in the wretched hut of a serf, Heimdal was offered boiled veal; and in Valhalla the boiled flesh of the hog Sæhrimni was served to the chosen warriors. Broths made from the various meats must have been a familiar dish; and the Vikings were also practised in methods of drying meat and fish. Game-birds, too, were an extra item in the Viking diet. The most common vegetables were cabbages and onions; and apples, berries, and hazel-nuts were abundant. Honey was much in use, largely as the basis for the manufacture of sweet fermented mead. The preservation of food was an important consideration for the Vikings, and for this purpose they learned to make use of ice, salt (from the sea or from burnt seaweed), and whey. In those countries remote from the sea but well forested, much of the Viking sustenance came from hunting elk, deer, wild boar, and bear. Hares, geese, and chickens were other popular

items on the menu, and, in the far north, reindeer and
bison. In spite of all these natural resources, however, many
areas of Scandinavia suffered such shortages of food, and
when crops failed, such conditions of famine, that it was
necessary for the people to make up the daily meal with seaweed, bark, and lichen.

EATING HABITS

Viking houses were furnished with tables and chairs, table-
cloths and plates; and for eating utensils there were spoons
and knives – but not forks. It seems to have been the Viking
custom to eat twice a day, one meal called *dagverðr* in the
morning, and one called *náttverðr* in the evening. King
Harald Hardrada's habit of eating only once a day attracted attention because it was so unusual. Of this somewhat tyrannical monarch it is related, in the *Flateyjarbók*,
that he was served first, as was only right and proper, but
by the time the rest of the company had been served he had
just about eaten his fill and thereupon rapped sharply upon
the table with his knife, as the signal for the food to be
cleared away. 'There were many,' is the rueful comment,
'who were by no means satisfied.'

PERSONAL CLEANLINESS

It has been much debated whether or not the Vikings were a
clean people. The sagas give the Icelanders and Norwegians a clean bill in this respect. One of the earliest sentences
in the *Hávamál* relates of a guest being met at the table by
his host 'with water, a towel, and a hearty welcome'. Later

on it says: 'Freshly washed and well-filled with food should
every man set off to the Thing, even if he is not too well
dressed.' One of the days of the week, Saturday (Old Norse
laugardagr), was named as the day for washing (*laug*
'bath'); the Icelandic scholar Skúli Guðjónsson notes a reference in the *Landnámabók* to Thorolf Mostrarskegg, who
believed that a certain mountain was holy, so that 'no one
should turn an unwashed face towards it'. A very different
account (see p. 265) is given of the Swedish Rus, who are
described by the Arab, Ibn Fadlan, as extremely dirty. On a
visit to the Volga region about 920, he found them (he declares), the most unclean of god's creatures. They did not
clean themselves after discharging their natural functions,
nor did they wash after a meal. 'They are as stray donkeys,'
he adds. Other Arab sources, however, are less critical. The
Danes in England appear to have been more careful of their
toilet, according to a literary source which says that they
combed their hair, had a bath on Saturdays, and changed
their linen frequently 'in order the more easily to overcome
the chastity of women and procure the daughters of noblemen as their mistresses'. All this evidence, such as it is, makes
a poor basis for generalization about the Vikings of Norway,
Iceland, Sweden, and Denmark. The probable truth is that
cleanliness was not an uncommon habit among the Vikings,
but that they practised it in moderation, and for special purposes. Whether they had real soap is not known; but
for washing their coarser clothes probably (as people
continued to do quite late in Iceland) stored up cow
urine, which contains the valuable cleansing element,
ammonia.

MEDICINE

The science of medicine must have been at a very crude stage, yet there is every reason to believe that these warlike people had developed some skill in the treatment of severe injuries. Skúli Guðjónsson, the Icelandic scholar already mentioned, has called attention to Snorri's famous tale of the death of Thormod Kolbrunarskald after the battle of Stiklestad in 1030, a tale which reveals some medical knowledge. (Thormod, it will be remembered, mortally wounded, pulls the arrow out of his chest and, observing the bits of flesh sticking to the barb, says: 'I still have fat round the roots of my heart!') Snorri's tale gives a description of the ways in which the wounded were treated in a barn after this battle. The women heated water (to sterilize it?) and dressed the wounds; then they prepared a porridge made of onions and other herbs, which the wounded man was induced to eat. If a smell of onions subsequently came from the wound in a man's belly it proved that his intestines had been pierced, which would inevitably mean death from peritonitis; in other words, a test meal was used to make a diagnosis, which is exactly what we do nowadays. This fact explains Thormod's cryptic remark when he is offered this porridge 'Take it away. I am not suffering from the porridge illness': i.e. his wound is not in his belly but in his heart.

GAMES

Board games were very popular among the Vikings (the story of the game of chess between Cnut the Great and Earl Ulf is well known). As early as c. A.D. 100 Tacitus had remarked upon the Germanic people's passion for gambling.

Chess reached Europe, via the Arabs, from India, and became widely popular in the north during late Viking times. Other board games were also favoured, such as draughts and fox-and-geese, and the Old Norse name for a gaming board, *taflborð*, was borrowed into Welsh. There have been archaeological finds of both boards and pieces. In the Gokstad ship (*c.* 900) a board was found marked out for a different game on each side; and during the American excavations at Ballinderry in Ireland in 1932, there came to light a well-preserved board, presumably for the fox-and-geese game, which is now in the National Museum at Dublin. It is decorated in a Norwego-Celtic style and is thought to have been made in the Isle of Man in the tenth century. There have been several finds of chess- and draughtsmen from the Viking period and early Middle Ages.

FAMILY LIFE

The Viking in peacetime seems to have had a strong liking for family life. Marriages were arranged by agreement between the families, conflict only arising if the young people's wishes differed from those of their kinsmen. The family was a powerful unit of protection within the larger, less clearly defined, community. A man stuck to his family in all circumstances, from them he got assistance and support in time of strife and trouble; in return it was his duty to help and support his kind. If he failed he could incur the worst possible consequences: ostracism, outlawry. But in this power of the family there was danger, too. An individual was not allowed to keep himself to himself, and duties might arise which would bring even a peace-loving man into grave difficulty. This is the reason why the *Hávamál* urges men to be prudent, vigilant, and well balanced, and to cultivate friendships – otherwise they will find themselves alone and without help when unforeseen dangers crop up. A man without a friend is like a naked fir tree, without bark or foliage, lonely on a barren hill. Therefore, always be on your guard, avoid arrogance towards men less important than yourself, do not try to foresee your fate, for it is best not to know it. Be guided by your own experience. 'Praise not the day until evening has come; a woman until she is burnt; a sword until it is tried; a maiden until she is married; ice until it has been crossed; beer until it has been drunk.' This pervasive prudence may indeed sometimes seem a stolid and negative virtue, but it clearly sprang from the hazardous conditions of Viking life.

The Vikings possessed a lively appreciation of satire, and were also very susceptible when it was applied to their own behaviour. The *Hávamál* uses it frequently: e.g. when it comments on the thrifty hospitality which 'welcomes me as a guest only if I need nothing to eat or if two hams still hang from my host's roof after I have eaten one'. The Vikings had a keen eye for the oddities and frailties of their neighbours, a characteristic illustrated by their extreme fondness for descriptive nicknames, not least for kings and nobles: Harald Bluetooth, Swein Forkbeard, Harald Fine-hair, Harald Hardrada ('the tyrant'), Eric the Victorious, Magnus the Good, Thorkel the Tall, Ragnar Lodbrok ('with hairy trousers'). Many of these appellations refer to some physical deformity: Sigurd Snake-in-the-eye, Ivar the Boneless; as well as other nicknames such as 'cat-back', 'crooked foot'. One of the oddest of these is 'juice head'. Whether this referred to eczema on the face and head, or to a man who liked sucking the juices of vegetables (i.e. a vegetarian), is a speculation which cannot be settled. Nicknames, again, often developed from a memorable situation in which a man had been involved. There was also

frequently an element of satirical paradox in the nickname,
as Finnur Jónsson has pointed out: thus Thord the Short is
known to have been exceptionally tall, and another Viking,
who was worried about his very dark complexion, was
known as 'the Fair'.

THE VIKINGS ABROAD

Thus equipped materially and spiritually, did the Vikings
set out on their campaigns, taking with them their culture,
skills, laws, and beliefs to their newly-founded foreign communities in the west and east, among the Irish, Anglo-
Saxons, Franks, and Slavs, and upon the remote Atlantic
islands. On the Atlantic islands, of course, they had no
rivalry or competition to meet, and could transplant their
culture straight from their homeland to virgin soil. However it was a very different matter to assert their culture in
well established foreign communities which already had
their own ways of life and, indeed, in most cases an equal or
superior culture. In these circumstances, did the Vikings
make any notable impression on the foreign community?
Did they make a permanent contribution, or an ephemeral
one?

IN IRELAND

In Ireland the Norwegians encountered a community
divided into numerous small kingdoms, politically independent units which were unable to organize a consolidated
military resistance. They encountered, too, a Christian
Church many centuries old, independent of Rome, fortified

by its own separate traditions and practices, and concentrated in numerous monasteries. And, finally, they came up against a people of fanatical and uncompromising temperament who had no inclination for peaceful coexistence with strangers. The Norwegians, on the other hand, were a tough people who preferred brute force to diplomacy, and thus there was no prospect of any fusion of cultures between them and the Irish. It was not, indeed, until the Viking period was over, at the end of the twelfth century, that there seemed to occur any such integration of cultures; but then came the English – the Anglo-Saxon–Norman fusion – called in by the Irish themselves, to begin their command which was to last more than seven centuries.

Although the Norwegians achieved no real colonization in Ireland, and did not succeed in the protracted occupation of substantial areas of the Irish interior, there is no doubt that their centuries of settlement along the coastal areas left a marked influence upon the country. They established a series of fortified harbours in the east, south, and west, at such places as Dublin, Wexford, Waterford, Cork, and Limerick, and round these prosperous trading centres the country was occupied by Norwegian settlers. The reason why no such coastal towns were founded in northern Ireland – the direction from which the Norwegians came – must be that Ireland was not the main goal of their ambitions, and that they wanted to press on to the coastal countries of western Europe. For these further trading ventures the southern tip of Ireland was, of course, a better springboard than the northern end, which faced the grey and desolate Atlantic Ocean. These coastal towns prospered as centres of trade; Dublin became wealthy; and when in 968 the Irish captured the Norwegian town of Limerick, they took a rich plunder of gold, silver, satins, and silks. The Norwegians taught the Irish a great deal about shipbuilding and navigation, and they managed to a certain extent to establish contacts between their coastal settlements and the Irish interior.

IN ENGLAND

A different situation developed in England, especially within the Danelaw where permanent colonization left distinct traces. For one thing there was the administrative division of the country into 'hundreds' and 'wapentakes'. A 'hundred' must have been a district which represented a hundred of something or other: warriors, perhaps, or ploughs; 'wapentake' refers to the Thing itself, the assembly where decisions were confirmed by the brandishing of arms (*vápnatak*). From this 'wapentake' came to mean the area covered by the members of the Thing, the district whence they came. The word 'hundred' is perhaps an Old English (common Germanic) term, but 'wapentake' is Danish, although the two terms seem to have become synonymous. The great English historian, Sir Frank Stenton, notes that as late as the eleventh century Anglo-Saxon sources could use either word for a single district. Danish influence can also be traced in legal codes and institutions. In the Danelaw, for example, the size of the fine imposed for murder varied according to the status of the victim, while elsewhere in England it was assessed according to the status of the victim's master, a difference which illustrates the Nordic conception of free men's equality. The swearing-in of juries, unknown in Anglo-Saxon rules of law, possibly originates with the Danes in the Danelaw, where twelve thegns (thanes) in each wapentake were called to take their solemn oath not to accuse an innocent man or to protect a guilty one. Furthermore, these enactments in the Danelaw, preserved in the so-called code of Æthelred II, affirmed that the verdict of eight of the twelve thanes would be accepted – the first example in England, says Stenton, of the principle of a majority verdict by juries.

The backbone of these Danelaw communities was of free but poor men. These *sokemen*, as they are called, owed certain obligations to the large estate owners, both in service and in dues, but the soil they occupied was their own property. This fundamental condition of the Danelaw society has been described as peasant aristocracy, and it is clearly reflected in the *Domesday Book* of William the Conqueror, where many Danish place-names (ending in -by and -thorp, etc.) are to be found. The Danish place-names of the Danelaw preserve the memory of the Danish peasant population which settled there, just as the Norwegian place-names which survive in the north and north-west of England provide a similar testimony to the Norwegian settlements in those regions. The Danish Viking came to England sword in hand, but he came to stay and to wield the plough and till the ground. He doubtless dispossessed some of the native population, but there is no evidence that he sought to exterminate it. He brought his language with him, his laws, and ways of life, and their effect was felt far into the Middle Ages; it was a long time before the Viking laws and customs became assimilated into the feudal system. The one part of their inheritance which the Vikings abroad quickly abandoned was their pagan religion, despite such instances of the opposite as the behaviour in Ireland, around 840, of the pagan fanatic, Turgeis. The pagan faith must have been weak, or the religion it found abroad too strong, for in Ireland, England, France, and Russia the Vikings were not long in adopting Christianity, sometimes no doubt for political reasons, as when Rollo in Normandy accepted the new faith in 912.

IN NORMANDY

Normandy, granted in 911 to Rollo at the head of a
Nordic army, was for the next two to three hundred years a
mixed Nordic–Frankish duchy. Its further development was
very different from that of the Danelaw in England. Its close
proximity to the Frankish and German Empires exposed it
to the influence of their feudalism, a principle fundamen-
tally different from the Scandinavian pattern of government; and the colonizers of Normandy had to accept the
inevitable. Rollo seems to have discerned this necessity of
compounding with an unfamiliar feudalism – and by his
opportunism established himself as sole ruler, and future
dukes of Normandy as absolute overlords. During the time
of Rollo and his successors nothing is heard of Things or
similar assemblies of free and equal men, and very little of
any of the standard Scandinavian practices of government.
'Hundreds' did not exist in Normandy. The duke and his
notables retained full power in a centralized and militarized
administration. There is a story characteristic of this state of
affairs, which recounts how, about the year 1000, the
peasants of Normandy summoned an assembly to demand
their rights to use the country's woods, lakes, and rivers.
Duke Rollo sent his uncle, Count Rudolph, to round up
these peasant delegates, mutilate them all by chopping off a
hand and a foot, and send them back to their villages to
prove who actually held sway over the woods and waters. It
is not reported that these unfortunates were the original
Frankish inhabitants. Very likely the Scandinavian peasants,
too, were among the victims of this savage lesson to prove
who held the final powers in Normandy. The only assemblies permitted in the dukedom were gatherings of the civil
and ecclesiastical members of the duke's court. Even if
feudalism was not yet fully developed during the tenth and
eleventh centuries it was well on its way. If the warriors in

the familiar story who cried 'We are all equals' were Rollo's men, they were soon to learn a different motto.

In Normandy, as in the Danelaw, the Vikings left tokens of their presence in many place-names: such suffixes as *-bec, -bu, -digue, -tot,* are pure Norse (*bekkr, bu, dìk, topt*), and so are *-torp,* and *-tved;* and first elements of names ending in *-ville* and *-tot.* Most of these Scandinavian place-names in Normandy seem to be of Danish origin, but several are Norwegian. It is not certain whether Rollo himself was Danish or Norwegian. Later Norse sources assert he was from Norway, but earlier sources (such as the Frankish Dudo, who was born around 960) say he was Danish. All things considered, the strong development of feudalism in Normandy does not quite obscure the impression made on the country by the Vikings.

IN RUSSIA

In considering the impact made by the Swedish Vikings in the east, we must bear in mind that their predominant motive was the expansion of trading interests. The Swedes did not penetrate Russia with the intention of conquest and settlement, as the Danes did England and France; they set out to establish and maintain extensive trade-routes. These ventures somewhat resemble the Norwegian settlements in Ireland, which, as we have seen, were trading-posts surrounded by narrow areas of colonization. Whereas the Norwegians in Ireland established their trading centres on the coasts, Swedes in the east did this in the interior and on rivers. Thus, at certain periods, Novgorod, Smolensk, and Kiev were no doubt Slav towns commanded by Swedish garrisons; the large burial ground at Gnezdovo, near Smolensk (to which I shall return later), seems to indicate

the presence of Swedish warriors and merchants at this
flourishing and active military base. But there were not
created in Russia – at least not on any significant scale –
those permanent agrarian colonies which were developed in
the Danelaw and Normandy. The trade-routes were too extensive, the countries which would have had to be pacified
were too vast. There was, too, the same difficulty as in Ireland concerning assimilation with a native population of
different stock and language – there Celtic, here Slav –
whereas in England the Anglo-Saxons were at least a Germanic stock related to the Viking invaders. By the end of the
Viking period, it is fair to say, the extensive Swedish trade-
routes from the motherland to the Byzantine world were
abandoned, the kingdom of Kiev and the west Russian
towns resumed their Slav nature, and before long the
Swedish infiltration of these distant lands became simply a
chapter of history. In northern Russia (the Ladoga region),
however, in Finland, and in the northern Baltic countries,
Swedish colonization was maintained throughout the
twelfth and thirteenth centuries.

There seems slightly more evidence of the degree of assimi-
liation which occurred between the Vikings and the people
with whom they came into contact in Russia than there is of
the same thing in western Europe. There is archaeological
testimony provided by the Norse graves discovered in
Russia, which reveal a mixture of Nordic, Slav, and oriental; and there is literary testimony provided by two Arab
writers of the tenth century, Ibn Fadlan and Ibn Rustah –
the former telling us of the Swedish Rus of the Volga, and
the latter of those in what was presumably western Russia.
Ibn Fadlan says:

I saw the Rus when they arrived on their trading mission and
anchored at the River Atul [Volga]. Never had I seen people
of more perfect physique; they are tall as date-palms, and red-
dish in colour. They wear neither coat nor mantle, but each

man carries a cape which covers one half of his body, leaving one hand free. Their swords are Frankish in pattern, broad, flat, and fluted. Each man has [tattooed upon him] trees, figures, and the like from the finger-nails to the neck. Each woman carries on her bosom a container made of iron, silver, copper, or gold – its size and substance depending on her man's wealth. Attached to the container is a ring carrying her knife which is also tied to her bosom. Round her neck she wears gold or silver rings; when a man amasses 10,000 *dirhems* he makes his wife one gold ring; when he has 20,000 he makes two; and so the woman gets a new ring for every 10,000 *dirhems* her husband acquires, and often a woman has many of these rings. Their finest ornaments are green beads made from clay. They will go to any length to get hold of these; for one *dirhem* they procure one such bead and they string these into necklaces for their women.

They are the filthiest of god's creatures. They do not wash after discharging their natural functions, neither do they wash their hands after meals. They are as stray donkeys. They arrive from their distant lands and lay their ships alongside the banks of the Atul, which is a great river, and there they build big wooden houses on its shores. Ten or twenty of them may live together in one house, and each of them has a couch of his own where he sits and diverts himself with the pretty slave-girls whom he has brought along to offer for sale. He will make love with one of them in the presence of his comrades, sometimes this develops into a communal orgy, and, if a customer should turn up to buy a girl, the Rus will not let her go till he has finished with her.

Every day they wash their faces and heads, all using the same water which is as filthy as can be imagined. This is how it is done. Every morning a girl brings her master a large bowl of water in which he washes his face and hands and hair, combing it also over the bowl, then blows his nose and spits into the water. No dirt is left on him which doesn't go into the water. When he has finished the girl takes the same bowl to his neighbour – who repeats the performance – until the bowl has gone round to the entire household. All have blown their noses, spat, and washed their faces and hair in the water.

On anchoring their vessels, each man goes ashore carrying bread, meat, onions, milk, and *nabid* [beer?], and these he takes to a large wooden stake with a face like that of a human being, surrounded by smaller figures, and behind them tall poles in the ground. Each man prostrates himself before the large post and recites: 'O Lord, I have come from distant parts with so many girls, so many sable furs (and whatever other commodities he is carrying). I now bring you this offering.' He then presents his gift and continues 'Please send me a merchant who has many *dinars* and *dirhems*, and who will trade favourably with me without too much bartering.' Then he retires. If, after this, business does not pick up quickly and go well, he returns to the statue to present further gifts. If results continue slow, he then presents gifts to the minor figures and begs their intercession, saying, 'These are our Lord's wives, daughters, and sons.' Then he pleads before each figure in turn, begging them to intercede for him and humbling himself before them. Often trade picks up, and he says 'My Lord has required my needs, and now it is my duty to repay him.' Whereupon he sacrifices goats or cattle, some of which he distributes as alms. The rest he lays before the statues, large and small, and the heads of the beasts he plants upon the poles. After dark, of course, the dogs come and devour the lot – and the successful trader says, 'My Lord is pleased with me, and has eaten my offerings.'

If one of the Rus falls sick they put him in a tent by himself and leave bread and water for him. They do not visit him, however, or speak to him, especially if he is a serf. Should he recover he rejoins the others; if he dies they burn him. If he happens to be a serf, however, they leave him for the dogs and vultures to devour. If they catch a robber they hang him in a tree until he is torn to shreds by wind and weather.

There follows a description of a chieftain's funeral (see pp. 301), and then Ibn Fadlan continues:

It is customary for the king of the Rus to have a bodyguard in his castle of 400 reliable men willing to die for him. Each of these has a slave-girl to wait on him, wash him, and serve him, and another to sleep with. These 400 sit below the royal throne: a large and bejewelled platform which also accommodates the forty slave-girls of his harem. The King frequently has public intercourse with one of these. He does not bother to leave his throne when he wants to make water, he has a basin brought to him for the purpose; and when he wants to go riding his horse is led up to him, and on his return the horse is brought right up to the throne. He has a deputy to lead his armies in battle, fight his enemies, and hold audiences with his subjects.

This Ibn Fadlan was a member of a diplomatic delegation sent in 921-2 from the Baghdad Caliphate to Bulgar on the Volga. His account of his personal experiences creates the impression that the Rus of the Volga region were an organization of dealers in furs and slaves, a pretty rough lot in both sexual and hygienic matters. Whether their women were Scandinavian or not we do not know; but what emerges from Ibn Fadlan's commentary is that, in general, these Rus retained their Swedish manners and observances in such matters as weapons, punishments, ship-burials,and religious sacrifices. They seem, on the other hand, to have come under foreign influence in matters exemplified by the overloading of their women with jewellery and the dead chief's costume (see p. 302). Whether in other ways, such as their treatment of the sick and their tattooing (if it is tattooing), they followed Swedish or Slav practice, we do not know. What seems, however, to indicate the beginning of assimilation (to a foreign [Turkic] custom) is the description of the Rus King's household, a crude mixture of *hirð* and harem.

Ibn Rustah, astronomer and geographer, seems to have been writing twenty or thirty years later than Ibn Fadlan. About the Rus folk he says:

They stay on an island (or peninsula) in a lake, an island covered with forest and brush, which it takes three days to walk round and which is marshy and unhealthy. They have a prince

called Haqan-Rus. They sail their ships to ravage as-Saqaliba
[the surrounding Slavs], and bring back captives whom they
sell at Hazaran and Bulgar [both towns on the Volga]. They
have no cultivated fields but depend for their supplies on what
they can obtain from as-Saqaliba's land. When a son is born
the father will go up to the newborn baby, sword in hand;
throwing it down, he says; 'I shall not leave you any property:
you have only what you can provide with this weapon!' They
have no estates, villages, or fields; their only business is to trade
in sable, squirrel, and other furs, and the money they take in
these transactions they stow in their belts. Their clothes are
clean and the men decorate themselves with gold armlets. They
treat their slaves well, and they wear exquisite clothes since they
pursue trade with great energy. They have many towns. They
deal firmly with one another; they respect their guests and are
hospitable and friendly to strangers who take refuge with them
and to all those who usually visit them. They do not allow any-
body to molest their guests or do them any harm, and if some-
body dares insult them or do them any injustice they help and
defend them. They use Sulaiman swords. If a group of them is
challenged to battle, they stick together as one man until victory
has been achieved. If two men quarrel, their case is considered
by the prince, in whose presence they both plead their cause, and
if they agree about his ruling his decision stands, but if they
do not agree he tells them to settle their dispute with their
swords – and may the sharpest sword win! The fight takes place
in the presence of the contestants' kin who stand with swords
drawn; and the man who gets the better of the duel also gets
the decision about the matter in dispute.

There are *atibba* (medicine men) who wield great power; they
act as if they own everything. They tell the people exactly what
offerings of women, men, and cattle to make to their creator.
When the medicine man has given his orders there is no way
of evading them. The *attiba* then takes the offering, human or
animal, and hangs it from a pole till all life has expired, saying
'This is a sacrifice to God.' – They are courageous in battle and
when they attack another tribe's territory they persist until they
have destroyed it completely. They take the women prisoners

and make the men serfs. They are well built and good looking and daring, but their daring is not apparent on land ; they always launch their raids and campaigns from ships. They wear full trousers (about 100 ells of fabric a pair), and when they put them on, they roll them up to the knees and fasten them there. When they want to relieve themselves they go out in groups of four, taking their swords along, so as to protect each other. There is little security among them, and much deceit, and even a man's brother or comrade is not above killing and plundering him if he can.

Ibn Rustah's account of the Rus concludes with the short remark on the funerals of their notables (see p. 305). There is nothing which suggests that Ibn Rustah was an eyewitness of what he relates, but, although his stories are doubtless based on other sources, they bear a stamp of reality and reliability. The island on which he says the Rus established themselves is thought by many scholars to have been Novgorod which is likely enough but not susceptible of proof. There is special significance in his assertion that the Rus were not an agrarian people, that they had no fields nor villages but many towns, that is to say they were concentrated in fortified garrison towns of which the remains have been found in great numbers, for instance, in the province of Smolensk. He mentions specifically the principal commodities they dealt with : slaves – taken from the neighbouring Slav tribes and brought to the markets of the Volga – and furs. He does not suggest any pronounced non-Nordic characteristics among them, except the oriental swords and baggy trousers. Everything else described is Nordic enough ; hospitality, courage, settling disputes by single combat, human and animal sacrifices, handling of ships, and burial customs. We get no impression of solidly established governments ; they came later. In the middle of the tenth century the organization was essentially that of a trading company. Their position and activities were compared, indeed, to

those of the Jews, by Ibn Horradadbeh who wrote, in
the 840s, the earliest Arab account of the Swedes. It must
have taken these Swedish Viking merchants a century
or more to lay even the foundation of a solid political
state.

CHAPTER FOURTEEN

Religious Beliefs and Burial Customs

In the great poems of the *Elder Edda*, particularly *Völuspá* ('The Sibyl's Prophecy'), and in *Gylfaginning* ('The Deluding of Gylfi'), where the Christian writer Snorri Sturluson, drawing on a number of sources, recreates the religious beliefs of his pagan ancestors, Icelandic literature gives us a splendid and highly-coloured picture of the old religion of Scandinavia. It is not a simple and terse account of noble beliefs. On the contrary. Ancient myths, tales, and traditions of widely different sorts and places of origin, beliefs and ways of thought both old and new, native and foreign, are all combined by Snorri's great sense of composition and story-telling into an imposing whole. We are told of the creation and the ultimate end of the world, the battles of the gods and the giants, and the Norse pantheon, with its two categories of gods: the *Æsir* and the *Vanir*. In the centre lies the home of the gods, Asgard, where the mighty Odin has his great hall Valhalla with its 640 doors, and his throne Hlidskjalf from which he can survey all creation. This heaven of the gods is separated from the earth by the bridge Bifröst, the trembling rainbow; the disc of the earth is surrounded by the great ocean, home of the Midgard serpent, and on its farthest shore lie the mountains of the giants, Jötunheim, where stands their citadel Utgard. Beneath the disc of the earth lies Hel, the land of the dead.

What we learn about the great ash-tree Yggdrasil, itself a world of good and evil, of joy and sorrow, sounds like a song from a completely different world. Yggdrasil is gigantic; its crown reaches the sky, its branches cover the earth, its three roots stretch out to Hel, to Jötunheim and beneath Midgard, the home of mortals. At the foot of Yggdrasil are two wells, one belonging to Mimi, god of wisdom, the other to Urd, goddess of destiny. In the branches of the tree sits the eagle, and between its eyes perches a hawk, bleached by weather and wind. A serpent gnaws at the root of the tree, and between it and the eagle a chattering squirrel runs to and fro carrying words of evil. Four deer nibble away at the young shoots of the tree, and its sides are rotting away. 'The ash-tree Yggdrasil suffers and endures more than men realize!' But the Norns give solace and renewal at Urd's well, from which they pour water daily on Yggdrasil so that it shall not wither. The bees are nourished by Yggdrasil's honey-dew. At a holy place by Urd's well the gods meet for their Thing, and here live the three highest of the Norns, the goddesses of past, present, and future, who are called Urd, Verdandi, and Skuld. In the centre of the world above the humans are the abodes of the gods, where live the two races of gods, the *Æsir* and the *Vanir*. We shall return later to this Nordic pantheon; meanwhile let us look briefly at the Nordic conception of the end of the world – Ragnarök.

Nothing lasts for ever, and when the gods have fulfilled their destiny the end of all things will arrive. This is the event so graphically related in *Völuspá* and in Snorri's tale. The first sign of the approaching end will be the coming of dreadful and horrible events and desperate desires – 'sword-time', 'wolf-time', fratricide, and incest. The cocks will crow in Odin's hall, in Hel, and in the sacrificial groves. Horror and eeriness grow. It is the time of the giant monsters; the hound of Hel, Garm, will howl, the wolf Fenri is freed from his chains, and its jaws stretch from earth to heaven. The Midgard serpent will whip the ocean into foam and spew venom upon the earth. The giant Hrym will cross the seas in his ship Naglfar, built from dead men's nails, and the sons of Muspel will sail forth with Loki as their leader. The tree Yggdrasil will tremble, the sky split asunder, the rocks roll down; in Jötunheim there will be rumbling, the dwarfs will whimper. Odin will be on the watch, Heimdal will blow his horn, the bridge Bifröst will break, and the giant Surt will advance, spouting fire. Then will come the final battle between gods and monsters. The wolf Fenri devours Odin, but is then slain by his son, Vidar, who smashes the brute's jaws with his heavy shoe. Thor kills the Midgard serpent, but after walking nine paces falls dead, poisoned by its venom. Ty and the hound Garm kill each other; so do Heimdal and Loki. Surt kills Frey and burns up everything with his flames. The sun turns black; the stars disappear. Yet hope survives; the earth rises again from the ocean. The two guiltless *Æsir* gods, Baldr and Höd, return; and in the golden hall, Gimli, the sinless live on. The eagle flies again above the thundering waterfall, the sun shines once more upon a newborn world. Although Christianity is not named, this tale implies the emergence of a new triumphant faith for a newly created humanity. It is a drama of death and resurrection.

THE GODS

Nordic religion, like the Egyptian, Greek, and Roman, was polytheistic. There were numerous gods, each governing a particular human need or action. In this hierarchy the gods varied considerably in power and status: some were at the height of their power, others apparently were aged and half forgotten; some stood high in the table of precedence, others were secondary figures. Let us look here at the principal deities in Asgard.

Odin

Supreme among them is Odin: a magnificent, dominating, demonic, and sadistic figure. He is consumed by his passion for wisdom; for its sake he sacrifices an eye, even hangs himself. Pitiless, capricious, heartless, he is the god of war and of the slain warriors. He owns the spear, Gungni, the self-renewing gold ring, Draupni, the fleet eight-footed horse, Sleipni. He is guarded by his two wolves and is brought news from everywhere by his two ravens. He communes with the head of the wise decapitated Mimi, he finds the runes and knows their secret power. He hunts by night, with his retinue, through mountains and woods; he appears to the doomed and on the battlefield as a tall one-eyed figure clad in a long cape and wearing a broad-brimmed hat. Odin is also the god of skalds: he governs the mystic ecstasy, the great pathos, the passion of the soul. He knows witchcraft and sorcery; he can fathom the soul's subtleties. He is the god of the great ones, an aristocrat, a dangerous god. He is sometimes called Universal Father, and justly, in so far as he takes the chair among the deities; but we must not take the words 'Universal Father' as denoting paternal tendencies and sympathy; with this meaning they do not apply to Odin. His human clientele consists of kings, earls, chieftains, magicians, and poets. The warriors who die in battle dedicated to him are carried by the valkyries to Valhalla, where they are enrolled in his immense corps, the *einherjar*, who will be at Odin's back at Ragnarök. To achieve his aim of gaining all wisdom and knowledge of all mysteries Odin stops at nothing in the way of deceit, cunning, and treachery, and if he is hard to others so also is he to himself. His characteristics cover a wide range: from cold cynicism to Dionysian enthusiasm, from ferocity to ecstasy.

Thor

Between Odin, greatest and most profound of the Nordic deities, and the next of the *Æsir*, the powerful red-bearded Thor with his goat carriage and mighty hammer, there is a considerable gap. Odin is the god of the great, while Thor is the god of the common man. The humour which is lacking in the descriptions of Odin is suitably prominent in the accounts of Thor.

Numerous legends and anecdotes are recounted of Thor the strong and faithful protector of the Viking peasant, and the superb fighter who finds no lack of targets for his hammer among the giants. When he races across the clouds with his team of he-goats, the thunder rumbles, and when he goes forth with his hammer, Mjöllni, in his hand, he is irresistible. He does not practise cunning and stratagems, and although he is often outwitted by the tricks of the giants he always wins in the end. The Northerners invented many vivid stories of his deeds: he wrests the great beer cauldron from the giants; he wins back the stolen hammer; fishes for the Midgard serpent; encounters strange adventures with Utgardaloki, king of the giants, whom he visits accompanied by the clever, but in this case rather helpless, Loki.

Thor was quick-tempered, but equally easily pacified. The Viking peasant understood and appreciated him. He was not merely the subject of entertaining tales round the fire in the evening; he was the helpful deity who made the crops grow, the god of agriculture (except perhaps in Norway). For this reason, because he was so involved in the daily life of the people, he seemed more real and important to the peasants than Odin himself. This is illustrated by the fact, related by Adam of Bremen, that it was Thor's effigy, not Odin's, which stood in the central position in the temple at Uppsala where the three principal gods, Odin, Thor, and

Frey, were worshipped. Thor was also called upon at weddings to bless the bride with fertility, and it is he and not Odin who is invoked on the rune-stones to consecrate the runes. When in late Viking times a symbol was needed to resist the potency of the Cross, the Vikings chose the hammer of Thor, not the spear of Odin. Thor was, finally, a more popular deity than Odin – his favour was sought not only by the farmer but by the blacksmith, the fisherman, the sailor; he was closer to the ordinary man than was the complex, unapproachable, and violent Odin.

Ty

Ty is a deity less clearly defined than the other two. We hear he is brave and virtuous, that he loses a hand when the wolf Fenri is bound, and that at Ragnarök he fights with Garm, the hound of Hel. Norse sources tell little more of him.

These three *Æsir*, Odin, Thor, and Ty, are by no means newcomers to the Germanic pantheon. All of them are mentioned, under Roman names, in Tacitus's famous book about the Germanic peoples, written about A.D. 100, where Mercury, Hercules, and Mars correspond respectively to Odin, Thor, and Ty, and where Mercury is said to be the principal Germanic god and the only one to whom human sacrifices are made. Mercury (and the Greek Hermes as well) has it in common with Odin to be guide of the dead, to wear a mantle and a broad hat, and to carry a stick (or spear). Beyond this, however, there is not very much resemblance between them; Mercury does not display the savagery so characteristic of Odin – an attribute derived by some scholars from the proximity of the East Germanic peoples to those wild Asiatic hordes which poured into Europe during the migration period. This Mongolian type of Odin may have travelled first to Sweden, and then to the rest of Scandinavia with the Gothic cultural connexions that linked the Black Sea to the Baltic. To compare Thor with Hercules is acceptable to a point, but does not account for the thunder or the hammer; Thor must have been an ancient god of agriculture and a thunder and rain god as well. Ty, again, is only the partial counterpart of Mars; his Norse name, *Týr*, *Tir*, or *Ti*, is cognate with the Latin Jupiter, the Greek Zeus, and the Indian Dyaus. He is really an archaic, later dethroned, King of Heaven. How old this trinity was among the Germanic peoples it is not possible to say (perhaps not very old); Caesar, as is well known, observed that the Germanic races worshipped natural forces – fire, the sun, and the moon. The Germanic peoples called days of the week after these gods: Tuesday (Ty), Wednesday (Odin), Thursday (Thor).

Baldr

A special place within the circle of the gods is taken by Baldr, the son of Odin and Frigg. Snorri tells of him this famous story: how the genial and friendly god met his tragic death from the arrow of mistletoe shot by his blind and innocent brother; how he was laid on the funeral pyre, how all nature lamented; how the gods tried to liberate him from Hel but were prevented by the machinations of the wicked Loki. The figure of Baldr is unique in Norse mythology and an enigma which scholars have not yet solved. Some suggest Christian influence from the legends of the Middle Ages; others observe similarities to Oriental myths of the god of fruitfulness, for whose death Nature weeps and laments; but these comparisons fail to account for the fact that in the Baldr myth the expected theme of resurrection is totally absent. The medieval Danish historian Saxo Grammaticus also tells the story of Baldr, but his material is quite different from Snorri's, and is not of great interest.

Compared with the trinity of Odin, Thor, and Ty, Baldr is a very young deity.

Viking art derives at least one of its themes from the Baldr myth – that of how the gods, trying to launch the heavy funeral ship on to the sea, have to send to Jötunheim for the witch Hyrrokkin, who comes riding on a wolf, with an adder for a bridle, and pushes the funeral ship into the water with a violence which shakes the earth and angers Thor. This event is depicted on a sculptured stone dated about 1000, from Skane. It shows the riding giantess, wearing a shift and a pointed hat, her snake tongue hanging out, the adder used as a bridle for her magnificent wolf which gallops along with jaws open, ears pointed, and a long tasselled tail. That vivid picture can be of no one but Hyrrokkin.

Heimdal

Heimdal is the god with the war-horn which sounds at Ragnarök. He is keen-eyed, vigilant, and alert, the watchman of the gods and the guardian of the bridge Bifröst. *Völuspá* calls human beings 'Heimdal's sons', and Heimdal is the wandering god who, in *Rigspula*, creates the three classes of society. He and Loki, old enemies, kill each other at Ragnarök. Apart from that, Heimdal is not very well defined in the circle of Norse gods.

Ull

The god of hunting is Ull, who excels at archery and at skiing. His status in the hierarchy is even more obscure than Heimdal's; there are no myths about him, and in late Viking times he remains very much a nonentity. However, his name forms an element in certain Scandinavian placenames, the evidence suggesting that he was known and worshipped in southern Norway and central Sweden; but not in

Denmark. The general conclusion is that by Viking times Ull was an old deity well on his way to oblivion.

The Vanir

Among the gods we meet are three who do not belong to the *Æsir* but to a different and apparently older race of gods called *Vanir*, representatives of a religion which in the Viking period was losing ground to that of the *Æsir*. These three were Njörd, Frey, and Freyja. According to Snorri the two races of gods came to terms after a battle and gave each other hostages. The three *Vanir* hostages who went to live in Asgard were those named above, and all three were deities of growth, conception, fertility, and sexual life. In other words old fertility gods, whom the *Æsir* did not succeed in replacing.

Njörd was the eldest of the three; in fact on his sister he begot Frey and Freyja. In the myths he is married to Skadi, a giantess who liked to live in the mountains, whereas Njörd preferred the shores and sea. He is the ruler of the winds and the god of seafaring people; he also gives wealth. The name Njörd is cognate with the Nerthus whom Tacitus names as the north-west Germanic goddess (not god) of fertility. A confusion of sexes like this is no rarity in the history of religion. There is undoubtedly some connexion between Njörd and Nerthus, and it is worthy of note, in passing, that (as Wessén has pointed out) Swedish place-names ending in -*njard* are feminine. Tacitus calls Nerthus 'Mother Earth'; she dwells in a grove 'on an island in the ocean'. Each spring she is driven by her priest around the island, with great ceremony, in a consecrated covered carriage drawn by oxen, and is everywhere received with the greatest delight. Weapons are laid aside and feasting is universal. Returned after the ceremonial visit, her carriage and the linen too are washed in secret in a lake by serfs, who, their task finished, are summarily drowned. Archaeologists are inclined to think, as we shall see again later, that this goddess of the Roman Age, this earth-goddess promoting fertility, existed in much earlier times in Scandinavia, probably as far back as the Bronze Age.

The strongest and most celebrated of the three *Vanir* in Asgard was Njörd's son, Frey, the god of sexual intercourse, whose statue in the temple at Uppsala was distinguished by a gigantic phallus. He appears to have inspired particular devotion in Sweden, as evidenced by erotic statuettes (Pl. 24B) and amulets, and by the tradition of carriage processions in the style of Nerthus. He was apparently popular also in Iceland, in Trondelag, and in Denmark. This god of fecundity and growth, rain and sunshine, is attended in Asgard by his sacred pig, Gullinbursti. There is a famous myth of Frey's passionate love for the giant's daughter, Gerd of the white arms. The worship of Frey may have reached Norway and Iceland from Jamtland, in whose central lake, Lake Stor (Störsjön), lie the islands of Norderön and Frösön (Njörd's Island and Frey's Island). In Iceland Frey is sometimes called 'the Swedish god' (*Svíagoð*).

The third of the Vanir is Freyja, Frey's sister and in every way his female counterpart. His name means 'lord', hers 'lady'. A goddess of love and fertility, she has in the *Edda* the reputation of being easy with her favours; for example, she is accused by Loki of being the willing paramour of gods and elves, and she is said to have bought her magnificent necklace, the *men Brísinga*, from four dwarfs at a disreputable price. She, too, possesses a carriage, but hers is drawn by cats (cf. the lion-drawn carriage of Cybele). Barren women invoked her blessing, and she was the death goddess not only of all women, but also of half the warriors slain in battle.

These three *Vanir* deities were no doubt very ancient gods; older than Odin and Thor, older even than Ty. The question arises: what gods did they dispossess when, possibly during the last few centuries B.C., they came to the Germanic peoples? The latter doubtless had their Nature gods, as Caesar noted, and it may be supposed that they also worshipped their old gods from the Bronze Age. We know from Bronze Age archaeological finds and rock drawings that they worshipped a god with large hands and bristling fingers, sometimes armed with an axe, who appears to have been the god of thunder; that they worshipped also a naked goddess adorned with a necklace, and a goddess seated in a carriage. The latter is evidenced in Early Iron Age discoveries – e.g. the carriage with women's belongings in it found at Dejbjerg in west Jutland. This carriage-driving goddess is possibly the same as Nerthus who, if the supposition is correct, must have derived from the Bronze Age. It is reasonable to surmise, in that case, that the naked goddess was a forerunner of Freyja. This cannot be accepted as certain, but it encourages the conclusion that the *Vanir*, partly superseded in Viking times by the rival *Æsir*, originated back in the Bronze Age, at least 500 years B.C.

Loki

The last of the *Æsir* in Asgard is Loki, half god and half devil, next to Odin the most singular and strange god. He is the offspring of a giant and in many ways a split personality. Though a giant's son and married to a giantess, Angrboda, by whom he has three fearful monsters, the Midgard serpent, the wolf, Fenri, and Hel, he lives with the *Æsir* and at one point became blood-brother of Odin, whose complex personality in many ways matches his own. Loki relishes satire but has no sense of humour; he is cunning and deceitful and lacks all capacity for friendship; his stinging words can hurt and strike, and his attacks on practically all the gods and goddesses are invariably vicious and cruel; he is always animated by self-interest.

Both the *Edda* and Snorri harp upon his unpleasant character and his perpetual malice. He is a sexual freak too, capable of giving birth to such oddities as Odin's eight-footed horse, Sleipni. Of his many misdeeds the most notorious is his instigation of the killing of Baldr – the crime which finally determines his fate. He tries to escape by changing himself into a salmon, but the *Æsir* capture him and fetter him to a rock underneath a serpent dripping poison. His second wife, Sigyn, manages to catch the venom, but whenever she misses a drop his trembling makes the earth quake. In this plight he survives until Ragnarök when, after getting free and joining forces with the enemies of the *Æsir*, he and Heimdal kill each other. In modern jargon Loki would be reckoned the psychopath among gods; on the basis of his feud with the gods, he has been compared with Prometheus and Satan: but he has none of the splendid defiance of the first named, and none of the fallen Lucifer's secret longings. He loves evil for its own sake; has a sharp eye for the vulnerable qualities of his enemies; and so nourishes his evil nature as to develop in himself every hue and aspect of sin. His weakness is his passion to see how deeply he can commit himself to evil without paying the price – and at last he goes too far and brings down catastrophe upon himself. In the Viking nature there must have been characteristics which account for the pleasure they took in the personality of this bizarre deity. Nations get the gods they deserve. Loki has features in common with the Mephistopheles of the Middle Ages – thus far one can point out a connexion with Christianity. Loki is not as old a figure as Odin, Thor, and Ty, and by no means as old as the *Vanir*. He is not truly a god at all, in the sense of being a figure whom men are impelled to worship. Rather is he a product of mythological speculation.

GODS AND PLACE-NAMES

Scandinavian place-names provide clues to the identity of the gods worshipped in various localities. Odin was known over a wide area, since place-names embodying his name* are scattered throughout the Norse lands, except Iceland. The name Thor is common over the whole of Scandinavia, including Iceland. In Norway and Sweden Thor often appears in combination with such elements as *-hof* ('temple'); but this is not the case in Denmark, where his name is commonly associated with *lundr* ('grove'). In Norway Thor is never linked with an agrarian element such as *-akr* ('field') or *-vin* ('meadow'), which suggests that here he was not such an agrarian deity as in Denmark and Sweden, nor in Iceland is Thor found with agrarian endings. Ty or Ti seldom appears in Norwegian or Swedish place-names, but is common in Denmark. Baldr's name turns up sporadically in all the Norse countries; and Heimdal's so infrequently as to lead to the conclusion that he enjoyed no cult at all. Ull is incorporated in many place-names in Norway and eastern Sweden, but not in Denmark. The names of the three *Vanir*, Njörd, Frey, and Freyja, are widespread: all three are abundant in Norway and in eastern Sweden as far north as Jamtland. In Denmark Njörd appears in place-names on Zealand and Fyn; Frey and Freyja also appear in these two islands as well as in southern Jutland. Judging from the place-names, Loki, like Heimdal, enjoyed no cult at all. In many places the word 'god' or 'holy' is used instead of any individual god.

These place-names often have as second element the object which is consecrated to the god. Endings such as *-hov* or *-hof* show that he had a house or temple; *-harg* or *-tuna* signifies his place of sacrifice; *-hylde* the base of an idol; *-vi*

---

* Incidentally, Swedish place-names ending in *-tuna* are never found in combination with the name of Odin.

the god's fenced-in sanctuary; -*ager* his cultivated field. Or
the god's name may be linked with some natural object
associated with him – a grove, hill, rock, lake, spring, bay,
island, etc.

FORMS OF WORSHIP

Little is known about the forms of worship of these deities,
or about their temples, although both archaeological and
literary sources give some information. The most famous
literary source is Adam of Bremen's famous description of
the most renowned temple of the north, that at Old Uppsala,
still flourishing when he wrote around 1070, as the centre of
paganism and strong resistance to Christianity. Here is his
account of it:

These people have a celebrated sanctuary called Uppsala, not
very far from Sigtuna and Birka. In this temple, entirely covered
with gold, are three idols which the people worship: Thor, as
the mightiest god, has his throne in the centre of the hall, and
Odin and Frey are on either side of him. Their fields of action
are the following: Thor, it is said, rules the air – thunder, lightning, storm, rain, fine weather, and the crops. The second, Odin
[i.e. fury], is the god of war who inspires men with courage to
fight their enemies. The third is Frey, who gives mankind peace
and sensuous pleasures. His idol, therefore, they endow with a
mighty phallus. Odin is represented as armed, in the fashion of
Mars; the sceptred Thor resembles Jupiter. Sometimes these
people also elevate men to the status of deities, and endow them
with immortality as a tribute to some great achievement of
theirs – the reward, according to St Ansgar's biography, which
was bestowed upon King Eric.
    Attached to the gods are priests who offer the people's sacri-
fices. If sickness or famine threaten they sacrifice to the idol
Thor; if war, to Odin; and if a wedding is to be celebrated they

sacrifice to Frey. There is also a festival at Uppsala every nine years, common to all the provinces of Sweden. Attendance at this event is compulsory and it is the universal practice for kings and peoples and everyone to send offerings to Uppsala and – a cruel thing – those who have become Christians may secure exemption on payment of a fine. The sacrifice on this occasion involves the slaughter of nine males of every creature, with whose blood the gods are placated. The bodies are hung in a grove near the temple, a sanctuary so holy that each tree is regarded as itself divine, in consequence of the death and decay of the victims. Dogs and horses hang there beside human beings, and a Christian has told me that he has seen as many as seventy-two carcases hanging there side by side. By the way, it is said that the songs sung during the ceremony are numerous and obscene, so that it is better to say nothing about them.

Some later additions to this account run thus:

Near this temple stands a huge tree, which stretches out green branches in summer and winter alike; what species nobody knows. There is also a spring there at which pagan sacrifices take place. A living man is plunged into it, and if he does not reappear it is a sign that the people's wishes will be fulfilled.

And further on:

A chain of gold surrounds the temple, hanging over the roof and greeting visitors from afar with its brightness, for the temple lies in a plain, as an amphitheatre surrounded by mountains.

A rather older literary source, the German Thietmar of Merseburg (c. 1000), describes a sacrificial feast held every nine years in January at Lejre on Zealand. Here, says Thietmar, in front of the people, ninety-nine human beings and ninety-nine horses, to say nothing of dogs and cocks, were sacrificed to the gods in order to protect the people against evil powers and atone for its sins. It is not clear whether this feast occurred during the time of the Vikings, or before.

A pagan sacrificial feast was called a *blót*. Snorri describes those held at Lade, in Trondelag: All the peasants had to attend, bringing beer and horseflesh. The walls of the temple were daubed outside and in, with the blood of the horses, and the flesh was cooked in fires built upon the floor of the temple and dedicated to Odin, Njörd, Frey, and the minor god Bragi before it was eaten. There is a famous story that the peasants of Trondelag forced the Christian king Hakon the Good to participate in such a feast, which he did only in part and with reluctance.

Not only the major gods but also the lesser deities, the *dísir* and *álfar* were celebrated with sacrifices. The *dísir* were mysterious female beings, related possibly to the *fylgjur* and the valkyries, and perhaps connected with Freyja in her capacity as goddess of the dead. It was wise to keep in with the *dísir*, and to remember them with sacrificial gifts, for they could foretell death and had also certain protective powers over houses and crops. The *dísir* were not always friendly powers, and it was important to treat them with a certain awe and respect, rather as one would respect the dead. In Viking times the *dísir* were worshipped at Uppsala at a large winter feast held in February at full moon. The *álfar*, or elves, were low-grade deities, not strictly gods at all, but figures who were worshipped within the home because of their protective powers. Sighvat, a Christian, who was skald to St Olaf, describes in his poem *Austrfararvísur* how he went to heathen Sweden and at night reached a closed house. From inside they answered his knocking by crying out that they were engaged in holy practices. 'Come no nearer, you miserable fellow,' exclaimed the woman. 'I fear Odin's wrath, we worship the ancient gods.' 'This wicked woman,' Sighvat writes, 'who would drive me away like a wolf, said she was preparing for *álfablót*.' On such occasions there was no scope for the traditional Nordic hospitality.

Another species of invisible beings who frequented human

habitations and with whom it was well to be on good terms, were the *vættir*, and further down the scale still, trolls and goblins, but these things were not actually worshipped.

A remarkable example of the survival in a remote area of a primitive cult is related in a tale called *Volsaþáttr* – 'the story of Völsi'. The scene is a lonely farm in northern Norway on which lived the farmer and his wife, their son and daughter, and their thrall and his wife. Völsi is the name given to the penis of a horse, carefully preserved in herbs by the wife and kept wrapped in a linen cloth. Every night the six of them pass this object from hand to hand, addressing it in short verses while doing so. This ceremony becomes their nightly habit until St Olaf and some travelling companions unexpectedly arrive on the scene, fling the pagan phallus to the dog, and teach Christianity to the benighted family. Such a medley of sexuality and magic was no doubt far from exceptional among the primitive Scandinavian peasants.

PLACES OF WORSHIP

Scattered through literature are references to heathen temples, sanctuaries, and sacrificial feasts, besides the accounts already quoted: Snorri's of the Trondelag *blót*, Adam of Bremen's of the temple at Old Uppsala, and Thietmar's of sacrifices at Lejre. The last, incidentally, can be related to the story in *Beowulf* of King Hrothgar's hall, called *Heorot* ('hart') in Lejre; and both are, no doubt, somewhat older than the Viking Age. What evidence, however, can archaeology offer of the temples, sanctuaries, or enclosed holy places? It is scanty, it must be admitted, and certainly not sufficient to enable reconstructions to be made. A good example is Ejnar Dyggve's excavation under the choir of the

Romanesque Church at Jelling* in south Jutland. Here Dyggve found the remains of a stave-church with a rectangular apse in the east, four great roof-posts forming a square in the middle of the church, and at the western end an open space enclosed by stones. He also found traces of a still older wooden building – the remains of a floor made of clay through which a great supporting beam had been embedded.

The first of these two finds is believed to be the church which King Harald Bluetooth built after his conversion to Christianity, while the older building is generally considered the remains of the heathen temple of his father Gorm. Sune Lindqvist similarly found traces of a temple below the stone church at Old Uppsala, though these were insufficient to justify the reconstruction of the famous temple which he has made. The remains are yet to be discovered which will provide us with the shape and plan of a heathen temple. Why are they sought for under the stone churches of the Middle Ages? The reason is that these are often found to have been built over older churches which, in their turn, may be presumed to have been put up on top of demolished heathen temples. In Iceland, certain long-houses with special end sections (for idols?) have been interpreted as temples, but with no certainty. At Jelling about ten years ago Dyggve identified a large triangular area, which had been surrounded by upright stones, presumably a *vé* or holy place. Similar enclosed triangular areas have been located by him elsewhere in Denmark. We shall return later in some detail to the difficult problem of interpreting the Jelling finds – mounds, *vé*, temple, stave-church, and rune-stones.

*This is, of course, the setting where two great mounds and two royal rune-stones stand.

IDEAS OF DEATH, AND BURIAL CUSTOMS

The Viking attitude towards death is to some degree disclosed through grave-finds. Hundreds of Viking graves have been unearthed (though fewer in Denmark and Jutland than in Norway and Sweden); but, far from presenting a uniform impression of the Viking idea of the after-life, they reveal a great complexity and variety of practice and belief. Both burial and cremation occur; burial occurred sometimes in large wooden chambers, sometimes in modest coffins; in a big longship or in a little boat, or sometimes in a symbolical boat made of stones or in a carriage. There are graves under huge mounds, and graves under ordinary flat fields, the grave-goods are sometimes rich, sometimes poor, and sometimes completely absent. There are two main reasons for such wide variation of practice. The first is that in pre-Viking – Merovingian – times burial customs varied between the three Northern countries and variations continued into the Viking period. The second reason is that the Viking religion was very indefinite in its doctrine about life after death. But let us consider these two points more closely.

Variations in Burial Customs

In Denmark in Merovingian times the tendency developed to provide only symbolic sacrificial offerings and grave-goods. Fragments of objects or symbolic miniatures were often used instead of genuine ones. In Norway and Sweden, on the other hand, this tendency was much rarer, and it was a frequent custom to leave rich and precious deposits with the dead. Another difference was that in Merovingian times in Norway and Sweden it was common to bury the dead man in his boat – whilst this practice was practically unknown in Denmark. In Sweden and Norway there are many traces of seventh- and eighth-century boat-burials; even when the boat was burned or has rotted away there are the tell-tale rivets to confirm that it existed. There is every reason to believe that these basic differences existing in the Scandinavian countries in the sixth, seventh, and eighth centuries, were maintained throughout the Viking era – in spite of the fact that during this period lavish and richly decorated graves occasionally appeared in Denmark.

One aspect of the Danish fashion for symbolic objects in burials occurs in Sweden and Norway – in boat-burials. There was probably a practical reason for this: a boat could not be spared, and so the dead man was put into a symbolic boat formed by an arrangement of stones. The impact of Christianity was a further factor in creating this complexity of Viking habits, for Christianity forbade the practice of cremation, and required a simple earth or wooden grave orientated east-west, and devoid of grave-goods. Christian practices are traceable in Denmark and Norway in the late Viking period, but hardly at all in Sweden, which was about a hundred years behind the other two countries in adopting the faith (after 1100). As regards cremation, in the Merovingian period this was much commoner in Sweden and Norway than in Denmark; but, just as cremation was not entirely unknown in Denmark, so earth-burials were by no means unknown in Sweden and Norway. In Norway there are many graves of Merovingian date, and Viking Age ship-burials where the corpses were buried without cremation. It would be untrue, therefore, to assume that cremation in itself denotes a particular religion. There are no hard and fast rules about Scandinavian funeral practices; numerous factors determined the methods adopted – local customs, wealth, social status, and the relative importance of Christian or pagan tradition.

Pagan traditions themselves, moreover, were by no means unanimous in this matter. What did the ancient family religion and the belief in the *Æsir* teach about life after death?

Where did the dead go? These questions were beyond most Vikings. The mythology recorded in the Eddic poems and in Snorri asserts that warriors slain in battle went either to Odin's Valhalla or Freyja's fortress. To the latter, also, went the women who died. Criminals, outlaws, and cowards presumably all went to Hel. How far did the Vikings really believe this? We can never know for certain, but it is customary among people who accept polytheism for the individual to select one god from the pantheon and entrust his fate entirely to the chosen deity. If this was not the case, what happened to all the people who were not criminals, warriors, or women; where did they go?

So much for the teachings of formal religion. Also having a strong hold on the mind and spirit of the Viking was the religion of the family. The family unit was indispensable in death as well as life: as after all it was the family which built and preserved the grave, mound, or cemetery, however the dead were disposed of. Here the family kept its dead, and here in a sense they lived on, even if they visited Valhalla or Heaven in between. Or the dead might live on within a holy mountain or hill near the ancestral farm. The dead were always with the family, and for that reason it was a family obligation always to maintain the grave or the burial mound in good order so that the departed would never feel so forsaken as to be obliged to become a vengeful ghost. A walker-after-death was terrible and dangerous, and the only course open to the relatives would be to break open his grave and kill him a second time. A. W. Brøgger believes that many of the grave entries which archaeologists have noted may be explained in this way: they were not always mere looting. A single explanation, covering all the different types of Viking burial, cannot be given, for the Vikings did not have a fixed, clear, generally accepted theory of the nature of the afterlife. This is why there are so many variations even within a single type of burial.

Consider, for example, the ship-burials of the high-born Vikings. After his death, the king or chieftain is enthroned in his vessel. What determines the next step? Is he to be cremated? Is the ship to be burned? Should a burial chamber be constructed within the ship? The answer to such questions must have been conditioned by what was considered to be the purpose of the burial. Would the deceased come sailing into the next world in his own vessel? Or was the main object to inter him in a suitable burial chamber, and to regard the ship only as grave-goods (as for example, in the ship-burial at Hedeby–Slesvig, where the ship stood upright on its keel above the deep burial chamber). On the other hand, the only known Danish ship-burial, at Ladby on Fyn, implies that the dead nobleman buried in it was to sail his vessel towards the south and the sun, to Valhalla, as the ship's anchor was stowed in the bows ready to be dropped when he reached his destination. A third variation is found in the case of the Norwegian Oseberg ship, whose stem was moored by a cable to a boulder, so that the dead person was regarded as safe in harbour until some distant day of departure to another world. Of the unburnt ship-burials the three great Norwegian examples, Tune, Gokstad and Oseberg, have preserved their ships. In the single Danish example, Ladby, only the lines of the ship remain in the earth.

The second form of interment for Scandinavian nobles was in a great wooden burial chamber, sometimes (like the ship-graves) covered with a huge mound of earth, sometimes laid under a flat field. The corpses were not cremated, and are often accompanied by their horses, dogs, weapons, and tools.

The common Danish type of grave (also found quite often in Norway) is the simple earth one in which the warrior is buried unburned with his weapons, and the woman with her jewellery. Corresponding to them in Sweden and Norway are cremation graves with or without a boat and with or without a low barrow; symbolic patterns of stones (boat-shaped, oval, or triangular) in the surface over the graves are very common. One interesting variant, from the fort of Fyrkat in Jutland, is that of a woman laid out in a carriage (similar in construction to the one found in the Oseberg ship) placed in the earth grave: a ritual which suggests that she was imagined to be riding to her final destination.

Major Burial Places

Three major Viking burial places have been located in Scandinavia at Birka, Hedeby, and Lindholm Høje. At Birka, in eastern Sweden, about 2,500 graves have been identified in various places round the town, and a thousand or so of these were examined by the archaeologist Stolpe in the 1870s and 1880s. The graves are of a wide variety of types: there are burials, and cremation graves, some with rich grave-goods, others poor. In the large burial chambers where the dead were not cremated the corpses are usually men, and they were laid there with their weapons, riding gear, food and drink, horse and dog – and sometimes with a woman as well, a wife or a serf. The greatest living specialist on Birka, Holger Arbman, has noted a peculiar burial chamber in which lay two women, one richly attired and the other lying in a strange, twisted position. He infers that the dead mistress was buried with a live serf who died from suffocation in the burial chamber, and he cites Ibn Rustah's evidence (see p. 305). Most of the women in Birka, with this exception, were buried in simple wooden coffins. There are many cremation graves at Birka, and these often contain traces of a boat given to the dead man as grave-goods. Christian influence is also extensive at Birka, evidenced partly by the absence of grave-goods in some graves, and partly by the occasional presence in graves of small crosses corresponding to the pagan hammers of Thor. With the tolerance which seems so characteristic of the Vikings, the Christian cross and the hammer of Thor are found in the same grave, as though these ancient people wished to secure the favour of both gods, disregarding the rivalry between them.

At Hedeby, in south Slesvig, the graves are found mainly inside the city walls, not outside as at Birka. Two cemeteries have been excavated, both in the south-west part of the city. The more northerly of these contained a large number of wooden coffins lying east-west; the southern cemetery, on the other hand, contained few graves, all of them burial chambers. There were no signs of cremation at either, and they contained both men's and women's bodies. In the coffin cemetery there were no grave-goods with most of the bodies; but some of the men had their weapons with them, and quite a lot of the women were buried with their possessions. The burial chambers were more richly furnished: the men sometimes with shields, spears, a wooden bucket, or bronze bowl, and the only woman there with her ornaments, knives, and keys. The coffin cemetery at Hedeby, which dates from the early ninth to the mid eleventh century, contains about 3,000 graves, of which 350 have been examined; it was the main burial place of the town. The other cemetery was small (only ten graves examined); it dates from c. 900 and was probably established by the Swedish conquerors of the city; its graves show close relationship to the chamber graves at Birka, although they are not so richly furnished.

Christian influence is difficult to observe in the Hedeby graves; even in the coffin cemetery the oldest graves (which face east-west) are thought to be older than the first arrival of Christianity in south Slesvig. Moreover, unburnt burials with scanty grave-goods are found in Denmark from the eighth century, long before the advent of Christianity in the north.

The third large Viking cemetery is at Lindholm Høje in northern Jutland, north-west of Aalborg's sister town of Nørre Sundby. Here, on a large hill partly covered with shifting sand, have been found: (a) a settlement-site dating from 400 to 800; (b) a burial place, south of the settlement, partly covered by the sand, and dating from between 650 and 1000; (c) a village, dating from 1000 to 1100, built partly on top of the sand-buried cemetery. Archaeologists have excavated large areas of the cemetery and found nearly 700 graves, most of them cremation graves. Th. Ramskou, who was in charge of these excavations, gives the following description of the cemetery:

The cremation graves are all alike, whether surrounded by stones or not. The burning of the bodies had evidently not taken place in the actual graveyard, but elsewhere, in a place still unknown to us, and the grave-goods – such as ornaments, glass beads, knives, spindles, whetstones, wooden boxes, draughtsmen, a dog, a sheep, and (more rarely) a horse or a cow – had been burned with the bodies. The ashes from the funeral pyre are taken to the cemetery, spread on a piece of ground about a yard across (a 'cremation-spot'), and covered with a thin layer of earth. A sacrificial vessel might be placed on top of the graves.

Many of these graves were surrounded by patterns of stones in various shapes – oval, round, square, or triangular. Most interesting of these are the pointed oval shapes, the so-called 'boat-shapes'. The notion behind this was evidently to provide the dead with a symbolic vessel, a representation of the ship instead of the ship itself which was too valuable to be spared for practical use. For this reason it seems unlikely that a real ship was burned on the funeral pyre. Ramskou has concluded from his examinations of the Lindholm Høje graves, that these stone arrangements were treated with scant piety by the community, and that the

stones were usually removed to be used for another burial.
It was only at the burial that these symbolic stones assumed
any significance; once their symbolic purpose was served,
and the spirit of the dead had begun its journey, the stones
were of no further importance. A considerable number of
ordinary unburned burials have also been found at Lindholm Høje. Seldom are weapons found within them (or in
the cremation graves), and there is no reason to assume
Christian influence on the burial customs. One interesting
feature of this site is that the eleventh-century village partly
built on top of the graveyard had contained rectangular as
well as elliptical houses of the Trelleborg type; more important still, it disclosed, for the first time in the history of
Danish village-building, an example of the four-element
farm plan.

Last but not least, there are the Viking graves at Jelling,
in south Jutland. In the tenth century this was the seat of the
powerful dynasty from which came Gorm, Harald Bluetooth, Swein Forkbeard, and Cnut the Great. In Jelling
there is a whole complex of archaeological monuments: (a)
two large earth mounds lying respectively north and south
of the Romanesque church; (b) two rune-stones, one raised
by the pagan Gorm for his queen Thyri, and one set up
by the Christian Harald for his parents, Gorm and Thyri;
(c) the remains of two wooden buildings beneath the choir
of the present Romanesque church, one of them probably
Harald's church and beneath it Gorm's heathen temple; (d)
the remains of a large triangular enclosure, formed of large,
unmarked stones (*bautasteinar*), a *vé* or pagan sanctuary.
Excavation of the two earth mounds has revealed in the
northern one a large wooden double burial chamber, which
had been broken into and pillaged of almost everything, including the skeletons. The southern one was found to be a
cenotaph (i.e. a memorial without a grave), which, however, contained a curious symbolic 'building' of slender

branches, and on top of which were the remains of what seems to have been a watch-tower. This mound covered the southern end of the above-mentioned *vé* or sanctuary, which was thus partly destroyed when the mound was built.

The chronological order of these Jelling remains and of the events connected with them can be given with some confidence. First came Gorm's *vé*, and associated with it the northern mound, the heathen temple, and the rune-stone set up to Queen Thyri. The next is Harald Bluetooth's contribution, including the introduction of Christianity and the destruction of the heathen elements; his stave church is built on the site of the heathen temple; a new mound (the southern one) is built on part of the pagan *vé*; the remains of Gorm and Thyri are taken from the northern grave chamber to the Christian church (*translatio*), and Harald's great Christian rune-stone is erected to his parents between the two mounds. The final development is the building of the now standing Romanesque stone church, so constructed that the square choir stands on the spot formerly occupied by the temple and thereafter by the stave church. We owe this disentanglement to the Danish archaeologist Ejnar Dyggve, who discovered, among other things, the triangular *vé*, examples of which he had also found elsewhere in Denmark. However, certain obscurities about this Jelling site remain. Why, for example, did the Christian King Harald build so heathen a memorial as a mound (the southern one), and whom does it commemorate? Another puzzle is the symbolic pattern of branches inside the mound. Cenotaphs are not unknown in the Viking period: there is the case of the greatest mound known in Norway, Raknehaugen, which also proved to contain no grave. Jelling is Denmark's greatest burial monument from Viking times; and King Harald's rune-stone is memorable for the last words of the inscription, 'and he made the Danes Christians', a glorious record of Christianity's official victory in Denmark.

Graves Outside Scandinavia

It is reasonable to inquire to what extent Viking graves
have been found outside Scandinavia. It would be strange if
we did not encounter them in either eastern or western
Europe; and of course we have found them both in Russia,
where large cemeteries have been excavated, and also in
western Europe, where thirty years ago Norwegian archaeologists, directed by Haakon Shetelig, undertook a systematic examination of museums and collections with the
object of establishing roughly the number of Viking graves
known in the west. The result of this research is given here
only briefly: in Scotland and the small islands off its west
coast thirty Norwegian Viking graves have been found, none
of them cremation graves, and most of them women's. A
couple were boat-graves. The Hebrides and Orkneys provide us with about the same number of this kind, again
mostly women's. One boat-burial had been found in the
Orkneys. The Shetlands produced a couple of women's
graves, neither of them cremations. In Ireland the main
location of Viking graves is on a large destroyed site near
Dublin (Kilmainham and Islandbridge). Here have been
found forty swords, thirty-five spearheads, twenty-five
shield-bosses, a few axes and arrowheads, and such women's
articles as ornaments, spindles, and keys. Other finds in
Dublin produced eight swords, seven spearheads, and a few
shield-bosses and arrowheads. Outside the Dublin area two
men's graves and two women's have been found – all of
them without trace of cremation. The Isle of Man has produced ten non-cremation graves, all of men; England sixteen similar graves, three of women.

In Continental western Europe only a few graves are
known: a man's (unburnt) at Antum near Groningen in
Holland; a woman's, also unburnt, at Pitres in Normandy;
and a cremated ship-burial in the Cruguel mound on the

Île de Groix off southern Brittany, opposite Lorient. This is the only known Viking cremation grave in western Europe. The race and sex of those who were buried in graves can be determined by the objects placed in these graves, but it is of course only possible to say that they are Scandinavian rather than Scottish, Irish, Anglo-Saxon, or Frankish; it is not possible to differentiate between Norwegian, Danish, and Swedish graves abroad, because their weapons, tools, and ornaments are so much alike. To a certain degree the nationality is suggested by the known spheres of interest of the Viking countries; in this way the Viking graves in Scotland, Ireland, the Isle of Man, and north-west England are likely to be Norwegian; those in the Danelaw and in eastern and southern England, Danish; those in northern England and France either Norwegian or Danish. This does not exclude the possibility that some of the graves may have been Swedish, but it is not possible to prove it.

In eastern Europe it can be similarly assumed that Viking graves are predominantly Swedish. In contrast to those in the west, the Viking graves in Russia usually show signs of cremation. To the south and south-east of Ladoga are several large mounds (of the 'Volkhov' type) covering cremation graves, and besides these there are hundreds of smaller mounds ('Finnish' type), some containing unburned burials and others cremation graves. Most of these graves, of both types, are without doubt relics of the Swedish Vikings. Farther south in Russia, at Yaroslav, north-east of Moscow, there are two large mound-cemeteries containing both cremation and non-cremation graves, the contents of which have strong Nordic characteristics. In the province of Vladimir, east of Moscow, there are very large cemeteries also, but here the Nordic elements in the graves are much less evident and indicate no more than a modest Swedish influence upon a Slav environment. Novgorod, in western Russia, seems to have been essentially a Slav town, and

there are few Scandinavian finds there; but the situation is
different farther south at Smolensk, Chernigov, and Kiev.
West of Smolensk, at Gnezdovo, is Russia's largest prehistoric burial place, containing over 3,000 mounds. Several
hundred of these were examined by Russian archaeologists
in the 1870s and 1880s, and a further forty in 1949. Cremation was the most frequent burial custom, and the objects
buried with the dead varied a great deal in quantity. The
Russian scholar Avdusin regards this burial place as partly
– perhaps mainly – Slav, but with numerous Swedish elements. The Swedish archaeologist, Holgar Arbman, on the
other hand, deduces, from the fact that most of the contents
of the graves are Swedish, that it was the tenth-century
cemetery of a large Swedish colony of warriors and merchants, which seems logical; the presence of Slav elements is
not very surprising in a colony set in the middle of Slav
territory.

In and around Chernigov, north-east of Kiev, are many
more mounds. The largest, about 30 ft by 120 ft, called
'Tjernaja Mogila', was excavated in the 1870s, and proved
to contain in its centre an unburned wooden burial house in
which were the skeletons of two men and a woman, surrounded by a quantity of objects, some Swedish (including a
sword), but mainly Slav and Persian. The clothes, too, and a
conical helmet, were Slav. Another large mound on this site,
dated to the tenth century, proved to contain a similar unburned burial. Such graves as these may very well have been
made for Swedish noblemen who had become partly assimilated into their Slav environment, for the clothing (as
Arbman points out) bears a close resemblance to that described below by Ibn Fadlan as being used in the burial of a
certain Swedish chieftain. The Swedish Rus appear to have
become more and more influenced by Slav dress and equipment the farther south they went. Finally a number of
tenth- and eleventh-century graves, men's and women's,

have come to light at Kiev, mostly unburned burials, and again indicating in the funeral objects a degree of assimilation between Swede and Slav.

In Poland too, there are some traces of Slav-influenced Swedish Vikings. Near Lodz, at Lutomiersk, under a Jewish cemetery, were found 125 graves, mainly unburned, and consisting, as a rule, of deep wooden chambers, some of them containing rich grave-goods (such as riding gear) of mixed Scandinavian, Slav, and Dnieper-Swedish origin. On the whole, these remains date from the early part of the eleventh century.

What archaeologists have discovered about Viking graves and burial customs in eastern Europe strengthens our general impression of shifting and vague beliefs about death and after-life. Literary sources too can throw some light on the subject. There is a contemporary eyewitness account of a Swedish ship-burial and cremation, which took place by the river Volga in 922. The narrator is the Arab ambassador, Ibn Fadlan, who writes:

I had been told that when their chieftains died cremation was the least part of their whole funeral procedure, and I was, therefore, very much interested to find out more about this. One day I heard that one of their leaders had died. They laid him forthwith in a grave which they covered up for ten days till they had finished cutting-out and sewing his costume. If the dead man is poor they make a little ship, put him in it, and burn it. If he is wealthy, however, they divide his property and goods into three parts: one for his family, one to pay for his costume, and one to make *nabid* [probably a Scandinavian type of beer] which they drink on the day when the slave woman of the dead man is killed and burnt together with her master. They are deeply addicted to *nabid*, drinking it night and day; and often one of them has been found dead with a beaker in his hand. When a chieftain among them has died, his family demands of his slave women and servants: 'Which of you wishes to die with him?' Then one of them says: 'I do'; and having said that the person

concerned is forced to do so, and no backing out is possible. Even
if he wished to he would not be allowed to. Those who are
willing are mostly the slave women.

So when this man died they said to his slave women: 'Which
of you wants to die with him?' One of them answered, 'I do.'
From that moment she was put in the constant care of two other
women servants who took care of her to the extent of washing
her feet with their own hands. They began to get things ready
for the dead man, to cut his costume and so on, while every day
the doomed woman drank and sang as though in anticipation
of a joyous event.

When the day arrived on which the chieftain and his slave
woman were going to be burnt, I went to the river where his
ship was moored. It had been hauled ashore and four posts were
made for it of birch and other wood. Further there was arranged
around it what looked like a big store of wood. Then the ship
was hauled near and placed on the wood. People now began to
walk about talking in a language I could not understand, and
the corpse still lay in the grave; they had not taken it out. They
then produced a wooden bench, placed it on the ship, and
covered it with carpets of Byzantine *dibag* [painted silk] and
with cushions of Byzantine *dibag*. Then came an old woman
whom they call 'the Angel of Death', and she spread these
cushions out over the bench. She was in charge of the whole
affair from dressing the corpse to the killing of the slave woman.
I noticed that she was an old giant-woman, a massive and grim
figure. When they came to his grave they removed the earth
from the wooden frame and they also took the frame away.
They then divested the corpse of the clothes in which he had
died. The body, I noticed, had turned black because of the
intense frost. When they first put him in the grave, they had
also given him beer, fruit, and a lute, all of which they now
removed. Strangely enough the corpse did not smell, nor had
anything about him changed save the colour of his flesh. They
now proceeded to dress him in hose, and trousers, boots, coat,
and a mantle of *dibag* adorned with gold buttons; put on his
head a cap of *dibag* and sable fur; and carried him to the tent
on the ship, where they put him on the blanket and supported

him with cushions. They then produced *nabid*, fruit, and aromatic plants, and put these round his body; and they also brought bread, meat, and onions which they flung before him. Next they took a dog, cut it in half, and flung the pieces into the ship, and after this they took all his weapons and placed them beside him. Next they brought two horses and ran them about until they were in a sweat, after which they cut them to pieces with swords and flung their meat into the ship; this also happened to two cows. Then they produced a cock and a hen, killed them, and threw them in. Meanwhile the slave woman who wished to be killed walked up and down, going into one tent after the other, and the owner of each tent had sexual intercourse with her, saying: 'Tell your master I did this out of love for him.'

It was now Friday afternoon and they took the slave woman away to something which they had made resembling a door-frame. Then she placed her legs on the palms of the men and reached high enough to look over the frame, and she said something in a foreign language, after which they took her down. And they lifted her again and she did the same as the first time. Then they took her down and lifted her a third time and she did the same as the first and the second times. Then they gave her a chicken and she cut its head off and threw it away; they took the hen and threw it into the ship. Then I asked the interpreter what she had done. He answered: 'The first time they lifted her she said: "Look! I see my father and mother." The second time she said: "Look! I see all my dead relatives sitting round." The third time she said: "Look! I see my master in Paradise, and Paradise is beautiful and green and together with him are men and young boys. He calls me. Let me join him then!"'

They now led her towards the ship. Then she took off two bracelets she was wearing and gave them to the old woman, 'the Angel of Death', the one who was going to kill her. She next took off two anklets she was wearing and gave them to the daughters of that woman known by the name 'the Angel of Death'. They then led her to the ship but did not allow her inside the tent. Then a number of men carrying wooden shields and sticks arrived, and gave her a beaker with *nabid*. She sang over it and emptied it. The interpreter then said to me, 'Now

with that she is bidding farewell to all her women friends.' Then
she was given another beaker. She took it and sang a lengthy
song; but the old woman told her to hurry and drink up and
enter the tent where her master was. When I looked at her she
seemed completely bewildered. She wanted to enter the tent and
she put her head between it and the ship. There the woman took
her head and managed to get it inside the tent, and the woman
herself followed. Then the men began to beat the shields with
the wooden sticks, to deaden her shouts so that the other girls
would not become afraid and shrink from dying with their
masters. Six men entered the tent and all of them had intercourse
with her. Thereafter they laid her by the side of her dead
master. Two held her hands and two her feet, and the woman
called 'the Angel of Death' put a cord round the girl's neck,
doubled with an end at each side, and gave it to two men to
pull. Then she advanced holding a small dagger with a broad
blade and began to plunge it between the girl's ribs to and fro
while the two men choked her with the cord till she died.

The dead man's nearest kinsman now appeared. He took a
piece of wood and ignited it. Then he walked backwards, his
back towards the ship and his face towards the crowd, holding
the piece of wood in one hand and the other hand on his buttock;
and he was naked. In this way the wood was ignited which they
had placed under the ship after they had laid the slave woman,
whom they had killed, beside her master. Then people came with
branches and wood; each brought a burning brand and threw
it on the pyre, so that the fire took hold of the wood, then the
ship, then the tent and the man and slave woman and all. Thereafter a strong and terrible wind rose so that the flame stirred and
the fire blazed still more.

I heard one of the Rus folk, standing by, say something to my
interpreter, and when I inquired what he had said, my interpreter answered: 'He said: "You Arabs are foolish."' 'Why?'
I asked. 'Well, because you throw those you love and honour
to the ground where the earth and the maggots and fields devour
them, whereas we, on the other hand, burn them up quickly
and they go to Paradise that very moment.' The man burst out
laughing, and on being asked why, he said: 'His Lord, out of

love for him, has sent this wind to take him away within the hour!' And so it proved, for within that time the ship and the pyre, the girl and the corpse had all become ashes and then dust. On the spot where the ship stood after having been hauled ashore, they built something like a round mound. In the middle of it they raised a large post of birch-wood on which they wrote the names of the dead man and of the king of the Rus, and then the crowd dispersed.

Ibn Fadlan was a sharp observer and a good narrator, who gives the impression of not being prone to exaggeration. I see no reason to disbelieve his eyewitness account or the interpretations he put on what he witnessed. One significant piece of information he provides is that the Vikings built a memorial mound, a cenotaph, and gave it a runic inscription on a piece of wood, suitable stones evidently not being available in the vicinity. It was apparently thought right that the dead man, although in Paradise, should have a place of his own on earth. Similar empty memorial mounds are known in the Viking homelands as we have seen.

Some time after Ibn Fadlan, about the middle of the tenth century, another Arab writer, Ibn Rustah, has this to say about the Rus:

When one of their notables dies, they make a grave like a large house and put him inside it. With him they put his clothes and the gold armlets he wore and, moreover, an abundance of food, drinking bowls, and coins. They also put his favourite wife in with him, still alive. Then the grave door is sealed and she dies there.

This comment fits in with the archaeological evidence of the Birka grave mentioned above; and also of the grave mound at Chernigov.

THE COMING OF CHRISTIANITY

The various burial rites of the Vikings reveal just how vague
and complex were their religious beliefs. In due course those
beliefs were bound to be supplanted by the clarity of the
Christian faith. A religion which offers the common man
vague and contradictory concepts of the after-life is not a
potent one and this is the case with all polytheistic faiths.
The belief in the *Æsir* with its many gods was doubtless
tolerant of foreign influences, and if one more god was
offered the Vikings, such as 'the White Christ', they saw no
reason why they should not, so to speak, give him a trial
along with the others. When St Olaf ordered the Viking
Gaukathori to adopt Christianity, the man philosophically
replied, 'If I must believe in a god it is no worse to believe
in the White Christ than any other . . .' – a remark which
may, however, merely mean that Gaukathori was an atheist.
A better example, therefore, is Helgi the Lean. In *Landnámabók* it is said of him that 'he was very mixed in his faith;
he believed in Christ, but invoked Thor in matters of seafaring and dire necessity'. The *Æsir* religion was an aristocratic one, and had little to give the ordinary man by way of
an after-life. And consequently in the end he turned to the
purposeful monotheism of Christianity, with its hope and
help for all. So Christianity triumphed.

Yet this new faith did not effect a rapid conquest. When
the Viking period began, about 800, the whole of the North
was pagan. It took 150 years to bring Denmark to Christianity, 200 for Norway and Iceland, and more than 300
years for Sweden. Why did it take so long for the well-
organized Roman Church – with its powerful missionary
activity and its tactical wisdom in seeking always to convert
first of all the upper ranks of society – to supplant the easy-
going dynasty of the Nordic gods? The answer is that the
real strength of the old religion resided in such traditional

elements as the fertility rites and practices. A change of gods at the summit of society might occur easily enough; but lower down the scale there was a natural resistance to any new religion which sought to interfere with old religious habits and observances, based on experience of life's needs and the whole of existence, dating back thousands of years. Any changes at this level of society took a long time; and indeed the acceptance of Christianity in the North, as in the rest of Europe, only began to make real progress as and when Christianity took over old superstitions and usages and allowed them to live under a new guise.

Christianity in Denmark

In Denmark the development of Christianity began when, in 823, Archbishop Ebo of Reims was charged by the Emperor and the Pope to convert the heathen land of Denmark. The first real success was not until 826, when the Jutish pretender to the throne, Harald, was converted by the Emperor, Louis the Pious, and the Frankish monk Ansgar. Very little came of this, as soon both Harald and Ansgar were banished. It was not until several years later, in 849, when Ansgar was Archbishop of Hamburg, with his see at Bremen, that real progress began, during the reigns of Harik the Elder and his successor Harik the Younger at Hedeby. Ansgar was permitted to build a church at Hedeby (the remains of which have not yet been found); and after a brief interlude of anti-Christian sentiment about 854 – during which the heathen Earl Hovi, after Harik the Elder's death, closed the church – Christianity revived and made good progress under Harik the Younger. Many people were baptized; many others accepted the *prima signatio* of the cross, as a preliminary to baptism, and another church was built, at Ribe.

The kings themselves, however, held back. Neither of the

Hariks was baptized, despite an urgent appeal from the Pope (sent on Ansgar's initiative in 864) in such terms as: 'Desist from worshipping false gods and serving the devil, for your gods are made with human hands and are deaf, dumb, and blind. What salvation can they bring you, they who being senseless cannot save themselves?' These exhortations were frequent. In 723 Boniface, the missionary of Germany, was told by Bishop Daniel of Winchester to use the following argument in reasoning with a heathen: the old pagan gods are themselves born and created, but who created the world before they came into existence? – And the monk Hucbald (c. 900) used an exhortation of which the purport was: 'God has created us, not we ourselves; but the idols you revere are made of gold, silver, copper, stone, or wood; they do not truly live, nor move, nor feel, because they are made by mankind and cannot help others or themselves.'

Ansgar died in 865, and apart from the forcible conversion of the Swedish king Gnupa, at Hedeby, by the German conquerers, little is heard of the progress of Christianity in Denmark for about a century. In 960, however, occurred the episode – related by a contemporary, the Saxon Widukind – of the priest Poppo, whose valiant effort converted Harald Bluetooth to Christianity. The Danes admitted, says Widukind, that Christ was a god, but asserted that other gods were greater, their signs and wonders mightier. No, said Poppo; God the Father, the Son, and the Holy Ghost were the one God: the rest were merely idols. King Harald ('Keen to listen but slow to utter') asked Poppo if he would subject this bold assertion to God's own judgement. Poppo immediately agreed, and the next day the king had a bar of iron made red hot and told Poppo to hold it as a token of his faith. Poppo took the glowing bar and carried it about for as long a time as the king wanted, whereafter he showed his undamaged hand and convinced all the bystanders. The

king was convinced and determined from now on to ac-
knowledge Christ as his only God. The Greater Jelling
rune-stone bears an inscription which shows that Harald
regarded himself as responsible for introducing Christianity
into Denmark. His son, Swein Forkbeard, conqueror of
England, proved an indifferent Christian, but Swein's son,
Cnut the Great, was ardent in the new faith. By the eleventh
century Christianity had taken firm root in Denmark, and
King Swein Estridsson (1047–76) devoted his long reign to
trying to liberate the young Danish church from the domination of the German bishopric at Bremen, an achievement
which did not, in fact, occur until later. In general it may be
asserted that Christianity was established in Denmark with
effective assistance from the monarchy, but not by royal
compulsion.

Christianity in Norway

In Norway the first Christian king was Hakon the Good,
son of Harald Finehair. He died in 960, about the same
time as Poppo achieved his spectacular miracle, but Hakon's
personal belief by no means implied that Norway had been
converted to the faith. He had been educated by the Anglo-
Saxon king, Athelstan, and he brought the new religion to
Norway from England. The people protested and rejected
Hakon's missionaries, and the king was either not strong
enough to compel conversion or too wise to want to; indeed,
when he died, he was given a heathen funeral. His successor,
Harald Greycloak, laboured diligently (according to
Snorri) for Christianity, but without notable success, and
Norway's next ruler, Earl Hakon of Lade (975–95), was a
confirmed heathen and a devotee of Thor. Norway's con-
version was brought about finally by the two Olafs, Olaf
Tryggvason (995–1000), and St Olaf (1014–30), whose per-
suasive efforts were violent and cruel. It is characteristic

that Olaf Tryggvason, wanting to abuse the Swedes before the battle of Svöld (where he met his death), derided their heathen condition and advised them to stay at home and lick their sacrificial bowls. In the fifteen years after his death, when western Norway had been converted to Christianity by his terrorist methods, the rulers were Hakon of Lade's two sons, Eric and Swein. Both were Christians, but they were tolerant enough to allow others to go their own heathen ways. It was not until St Olaf assumed power that this tolerance vanished; under his hard hand the whole of Norway was converted, and Olaf became the saint that the young Norwegian church so desperately needed. In Iceland the conversion was swift. Missionary activities began seriously in 981 with Thorvald the Far-Travelled; and in the year 1000 Christianity became legally the faith of the country.

Christianity in Sweden

In Sweden Ansgar led the first Christian mission to Birka in 829 after a perilous journey in which he was nearly killed by pirates. He was well received by King Björn at Birka, and permitted to build a church, and after he had worked two years there, during which period the young Swedish church was incorporated into the Roman ecclesiastical system, he became bishop of Hamburg, with rights of jurisdiction over the Birka community. Such rights, however, were nothing but mere formalities; the Birka 'church' was weak and no serious impact was made, not even when Ansgar revisited the place in the middle of the century. The pagan religion remained intact. Later on, in the 930s, a further mission was dispatched, again from Hamburg, under Archbishop Unni, but this, also, was only an interlude. Thus at the beginning of the eleventh century, when Denmark and Norway had gradually accepted Christianity, Sweden was still a completely heathen country. The battle to convert Sweden now developed in earnest, and during the next hundred years its many Christian neighbours made strenuous efforts to bring about this change in Sweden. One of these neighbours was the north German Church centred on Hamburg – Bremen; another was the English Church which was active in Sweden as a consequence of the Danish conquest of England; and similar influences were brought to bear from Norway, Denmark, and France, and even from the Eastern Orthodox Church in Russia. Swedish paganism, however, proved a powerful enemy, and the battle swayed back and forth during the eleventh century. Adam of Bremen, in the 1070s, painted a gloomy picture of the persistent paganism. The great heathen temple at Old Uppsala, described by him, was still the citadel of the pagan Nordic religion, and indeed a base from which strong counter-attacks were launched upon Christianity. Yet several Swedish kings supported the Christians – Olaf Skotkonung, Önund Jacob, Emund, Stenkil – and under the first of these a bishopric was established from Hamburg–Bremen, at Skara in Vastergotland. Christian words and expressions on Swedish rune-stones reveal the slow penetration of Christianity, and in 1060 a special drive was planned by two bishops – Egino of Skane and Adalward the Younger of Sigtuna – including the proposal to demolish by force the heathen temple at Old Uppsala. King Stenkil sympathized but would not permit this forceful evangelism, and when he died in 1066 the heathens retaliated by driving out the Bishop of Sigtuna. The bishopric of Skara was vacant, and heathenism remained strongly entrenched not only in Uppland but also in Gotland and Smaland. By the end of the century we hear of the banishment of the Christian king Ingi and the domination of the pagan Blót-Swein – although this position was subsquently reversed. Conditions in Sweden at the beginning of the twelfth century were described by

the Anglo-Danish monk, Ælnoth of Canterbury, in these
words:

> As long as things go well and everything is fine, the *Svîar* and
> *Gautar* seem willing to acknowledge Christ and honour him,
> though as a pure formality; but when things go wrong – bad
> harvests, drought, tempests and bad weather, enemy attacks, or
> outbreaks of fire – they persecute the religion which they seem
> nominally to honour, and they do this not only in words but
> also in deeds; then they revenge themselves on the Christians
> and seek to chase them completely out of their country.

This picture characterizes the closing chapter of the religious war in Sweden. The temple at Uppsala probably disappeared early in the twelfth century. At the same time
the Swedish Christian church came under the authority of
the Danish archbishop of Lund, in Skane, and in this
way passed from the control of the German bishops. It is
surprising that Christianization took so long, for it was a
foregone conclusion that the dynamic and purposeful monotheism from the south would prevail over the stagnant polytheism of the north. Yet the long time it took to prevail
serves to remind us not to minimize the power of this
ancient polytheism which remained capable of, at least,
sporadic recovery and reassertion. There is much weight in
the conclusion some scholars emphasize: namely, that it
would be relatively easy for Christianity to prevail over
Nordic religious beliefs; but far more difficult to overcome
the complex culture beneath that religion – a culture so
rooted in ancient fertility magic – and even more difficult to
substitute an ethical formula about loving your neighbours
for the Nordic concepts of honour and family.

CHAPTER FIFTEEN

Poetry and the Viking Spirit

Obviously the Vikings had their ideas of the perfect man. This is presented to us in *Rígsþula*: the young Viking chief in all his glory, the blond earl with the piercing eyes, a fearless rider and hunter, skilled with all warlike weapons, the leader who wins men and conquers land and whose son becomes king. The picture is perhaps a bit cheap and flashy. A better impression of the Viking ideal is to be found in the heroic figures, both of the Norse tales and of Viking history. Some of these figures have their roots in Nordic soil, some in that of south Germany, but whatever their origin they were real and vital figures in the Viking imagination. Bjarki and Hjalti are two examples: both were faithful to death by the side of their slain king Hrolf. Other examples are: Starkad, the ruthless scourge of timidity; the wise Hamlet; the shrewd Ragnar Lodbrok; the proud and fated lovers Hagbard-Signy and Helgi Hunding's Slayer, Sigrun, whose loves endure beyond death. There is, too, the great tragedy of the Volsungs; with its fatal triangle of relationships between Sigurd, Brynhild, and Gudrun. How powerfully this Sigurd Fafni's Slayer caught the Norse imagination is shown by the many representations of this saga cycle, in stone and wood, from Sweden, Norway, and the Isle of Man. And let us not forget among the heroes Völund (Weland) the Great Avenger. In Scandinavian history there can be no doubt that Cnut the Great, Olaf Tryggvason, St Olaf, Harald Hardrada, and others were in their day invested with all the glory of popular heroes. These then are the

figures, whether of legend or history, which display those
attributes the Vikings most revered and sought to emulate:
courage, bravery, daring, abandonment to love, contempt
for death, munificence, strength of mind, fidelity; and, on
the other side of the balance, ruthlessness, vengeance,
derision, hate, and cunning. These are the ingredients with
which the Icelandic sagas of the Middle Ages, with their
great traditions, recreate the heroes of the vanished Viking
times.

The Norwegian and Icelandic skaldic poetry is an elaborate literary form, bound by rigid rules. Its complexity
parallels that of contemporary ornamental art. It makes use
of alliteration and also has internal rhyme within the verse
line. Its practitioners use picturesque circumlocutions, vivid
metaphors avoiding the common name for a thing, and the
complicated verse forms are built upon strict rules. It was not
easy to master the skald's difficult art. The circumlocutions
referred to – *kenningar* ('kennings') – were greatly admired
by the Scandinavians, who loved riddles and enigmas as
they did vividness of expression. The best kennings are not
merely an ingenious play on words but the poetic expression
of experience. Here are a few examples. The earliest known
Norwegian skald, the ninth-century Bragi the Old, describes
the row of shields on the sides of a longship as 'leaves on the
trees in the sea-king's forest'. Battle scenes are favourites
with the skalds. Battle is referred to as 'Odin's roaring
storm', 'the Valkyries' magic song', and 'the shout of the
spear'. The ship is called 'the steed of the waves', the sword
'the battle-storm's fish', the arrow 'the wounding bee'.
The greatest of all known Norse skalds, the Icelander Egil
Skallagrimsson calls the surf along Norway's rocky coast 'the
island-studded belt round Norway'; and to describe how his
friends inside this belt gave him silver bracelets he employs
such flowery images as 'they let the snow of the crucible
[silver] fall upon the hawk's high mountain [the arm]'.

It appears that in late Viking times nearly all the skalds were Icelanders. The last considerable Norwegian skald is Eyvind Skaldaspillir, whereas the greatest of the later skalds are Icelandic: the love-poet Kormak, and St Olaf's two court poets, Sighvat and Thormod. The latter was the man who coined the *bon mot* as he plucked an arrow from his heart at the battle of Stiklestad. Egil Skallagrimsson has an impeccable technique and a wide range of feeling, capable of expressing passion, terror, vengeance, and happiness; after his sons' death he wrote the poem 'On the Loss of his Sons' ('Sonatorrek'), in which initial hate and bitterness are compounded with a final calm and equanimity.

It is a tempting though dangerous exercise to compare Viking poetry with Viking decorative art. The unnaturalistic animal ornamentation of the early period around 800 was superseded (a) in the ninth century by a naturalistic animal style ('the gripping beast'), (b) in the tenth by the Jelling ribbon pattern, and (c) in the eleventh by the 'great beast' motif. What correspondence can be found with Viking poetry from the ninth to the eleventh centuries? The Norwegian scholar Hallvard Lie has attempted to trace a comparable development of metrical style, but the establishment of such parallels seems extremely difficult.

The greatest Icelandic poem to survive is *Völuspá* 'The Sibyl's Prophecy'. It surpasses all others in prophetic power and force, and has both tragic gloom and inspiring hope. It is a seer's vision of what was, is, and shall be. The *Æsir* are named rather than depicted in the poem. To the poet they are not the great end of existence; they must atone for their guilty acts. Above them is a greater force. The middle part of the poem describes Ragnarök, the end of the world, in a great series of visions. All is consumed by fire, but when the fires are burnt out a new sun will dawn and life will be renewed. *Völuspá* suggests that the religion of the *Æsir* had lost its power; it is clearly spiritually inadequate.

The poet is ready for a religious change, and it reveals the significant conviction that, when Ragnarök is over, there will be but one god, *the* Mighty one. Is this to be taken as a premonition, a whisper, of the coming Christian god? Manifestly, the creator of *Völuspá* was a profound thinker and a great poet.

The Viking spirit, however, involves more than the inspired expression of poets, and to understand its full meaning we must come down from poetic heights and see how that spirit was expressed in the everyday life and behaviour of the Vikings. We must look again, for instance, at a poem mentioned earlier, the *Hávamál* ('The Sayings of the High One'), though, truth to tell, the speaker is not so very high! The poem deals with ordinary people in their ordinary context. Not all of us are heroes or princes, and it gives us valuable clues to Viking conduct on the daily level. Here the accent is not upon legendary valour but on common sense, not upon princely generosity but on economical housekeeping; not on romantic passion but on abstinence, and respect for the neighbour's wife. The *Hávamál* is cool and sober – a primer of practical behaviour.

Using that great part of Norwego-Icelandic literature which presumably gives a true reflection of Viking life, scholars have tried to depict the Viking's own view of human existence, of the condition of man and his surroundings. The influential Danish scholar Vilhelm Grønbech emphasizes, from these sources, two outstanding characteristics of the Viking: first, his concern for honour (his own and his family's); and second his belief in luck in a man's life and undertakings.

The Viking took nothing more seriously than his family. It is a continuing institution, even though the individuals within it perish. It is the man's master, it can do without him, but not he without it. The members of it are bound to assist and, if need be, avenge each other, and the honour of the family is supreme. If a man commits a crime which involves expulsion from the family he has condemned himself to the worst of fates: to be an outcast; for no man can be an entity to himself, he is part of the fabric of a family. To belong to a family of high esteem is a rare blessing, but to belong to some family is a human necessity. Not to belong is to be the lowest of the species, the thrall, the man who can scarcely be said to have a soul.

If a man had luck his honour would flourish the better, honour signifying not fame or fortune but, rather, esteem and security. In all matters the honour of the individual was that of the family also; hence the importance of collective revenge for an injury done to one member of a family. The vengeance could mean either a killing or the payment of compensation by the guilty party. If compensation had to be paid it was important to strike the right balance: the price must not be too high, nor, on the other hand, so low as to make the injured family feel aggrieved. Abundant diplomatic skill was needed to strike a balance of this sort, and the resort to such oaths that, were the case reversed, the giving party would still find the proposed payment equitable. This fundamental principle of family responsibility and family obligation must have created a stubborn trait in the Viking character, as well as a check upon any individual's disposition to forgive an affront or a wrong: for there was no escape from the family.

The Viking maintained his status in the community not only by his acceptance of the family tie but also by acquiring a wide circle of friends. The *Hávamál* ceaselessly praises the virtues of friendship; loneliness was a dire fate, but to move among one's friends and receive their praise for one's actions was indeed a blessing. To the Viking acclaim was like rain upon a parched meadow. When a skald sang the praises of an earl, everyone heard it; and when the earl rewarded him with a gold ring, everyone saw it: mutual appreciation! Both were delighted – the earl by the fame of his deeds, the skald by the celebrity of his poetic skill. When Egil's furrowed brow was smoothed by the gift of a gold ring at the English court, it was not only the gold which pleased him but the public recognition of his poetic prowess. This kind of thing, however, had a drawback: it led to an exaggerated dependence on what people said about one, and also to an excessive regard for satirical comment. The Viking was desperately sensitive to satire, derision, and malicious gossip: afraid for himself, yet ready to inflict these barbs upon others; keen to discover the faults of others, to listen to cutting sarcasm. He was vulnerable to the malice he liked to bestow.

The Vikings were a complex people. Their roots lay in an ancient, non-feudal tradition of freedom, and for a long time they had been cut off in their remote northern lands from contact with the rest of Europe. They were self-conscious and naturally intelligent in a naïve way; more responsive to an opportunity for quick action than one for long-term perseverance; and endowed with a passion for daring ventures.

The impact of the Vikings was widespread, but only superficial. No doubt, they brought new impulses and ferments to Europe, but they effected no fundamental political transformation there. Finally, they were a people of marked artistic talents – of which they have left ample evidence in the discoveries of archaeology and in the great treasures of Icelandic literature.

The Vikings' Place in European History

The Viking raids were not migrations of whole peoples. Although they have been described as such, and even vaguely associated with the great European migrations of the fifth century, the Viking raids were not movements of people under pressure. During the entire period between 800 and 1100 there was no external pressure on the Scandinavians which could have created a migration: this element was not present in the expeditions from Denmark to England and Normandy, from Norway to Scotland and Ireland, from Sweden to Russia. The political pressure which sent Norwegians to Iceland was purely local and partial. In short, the causes of the Viking raids were entirely different from those which accounted for the movements in fifth-century Europe, and there is no connexion between these two historical phenomena.

It is one thing for Scandinavia to call the period between 800 and 1100 a period or epoch of history, but how are these words justified in the perspective of European history? Scandinavia is a small part of the continent: have the Viking raids and feats of colonization an importance which can entitle them to be regarded as an epoch in Europe's history?

In western Europe the Vikings did exert some lasting influence. As in still earlier periods, England was invaded from the continent on several occasions between 500 B.C. and A.D. 1100: by Celts, Romans, Anglo-Saxons, Danes,

Normans; and these invasions produced the racial amalgam of which the English people were created. Two of the five invasions occurred in the time of the Vikings; the fourth was a directly Scandinavian one, the fifth was indirectly so, and both were of substantial dimensions. This influence upon England is indeed a matter of European significance. In the east, the results of the Viking impact upon Russia cannot be regarded as so vital or permanent, because the proportion of the Viking newcomers to the native inhabitants was far less than in the west. Yet the Swedish infiltration was a not unimportant episode in the history of Russia. Upon central Europe, evidently, there was no Viking impact, mainly for mercantile reasons. The Viking continental trade-routes lay to the east, over Russia's immense plains and along her wide rivers, directly to the Byzantine and Arab markets; there were no impassable Alps to face, no powerful empires to cross. In the history of central Europe the phrase 'Viking Age' has no meaning. Southern Europe was not affected by the Vikings either. Although the small south Italian Norman kingdoms achieved some importance after Viking times during the Crusades, their relationship with the Vikings is a remote one. Although Byzantines and Arabs encountered the presence and influence of the Vikings, it cannot be maintained that the Volga trade of the Rus or the Norse bodyguard of the Byzantine Emperor are historically important enough to justify the term 'Viking period' in the history of those two great empires. As an epoch in European history, therefore, the term 'Viking Age' can only be taken in a limited sense. On balance, the term means more to Scandinavians than to other Europeans.

What did the Vikings give to Europe? What did they get from Europe? To begin with they dealt out the *dona Danao-rum*: destruction, rape, plunder, and murder; and later they expended their energy and blood on colonization. Otherwise, the Vikings could teach Europe nothing. On the other hand they derived much from Europe, although it took a long time for them to use what they had taken. It took them 300 years – strange to say – to learn to build in stone and brick instead of wood and clay. It took 300 years, too, for the new religion to penetrate all three Scandinavain countries. But when at last these material and spiritual cultural changes were complete, there began in Denmark, in the twelfth century, a remarkable period of church building during which the new technique and the new faith worked together. And Christianity revealed the same power in Norway and Sweden. When at last the Viking Age faded into history, the Vikings had received from Europe more than they had given; and the North that they left after them, animated by these European influences, had not been weakened, but changed, by being led into a new cultural life.

Select Bibliography

CHAPTER I

A. DOPSCH. *Wirtschaftliche und soziale Grundlagen der europäischen Kulturentwicklung aus der Zeit von Cäsar bis auf Karl den Grossen*, I and II. Vienna, 1923–4.

H. PIRENNE. *Mahomet et Charlemagne*. Brussels, 1935. English translation: *Mohammed and Charlemagne*, London, 1939.

H. PIRENNE. 'Un contraste économique: Mérovingiens et Carolingiens.' *Revue belge de philologie et d'histoire*, 1922–3.

W. VOGEL. *Die Normannen und das fränkische Reich bis zur Gründung der Normandie*. Heidelberg, 1906.

R. H. HODGKIN. *A History of the Anglo-Saxons*, II. Oxford, 1939.

B. NERMAN. *Grobin-Seeburg, Ausgrabungen und Funde*. Uppsala, 1958.

JOHANNES STEENSTRUP. *Normannerne*, I. Copenhagen, 1876. pp. 218 ff.

CHAPTER 2

JOHANNES STEENSTRUP. *Normannerne*, I–IV. Copenhagen, 1876–82.

A. BUGGE. *Vikingerne*, I and II. Christiania [Oslo], 1904–6.

E. WADSTEIN. *Norden och Västeuropa i gammal tid*. Göteborg, 1925.

T. D. KENDRICK. *A History of the Vikings*. London, 1930.

FRITZ ASKEBERG. *Norden och kontinenten i gammal tid*. Uppsala, 1944. (See especially about the word 'Viking', pp. 115 ff.)

H. ARBMAN and M. STENBERGER. *Vikingar i Västerled.* Stockholm, 1935.

H. ARBMAN. *Svear i Österviking.* Stockholm, 1955.

H. SWEET. 'King Alfred's Orosius.' *Early English Text Society,* 1883.

ALEXANDER SEIPPEL. *Rerum Normannicarum fontes Arabici.* Oslo, 1: 1876; 11: 1928.

G. JACOB. 'Arabische Berichte von Gesandten an germanische Fürstenhöfe aus dem 9. und 10. Jahrhundert'. *Quellen zur deutschen Volkskunde,* 1. Berlin-Leipzig, 1927.

H. BIRKELAND. 'Nordens historie i middelalderen efter arabiske kilder.' *Norske Videnskaps-Akademis skrifter.* Oslo, 1954.

A. ZEKI VALIDI TOGAN. 'Ibn Fadlān's Reisebericht.' *Abhandlungen für die Kunde des Morgenlandes,* Vol. XXIV 3. Leipzig, 1939.

ADAM BREMENSIS, magister. *Gesta Hammaburgensis ecclesiae pontificum.* ed. H. B. Schmeidler. Hanover-Leipzig, 1917.

CHAPTERS 3—5

J. H. HOLWERDA. *Dorestad en onze vroegste middeleeuwen.* Leiden, 1929.

F. M. STENTON. *Anglo-Saxon England.* Oxford, 1947.

VILHELM THOMSEN. *The Relations between Ancient Russia and Scandinavia and the Origin of the Russian State.* Oxford, 1877. Revised edition in Danish in the author's *Samlede Skrifter* 1. Copenhagen, 1919

W. J. RAUDONIKAS. *Die Normannen der Wikingerzeit und das Ladogagebiet.* Stockholm, 1930.

H. PASZKIEWICZ. *The Origin of Russia.* London, 1954.

A. STENDER-PETERSEN. *Varangica.* Aarhus, 1953.

A. STENDER-PETERSEN. 'Das Problem der ältesten Byzantinisch-Russisch-Nordischen Beziehungen.' *Relazioni,* Vol. III: *Storia del Medioevo,* pp. 165 ff., ed. *Comitato internaz. di scienze storiche, X congresso internaz.* Rome, 1955.

JOHANNES STEENSTRUP. 'Normandiets Historie under de syv første Hertuger 911–1066' (with a summary in French). *Det kgl. danske Vidensk. Selsk. Skrifter*, 7. Række. Copenhagen, 1925.

JEAN ADIGARD DES GAUTRIES. *Les noms de personnes scandinaves en Normandie de 911 à 1066.* Lund, 1954.

EJNAR DYGGVE. 'The Royal Barrows at Jelling.' *Antiquity*, 88. December 1948, pp. 190 ff.

EJNAR DYGGVE. 'Gorm's Temple and Harald's Stave-Church at Jelling'. *Acta Archaeologica*, Vol. XXV. 1954, pp. 221 ff.

H. SHETELIG. 'An Introduction to the Viking History of Western Europe.' *Viking Antiquities in Great Britain and Ireland.* ed. by H. Shetelig. Part I, Oslo, 1940.

P. DU CHATELLIER and L. LE PONTOIS. 'La sépulture scandinave à barque de I'Île de Groix.' *Bulletin de la Soc. Arch. du Finistère*, Vol. XXXV. Quimper, 1908.

J. STEFANSSON. 'Vikings in Spain.' *Saga-Book of the Viking Club*, VI, 1909.

K. GJERSET. *History of Iceland.* London, 1924.

P. NØRLUND and M. STENBERGER. 'Brattahlid. Researches into Norse Culture in Greenland.' *Meddelelser om Grønland*, Vol. 88 : 1. Copenhagen, 1934.

LIS JACOBSEN. *Svenskevældets fald.* Copenhagen, 1929.

T. J. ARNE. 'Le Voyage d'Ibn Fadlan à Bulgar.' *Fornvännen.* Stockholm, 1941.

T. J. ARNE. 'Die Varägerfrage und die sovietische Forschung.' *Acta Archaeologica* XXIII. Copenhagen, 1952.

W. HOVGAARD. *The Voyages of the Norsemen to America.* New York, 1915.

H. HERMANSSON. 'The Problem of Wineland.' *Islandica*, Vol. 25. 1936.

J. BRØNDSTED. 'Norsemen in North America before Columbus.' *Smithsonian Institution, Annual Report* 1953. Washington, 1954, pp. 367 ff.

CHAPTERS 6 and 7

JAN PETERSEN. 'De norske vikingesverd. En typologisk-kronologisk studie over vikingetidens vaaben.' *Videnskaps-selskapets skrifter* II. Hist.-filos, klasse no. 1. Oslo, 1919.

JAN PETERSEN. *Vikingetidens smykker*. Stavanger, 1928.

JAN PETERSEN. 'Vikingetidens redskaper' (with a summary in English). *Skrifter utgitt av Det norske Videnskaps-Akademi i Oslo* II Hist.-filos. klasse no. 4. Oslo, 1951.

G. A. NORDMAN. 'Vapnen i Nordens forntid.' *Nordisk Kultur*, Vol. XIIB, Vaaben, pp. 46 ff. Stockholm-Oslo-Copenhagen, 1943.

ADA BRUHN HOFFMEYER. *Middelalderens tveæggede sværd* I–II. Copenhagen, 1954 (with a summary in English).

P. PAULSEN. *Axt und Kreuz bei den Nordgermanen*. Berlin, 1939.

D. SELLING. *Wikingerzeitliche und frühmittelalterliche Keramik in Schweden*. Stockholm, 1955.

BJØRN HOUGEN. 'Osebergfunnets billedvev.' *Viking*, Vol. IV. Oslo, 1940.

AGNES GEIJER. 'Die Textilfunde aus den Gräbern. '*Birka*, Untersuchungen und Studien*, Vol. III. Uppsala, 1938.

SUNE LINDQVIST. *Gotlands Bildsteine*, I–II. Stockholm, 1941–2.

K. FRIIS JOHANSEN. 'Le trésor d'argenterie de Terslev.' *Mémoires de la société royale des antiquaires du Nord.* 1908–13, pp. 329 f.

R. SKOVMAND. 'Les trésors danois provenant de l'époque des vikings et du Moyen Âge le plus ancien jusqu'aux environs de 1150.' *Aarbøger for nordisk Oldkyndighed og Historie*, 1942, pp. 1 ff.

s. GRIEG. 'Vikingetidens skattefund.' *Universitetets oldsaksamlings skrifter*, Vol. II. Oslo, 1929.

M. STENBERGER. *Die Schatzfunde Gotlands der Wikingerzeit.* Vol. II *Fundbeschreibung und Tafeln*, Lund, 1947; Vol. I *Text*, Stockholm, 1958.

CHAPTER 8

H. SHETELIG. 'Tuneskipet.' *Norske Oldfunn.* Vol. II. Christiania [Oslo], 1917.

N. NICOLAYSEN. *Langskibet fra Gokstad ved Sandefjord.* Christiania [Oslo], 1882.

A. W. BRØGGER, HJ. FALK, S. GRIEG & H. SHETELIG. *Oseberg funnet. Utgitt av Den norske stat*, Vols. I–IV. Christiania [Oslo], 1917–1928.

A. W. BRØGGER and H. SHETELIG. *Vikingeskipene. Deres forgjengere og etterfølgere.* Oslo, 1950. English Translation: *The Viking Ships, their ancestry and evolution.* Oslo, 1953.

THORLEIF SJØVOLD. *Oseberg funnet og de andre vikingeskipsfunn.* Oslo, 1957.

H. MÖTEFINDT. 'Der Wagen im nordischen Kulturkreise zur vor- und frühgeschichtlichen Zeit.' *Festschrift Eduard Hahn*, 1917, pp. 209 ff.

GÖSTA BERG. 'Sledges and Wheeled Vehicles.' *Nordiska Museets Handlingar*, no. 4. Stockholm, 1935, pp. 65 and 155 f.

SUNE LINDQVIST. 'Färdesätt och färdemedel.' Quoted in the author's book: *Svenskt forntidsliv.* Stockholm, 1944, pp. 248 ff.

CHAPTER 9

SOPH. MÜLLER and C. NEERGAARD. 'Danevirke, archæologisk undersøgt, beskrevet og tydet.' *Nordiske Fortidsminder* I, Copenhagen, 1903.

H. JANKUHN. *Die Wehranlagen der Wikingerzeit zwischen Schlei und Treene.* Neumünster, 1937.

H. JANKUHN. *Die Ausgrabungen in Haithabu (1937-9).* Berlin, 1943.

H. JANKUHN. *Haithabu, ein Handelsplatz der Wikingerzeit.* Neumünster, 1956.

H. JANKUHN. 'Die Frühgeschichte vom Ausgang der Völkerwanderung bis zum Ende der Wikingerzeit.' *Geschichte Schleswig-Holsteins,* Vol III. Neumünster, 1955-7.

H. JANKUHN. 'Die frühmittelalterlichen Seehandelsplätze im Nord- und Ostseeraum.' *Vorträge und Forschungen,* Vol. IV. Lindau, 1958.

VILH. LA COUR. *Danevirkestudier. En arkæologisk-historisk Undersøgelse.* Copenhagen, 1951.

OTTO KUNKEL and K. A. WILDE. *Jumne, 'Vineta', Jomsburg, Julin: Wollin.* Stettin, 1941.

B. EHRLICH. 'Der preussisch-wikingische Handelsplatz Truso.' I. *Balt. histor. Kongress.* Riga, 1938.

H. ARBMAN. *Birka, Sveriges äldsta handelsstad.* Stockholm, 1939.

H. ARBMAN. *Birka, Untersuchungen und Studien,* Vol. I. Stockholm, 1943.

H. ARBMAN. in *Situne Dei, Sigtuna fornhems årsbok,* Sigtuna, 1942.

H. ARBMAN. 'Hague-Dike. Les fouilles en 1951 et 1952.' *Meddelanden från Lunds Univ's. hist. museum.* Lund, 1953.

POUL NØRLUND. 'Trelleborg.' *Nordiske Fortidsminder* IV I. Copenhagen, 1948 (with a summary in English).

C. G. SCHULTZ. 'Vikingetidshuset paa Trelleborg,' *Fra Nationalmuseets Arbejdsmark,* 1942, pp. 17 ff.

PALLE LAURING and A. HOFF-MØLLER. 'Trelleborghusets rekonstruktion.' *Aarbøger for nordisk Oldkyndighed og Historie,* 1952, pp. 108 ff. (with a summary in English).

J. LARSEN. 'Rekonstruktion af Trelleborg.' *Aarbøger for nordisk Oldkyndighed og Historie*, 1957 pp. 56 ff. (with a summary in English).

C. G. SCHULTZ. 'Aggersborg. Vikingelejren ved Limfjorden.' *Fra Nationalmuseets Arbejdsmark*, 1949, pp. 91 ff.

H. P. L'ORANGE. 'Trelleborg–Aggersborg og de kongelige byer i Østen.' *Viking*, Vol. XVI, 1952, pp. 307 ff.

CHAPTERS 10—12

Nordisk Kultur Vol. XXIX, *Mønt.* Denmark: G. Galster pp. 141 ff.; Sweden: B. Thordeman pp. 7 ff.; Norway: Hans Holst pp. 95 ff. Stockholm-Oslo-Copenhagen, 1936.

A. W. BRØGGER. 'Ertog og øre. Den gamle norske vegt.' *Videnskapsselskapets skrifter*, Vol. II. Hist.-filos. klasse no. 3, Christiania [Oslo], 1921.

T. J. ARNE. 'La Suède et l'Orient.' *Archives d'études orientales publiées par J. A. Lundell*, Vol. VIII. Uppsala, 1914.

Nordisk Kultur, Vol. VI, *Runerne*, pp. 83 ff. (Magnus Olsen, J. Brøndum-Nielsen, Otto v. Friesen). Stockholm-Oslo-Copenhagen, 1933.

LIS JACOBSEN and E. MOLTKE. *Danmarks Runeindskrifter.* Copenhagen, 1942.

Norges innskrifter med de yngre runer, Vol. I ff., ed. Magnus Olsen. Oslo, 1944 ff.

Sveriges runeinskrifter, Vol. I ff., ed. Søderberg, Brate, Wessén, Kinander, Jungner. Uppsala, 1900 ff.

A. BÆKSTED. *Målruner og troldruner. Runemagiske studier* (with a summary in English). Copenhagen, 1952.

E. WESSÉN. 'Om vikingatidens runor.' *Filologiskt Arkiv* VI (with a summary in German). Stockholm, 1957.

E. WESSÉN. 'Runestenen vid Röks kyrka.' *Kungl. Vitt. Hist. och Antikvitets Akademiens Handlingar*, filol.–filosof. serien. Stockholm, 1958.

P. KERMODE. *Manx Crosses.* London, 1907.

H. SHETELIG. 'Stil– og tidsbestemmelser i de nordiske korsene paa øen Man.' in *Opuscula archaeologica Oscari Montelio dicata*. Stockholm, 1918.

The Guildhall runestone: *Vict. Hist. Co. London*, I, pp. 167 ff.

The Berezanj runestone: H. Arbman. *Svear i Østerviking*. Stockholm, 1955, p. 153, cf. p. 159.

SOPHUS MÜLLER. *Die Thier-Ornamentik im Norden*. Hamburg, 1881.

H. SHETELIG. *Osebergfunnet*, Vol. III, Christiania [Oslo], 1920.

JOHANNES BRØNDSTED. *Early English Ornament*. London, 1924.

Nordisk Kultur, Vol. XXVII, *Kunst*, pp. 124 ff. (Jan Petersen, Sune Lindqvist, C. A. Nordman). Stockholm-Oslo-Copenhagen, 1931.

H. ARBMAN. *Schweden und das karolingische Reich*. Stockholm, 1937.

H. ARBMAN. 'The Skabersjö Brooch and some Danish Mounts.' *Meddelanden från Lunds Univ. Hist. Mus.* 1956, pp. 93 ff.

N. ÅBERG. '*Keltiska och orientaliska stilinflytelser i vikingatidens nordiska konst*.' *Kungl. Vitt. Hist. Antikv. Handlingar*, Stockholm, 1941 (with a summary in English).

G. ARWIDSSON. *Vendelstile, Email und Glas*. Uppsala, 1942.

J.-E. FORSSANDER. 'Irland–Oseberg.' *Meddelanden från Lunds Univ. Hist. Mus.* 1943, pp. 294 ff.

SUNE LINDQVIST. 'Osebergmästarna.' *Tor*, Uppsala, 1948.

T. D. KENDRICK. *Late Saxon and Viking Art*. London, 1949.

H. SHETELIG. 'The Norse Style of Ornamentation in the Viking Settlements.' *Acta Archaeologica*, 1948.

H. SHETELIG. *Classical Impulses in Scandinavian Art from the Migration Period to the Viking Age*. Oslo, 1949.

H. SHETELIG. 'Religionshistoriske drag fra vikingetidens stil-historie.' *Viking*, 1950.

W. HOLMQVIST. 'Germanic Art During the First Millennium. A.D.' *Kungl. Vitt Hist. och Antikv. Handlingar.* Stockholm, 1955.

SUNE LINDQVIST. *Gotlands Bildsteine*, Vol. I–II. Stockholm, 1941–2.

H. SHETELIG. 'Billedfremstillinger i jernalderens kunst.' *Nordisk Kultur*, Vol. XXVII, *Kunst*, pp. 214 ff.

CHAPTERS 13—15

ADAM BREMENSIS, magister. See above under Chapter 2.

P. V. GLOB. *Ard og plov i Nordens oldtid.* Aarhus, 1951 (with a summary in English).

BJØRN HOUGEN. *Fra seter til gård. Studier i norsk bosetninghistorie.* Oslo, 1947.

Nordisk Kultur, Vol. XVII, *Bygningskultur*: Sweden pp. 31 ff., Norway pp. 59 ff. (M. Stenberger); North-Atlantic islands pp. 108 ff. (Aa. Roussell). Stockholm-Oslo-Copenhagen, 1953.

AA. ROUSSELL. *Norse Building Customs in the Scottish Isles.* Copenhagen-London, 1934.

Forntida gårdar i Island. ed. M. Stenberger. Copenhagen, 1943 (with a summary in English).

P. NØRLUND. *Meddelelser om Grønland*, Vol. 76, 1930; Vol. 88, 1934 (Gardar, Herjolfsnes, Brattahlid).

R. MEISSNER. *Beiträge zur Geschichte der deutschen Sprache und Literatur*, Vol. 57, 1933 (ab. *Rígsþula*).

JEAN I. YOUNG. *Arkiv för nordisk filologi*, Vol. 49, 1933 (ab. *Rígsþula*).

K. V. AMIRA. 'Recht.' Paul, *Grundriss der germanischen Philologie*, 1913.

CL. V. SCHWERIN. *Germanische Rechtsgeschichte.* 1936.

V. GRØNBECH. *The Culture of the Teutons*, Vol. I–II. London-Copenhagen, 1931.

Anthropology. Denmark: *Acta Archaeologica*, Vol. VII, 1936, pp. 224 ff.; P. Nørlund, *Trelleborg*, 1948, pp. 112 ff.; Norway: K. E. Schreiner, *Crania Norvegica*, Oslo, 1946; Iceland: *Forntida gårdar i Island*, ed. M. Stenberger (pp. 227 ff., by Jón Steffensen). Copenhagen, 1943.

SK. V. GUDJONSSON. *Folkekost og Sundhedsforhold i gamle Dage.* Copenhagen, 1941.

A. BUGGE. *Vesterlandenes indflydelse paa nordboernes og særlig nordmændenes ydre kultur, levesæt og samfundsforhold.* Christiania [Oslo], 1905.

A. WALSH. *Scandinavian Relations with Ireland during the Viking Period.* Dublin, 1922.

F. M. STENTON. *Anglo-Saxon England.* Oxford, 1947 (pp. 495 ff., 'The Danelaw').

JOHANNES STEENSTRUP. See above under Chapters 3–5.

H. BIRKELAND. See above under Chapter 2.

JAN DE VRIES. *Altnordische Literaturgeschichte*, Vols. I–II. Berlin 1941–2.

F. JÓNSSON. *Den oldnorske og oldislandske litteraturs historie*, Vols. I–III. Copenhagen, 1920–4.

G. VIGFUSSON and F. YORK POWELL. *Corpus Poeticum Boreale, the Poetry of the Old Northern Tongue from the Earliest Times to the Thirteenth Century*, edited, classified, and translated with Introduction, Excursus, and Notes, Vols. I and II. Oxford, 1883.

A. HEUSLER. *Die altgermanische Dichtung.* Potsdam, 1941.

G. NECKEL. *Die altnordische Literatur.* Leipzig, 1923.

JAN DE VRIES. *Altgermanische Religionsgeschichte*, Vols. I and II. Berlin 1956–7.

FR. VON DER LEYEN. *Die Götter der Germanen.* Munich, 1938.

G. DUMÉZIL. *Loki.* (*Les Dieux et les hommes*, Vol. I.) Paris, 1948.

M. OLSEN. *Farms and Fanes of Ancient Norway. The Place-Names of a Country Discussed in their Bearings on Social and Religious History.* Oslo, 1928.

Nordisk Kultur, Vol. v, *Stednavne*. Stockholm-Oslo-Copenhagen, 1939.

S. K. AMTOFT. *Nordiske Gudeskikkelser i bebyggelseshistorisk Belysning*. Copenhagen, 1948.

NILS LID. 'Scandinavian Heathen Cult Places.' *Folk-Liv*, Vols. XXI and XXII. Stockholm, 1957–8.

F. STRÖM. 'Diser, nornor, valkyrjor, Fruktbarhetskult och sakralt kungadöme i Norden.' *Kungl. Vitt. Hist. Antikv. Akad. Handlingar*, filolog.-filosof. serien I (with a summary in German). Stockholm, 1954.

E. DYGGVE in *Acta Archaeologica*, 1954, and in *Antiquity*, 1948; see above under Chapter 3.

A. W. BRØGGER and H. SHETELIG. *Vikingeskipene*. Oslo, 1950, pp. 92 ff.

J. BRØNDSTED. 'Danish Inhumation Graves of the Viking Age.' *Acta Archaeologica*, Vol. VII, 1936.

TH. RAMSKOU. 'Viking Age Cremation Graves in Denmark.' *Acta Archaeologica*, Vol. XXI, 1950.

H. ARBMAN. *Birka, Untersuchungen und Studien*, Vols. I and II, *Die Gräber*. Stockholm, 1943.

H. JANKUHN. *Haithabu, ein Handelsplatz der Wikingerzeit*. Neumünster, 1956, pp. 104 ff.

TH. RAMSKOU. 'Lindholm, Preliminary Report.' *Acta Archaeologica*, Vol. XXIV, 1953. Ibid. 1955 and 1957.

Viking Antiquities in Great Britain and Ireland, ed. H. Shetelig. Oslo, 1940.

O. ALMGREN. 'Vikingatidens gravskik i verkligheten och i den fornnordiska litteraturen.' *Nordiska studier tillägnade Adolf Noreen*. Uppsala, 1904.

H. ARBMAN. *Svear i Österviking*. Stockholm, 1955, pp. 81 ff. (Gnezdovo).

H. LJUNGBERG. *Den nordiska religionen och kristendomen. Studier öter det nordiska religionsskiftet under vikingatiden*. Uppsala, 1938.

Index

More about Penguins
and Pelicans

For further information about books available from
Penguins please write to Dept EP, Penguin Books Ltd,
Harmondsworth, Middlesex UB7 ODA.

In the U.S.A.: For a complete list of books available from
Penguins in the United States write to Dept DG, Penguin
Books, 299 Murray Hill Parkway, East Rutherford, New
Jersey 07073.

In Canada: For a complete list of books available from
Penguins in Canada write to Penguin Books Canada Ltd,
2801 John Street, Markham, Ontario L3R 1B4.

In Australia: For a complete list of books available from
Penguins in Australia write to the Marketing Department,
Penguin Books Australia Ltd, P.O. Box 257 Ringwood,
Victoria 3134.

In New Zealand: For a complete list of books available from
Penguins in New Zealand write to the Marketing
Department, Penguin Books (N.Z.) Ltd, P.O. Box 4019,
Auckland 10.

'Ghosts of the past . . .'

The Celts

Nora Chadwick

Nora Chadwick, a Celtic scholar of international repute, describes in this Pelican the rise and spread of the Celts and their arrival in the British Isles in about the eighth century B.C. Her study of their history, religion, art and literature reveals those individualistic and imaginative qualities which have contributed so much to the world we live in today.

The Irish

Sean O'Faolain

Many racial, religious, social, and intellectual strands have, over the centuries, been woven into the cloth of Irish genius, and it is Sean O'Faolain's achievement to have disentangled these in a classic study.

'A creative history of the growth of a racial mind' – this is Sean O'Faolain's own description of a book in which he has no truck with political events, wars, or rebellions and rejects the popular Irish notion of 'seven hundred years of slavery'.

The Anglo-Saxons

David Wilson

'The best introduction to Anglo-Saxon archaeology yet written' – *Medieval Archaeology*

The Anglo-Saxons presents a brief but very comprehensive view, based on the archaeological material, of life in England between the fifth and eleventh centuries. A short outline of the pagan and Christian epochs introduces chapters on the daily life of the people, on art, weapons and warfare.

Of men and Gods . . .

Gods and Myths of Northern Europe

H. R. Ellis Davidson

Tiw, Woden, Thunor, Frig . . . these ancient northern
deities gave their names to the very days of our week.
Nevertheless most of us know far more of Mars, Mercury,
Jupiter, Venus, and the classical deities. All these
northern deities were worshipped in the Viking Age, and
the author has endeavoured to relate their cults to daily
life and to see why these pagan beliefs gave way in time
to the Christian faith.

The Druids

Stuart Piggott

This modern study of the Druids has a double attraction.
Not only does Professor Piggott detail the little that can
be said with any certainty about this shadowy Celtic
priesthood; he also traces, through remarkably exact
stages, the evolution of a legend.

Posidonius and Julius Caesar and other classical writers
(not always objective) combine with ancient Irish texts to
supply the scanty written evidence: to this Stuart Piggott
adds his great knowledge of recent archaeological
discoveries about Celtic society before the impact of
the Romans.

Middle Eastern Mythology

S. H. Hooke

During the last half-century the discoveries of
archaeologists in the ancient Near East, now called the
Middle East, have created a widespread interest in the
ways of life and thought of the dwellers in that region,
and especially in their myths. For much of Greek,
Roman, and even Celtic mythology has its source in the
traditions and legends of the ancient Near East.